Bourgeois Coldness

Deft, and misleadingly straightforward, the question 'What is the self at sea?' effectively prefigures how Bourgeois Coldness *gathers a compelling account of the way in which bourgeois existence unfolds in a form that has always included both (European) society and the (American, African, Asian) colony. Foregrounding affect, this timely book provides an inestimable philosophical argument for the centrality of Blackness in critical examinations of capitalism's violence.* —Denise Ferreira da Silva

How does the bourgeois subject sail through a world of genocide, ecological devastation, the death of non-white people at sea, and a myriad of other forms of suffering and destruction? Henrike Kohpeiß plumbs the depths of the bourgeois soul to find an affective technique that allows this subject to remain unruffled: coldness. Elegant and erudite in equal measure, this book will stand as a landmark diagnosis of the practices of denial in our time. —Andreas Malm

Bourgeois Coldness

Henrike Kohpeiß

Translated from the German
by Grace Nissan

DIVIDED

Published in the United Kingdom by Divided in 2025.

Divided Publishing
Rue de Manchesterstraat 5
1080 Brussels
Belgium

Divided Publishing
Deborah House
Retreat Place
London E9 6RJ
United Kingdom

https://divided.online

First published in Frankfurt am Main in 2023 by Campus Verlag as *Bürgerliche Kälte. Affekt und koloniale Subjektivität.* Translated with the support of CRC Affective Societies, Freie Universität Berlin.

Funded by

Designed by Alex Walker
Printed by Printon, Tallinn

ISBN 978-1-7395161-2-3

Contents

New Black Music is this: Find the self, then kill it.

—Amiri Baraka, *Black Music* (1969)

Foreword and Acknowledgements

This book originates from another age – not long ago but entirely different in its affective and political conditions and – most importantly – in its sense of the future. Its writing between roughly 2018 and 2021 situates it deeply in the loneliness and timelessness of the pandemic years, but also in a newly awakened sense of what politics could be during the uprising of 2020.

I see *Bourgeois Coldness* as an invitation to meditate on the political conditions that have allowed for us to end up where we now are. Bourgeois coldness is a state of mind that lets reality be obscured by the belief that liberal democracy is exactly the end of history that one could hope for. This state of mind might be a partial explanation for the ubiquitous expressions of surprise and caught-off-guard-ness about the realities of fascism in 2025.

Who would have thought that the conditions would change so quickly? I don't think that anyone could have while remaining committed to a view of the world focused on liberation.

Since it first came out in German, this book has felt like my home – a material manifestation of what I believe to be true, and also a relief – since these beliefs now have a form and can be shared with others. The places the book has entered and the conversations it has offered me have surprised and delighted me and I cannot wait for more of them to unfold.

For this English edition, some sections from the German original have been cut, mostly in order to prepare the book for an international readership. Some of the extensive meditations on German public discourse as well as parts that introduce academic literature to a German-speaking audience which already circulates more broadly in English have therefore been removed. The part on the Aegean had an additional section on Odysseus' visit on the island of the Cyclops, which has not been included in the English version. Some sections of the German book refer to the specific political moment of the George Floyd uprising in 2020 and speculate on a different future than the one we are now already living. These parts have been cut, not in order to render speculation useless, but in order to give the aspects of futurity that, despite all still seem open, adequate space.

I am deeply grateful to and full of admiration for Grace Nissan, who has translated this book with a precision and love for German syntax that I did not know was possible. Their work of translation has included generously helping me to rethink the book in English, not least to keep it politically viable some years after its initial publication. Tremendous thanks go also to Eleanor Ivory Weber and Camilla Wills for taking no small risk in suggesting that I publish *Bourgeois Coldness* with Divided, and to Jacob Blandy for his careful copy-editing.

Boundless thanks are due to my doctoral advisors Jan Slaby and Ruth Sonderegger for the endless supply of energy that allowed me to finish the dissertation on which this book is based, and for their enthusiasm that keeps philosophy joyful. Nothing can be written if no one believes in it, and your trust has been essential.

Thanks to all the faithful and occasional visitors to the Affect and Blackness Reading Group for providing the intellectual space that made this work possible. Thanks to the students of philosophy at FU Berlin and Leuphana University Lüneburg for their curiosity, criticism and patience in the adventure of teaching. Thanks to Jan Slaby's research colloquium for the many years of continuity and generous thinking, and to the graduate programme Cultures of Critique at Leuphana

University Lüneburg for an exciting year. Thanks to the CRC Affective Societies and all its members for the opportunity to do research in dark times.

Thanks for discussion, commitment, time and encouragement: Marie Wuth, Heiko Stubenrauch, Nelly Y. Pinkrah, Isabel Mehl, Janna Hilger, Christian Schwinghammer, Jorinde Schulz, Fabian Bernhardt, Jonas Bens, Matthias Lüthjohann, Ana Makashvili, Karina Rocktäschel, Ulrike Geiger, Lester Spence, Emily Owens, Tyrone S. Palmer, Iris Dankemeyer, Millicent Churcher, Anthony Obst, Claas Oberstadt, Jason Bustos, Jandra Böttger, Janis Walter, siddhartha lokanandi, Oshrat Silberbusch, Susan Buck-Morss, Sami Khatib, Roberto Nigro, Andreas Malm, Sambojang Ceesay, Felix Werfel, Jonathon Catlin, Fumi Okiji, Eric Oberle, Bojana Cvejić, Marija Cetinić, Stefa Govaart, Jacob Blumenfeld, Daniel Loick, Robin Celikates and Anastasia Coope.

Thank you, Krischa Hasselbach for your clear view, Antonia Rohwetter for asking the right questions, Tamara Antonijević for insisting, Matthew James Milbourne for listening and for some of the best thinking. Thanks, Tim Vogel for cooperation and wisdom, Julia Novacek for solidarity, Maxi Wallenhorst for genuine interest. Thanks, Else Tunemyr for all the fun, Catalina Insignares and Carolina Mendonça for your ever-present spirits, Lara Kneesch for the beach, Helene Röhnsch for what never changes. Thank you, Caroline Elsen for growing up together, Anna von Glasenapp for the invincibility of laughter, Philipp Wüschner for your friendship to me and for the truth, Gerda Wendt-Kahl and Roy Kahl for a summer home, and Lotte Warnsholdt for saving my heart. Thanks, David Reiber Otálora, Christopher Weickenmeier and Aki for family.

Thank you, Johanna Malm for new places, Sam Nimmrichter for multilevel intelligence, Paolina Wandruszka for giving love and criticism in equal measure, Emmilou Rößling for loyalty and Vega for pizza, Duygu Ağal for never giving up, Hans Broich for all the help, Lama El Khatib for teaching me, Jonas von Lenthe for unwavering work, Nikhil Vettukattil for waiting for the book to come out. Thanks to those in New York who have made me feel like I belonged there when Grace and I were shaping the book: Oliver Silverman, Jochen Schmon, Athina Khalil, Valentina Desideri, Denise Ferreira da Silva, CRACS, everyone at Taaffe. I thank my parents, Anke Wendt-Kohpeiß and Ralph Kohpeiß, for exactly the right care, and my brother, Klaas Kohpeiß, for all the jokes and warmth.

I could not be without you all.

Henrike Kohpeiß
Berlin
July 2025

Introduction: The Self at Sea

And if we assume that this identity, this hardness, this opaqueness and impenetrability of this ego-authority is modelled on something external, we may reasonably conclude, without wasting too much time on idle speculations, that the hardness that characterises the will viewed as a strong ego has been derived from the hardness and impenetrability of things over which we have no control.
—Theodor W. Adorno[1]

It's difficult to live near the sea. It overwhelms. Well, not true. It owns. Your small life is nothing to it. —Dionne Brand[2]

The self and the sea have this in common: from up close they appear porous and transparent, but from a distance hard and opaque. Humans have tried to protect themselves from the overwhelming force of the sea since time immemorial; so too have they always wanted to rule over it. The infinite sea has thus been a stage for the subject since antiquity. In relation to the waves and the vast expanse, some construct themselves as seafaring heroes and saviours from the flood; others drown in the same waters. The sea elevates some, makes them unforgettable; others it buries, erases all traces of their existence. The sea can be a weapon and a mass grave. It holds the promise of eternal discovery, conquest and, depending on the swell, can be a friendly companion or an insurmountable obstacle. At sea, subjects and objects are separated – subjects survive despite poor visibility and big swells, objects are abandoned to the waves when things get choppy. Against the backdrop of ancient seafaring, colonial expedition, shipwrecks and fluid borders, the question remains: what is the self at sea?

The Bourgeois and Blackness

The self has been articulated in many ways throughout European history. One particularly prominent way is through the bourgeois subject. This book is about bourgeois subjectivity and its social, institutional and intellectual life in contemporary Western societies. This life is sustained through an affective structure I call 'bourgeois coldness'. In order to secure the survival of bourgeois society, subjects not only settle into the cold, they also use coldness deliberately as an affective social technique. A genealogy of coldness brings its colonial heritage to light. It manifests in a subject model that repeatedly contrasts a rational, European self to an irrational, colonised 'Other', even when it seeks to critically reflect on this juxtaposition. The entanglement of bourgeois subjectivity with the history of violence that this genealogy reveals diminishes the conceptions of humanism and causes them to rupture. Since the seventeenth century, the bourgeoisie have made fateful distinctions between humans and non-humans, subjects and objects, ownership of oneself and of property. In this book, the social and conceptual orders in which these differences have manifested appear in the process of decay.

'The bourgeoisie live on like spectres threatening doom.'[3] Theodor W. Adorno sees the bourgeoisie as elusive, time-transcending beings. They are undead presences whose vital sources never dry up – their perpetual existence is enigmatic. This ghostly form of existence is the reason Adorno and Max Horkheimer use the figure of Odysseus to describe the bourgeoisie. He is a figure situated long before the beginning of the bourgeois epoch and the emergence of modern capitalism.[4] The bourgeois way of life unfolds transhistorically and can be understood by tracing its structural characteristics in different historical constellations.

It is astonishing how successfully bourgeois society organises its own survival, although its overcoming is a political and cultural necessity. Its continued survival merits explanation. Because bourgeois forms of existence reproduce themselves both according to what can be expected as well as beyond it, examining them requires both historical and philosophical analysis. Bourgeois forms of life die hard – hence the assumption that they are based on elementary social techniques and attitudes. To better understand this persistence, we need to get to the root of the concept of the bourgeois and its normative implications.

The bourgeois does not merely mean the empirically defined social class of middle-class citizens, with their economic and social privilege. The history of bourgeois subjectivity is rooted in colonialism and bourgeois society as two major projects of equal precedence in European modernity. These unfinished projects affect all that they encounter: they must thus be evaluated according to their historical traces and effects. Evidence of colonial histories of violence will play only an occasional role here, despite the constant need for historical case studies. Of greater interest is the colonial, bourgeois present and future and the sites where interconnected exclusions and acts of violence unfold. My focus is on the structural continuities of the bourgeois self-understandings in which coloniality is still firmly inscribed today. Bourgeois politics bases itself on the pursuit of individual autonomy, meant to enable the fulfilment of high moral standards, based on the assumption that personal autonomy and moral competence are guiding principles for *every* social experience.

Bourgeois life goes beyond '2000 Marks net per month'[5] and the realisation of a set lifestyle. Bourgeois existence is at present an institutionally anchored and state-supporting way of life which has grown with capitalism, having laid claim to moral authority since the eighteenth century without interruption.[6] The continuity of bourgeois principles of order lends this topic relevance.

Bourgeois morality is committed to the equality of all human beings – albeit under its own premise – implemented in a colonial fashion, which includes an interpretive sovereignty over who qualifies as human and who does not. Frantz Fanon describes this strategy thus: 'The Western bourgeoisie, though fundamentally racist, most often manages to mask this racism by a multiplicity of nuances which allow it to preserve intact its proclamation of mankind's outstanding dignity.'[7] The differentiated nature of bourgeois world-views keeps its basic assumptions well hidden when it comes to who belongs to humanity and who does not. The bourgeois attitude maintains its credibility by demonstrating charity in a humanism where equality means self-reliance. 'Bourgeois ideology, however, which is the proclamation of an essential equality between men, manages to appear logical in its own eyes by inviting the sub-men to become human, and to take as their prototype Western humanity as incarnated in the Western bourgeoisie.'[8] Fanon in 1961 diagnosed the stubborn bourgeois capacity for moral and political hubris in the midst of the decolonial political movement. But who are the bourgeois subjects who protect the premises of their own hypocrisy today? What techniques have been developed over the course of the eighteenth, nineteenth and twentieth centuries to ensure ongoing self-preservation?

Bourgeois coldness refers to an affective strategy that offers an explanation for how this self-preservation works. Bourgeois coldness is one of the most advanced affective and aesthetic forms of preserving the structure of the colonial status quo. It creates an affective shelter in the world, unencroached upon by the immediate consequences of its many catastrophes. It functions like air conditioning – a complex technology which reliably stabilises the climate until those inside consider it natural. Bourgeois spaces – institutional and affective – stay cool and pleasant. But outside it's burning.

Adorno and Horkheimer recognise that the bourgeois is the bearer and beneficiary of coldness, extending it in all directions.[9] 'Connections with reason, liberality, and middle-class qualities do indeed extend incomparably further back than is assumed by historians.'[10] In this respect the bourgeois will prove to be a stubborn template of subjectivity.* The bourgeois depicts itself

* The German term *Bürgerlichkeit*, something like 'bourgeois-ness', describes not only a social economic position but also a lifestyle. The German *Bürger* means both 'citizen' and 'bourgeois', and the double bind of its usage is important for the argument of the book. But, in order to emphasise the origin of this concept in political economy, I mostly use 'bourgeois'. When the relationship to the state is the theme, 'citizen' has been used.

as perennially striving to come to terms with and to make reparations for its historical offenses, as well as to contemplate its privileges, but it fails in the last instance to succeed in the supposed goal of overcoming its injustices. The reason for the discrepancy between honest attempts at self-critique and political blindness is that the subject form of the bourgeois citizen seems incapable of abandoning its self-image as the spearhead of enlightenment. Therefore, the bourgeois subject constantly pursues new delimitations to protect its sovereignty against everything socially and aesthetically alien. The criteria for accepted and discarded social forms, as well as aesthetic ones, is constantly updated and varies on an affective and discursive level. To be valued by the bourgeoisie is no guarantee of fair treatment. This observation is important for recognising the interplay of capitalist, patriarchal and colonial affects in everyday interactions, so as not to take the bourgeoisie at its own word. What is deeply inscribed in the judgement of every bourgeois, as representatives of Western civilisation, is the devaluation of that which does not want to be – or cannot be – part of this form of society. Where bourgeois citizens have been observed for centuries, from close, local proximity and at the same time from a great social distance, these inscriptions become apparent.

Bourgeois existence is built on a history of exclusion. Those who are subjected to it, and the social positions they occupy, form the contrast to this ghostly bourgeois existence. Much about the bourgeois subject and its shadows can be learned from these people and from the conditions they have been forced into. Addressing the position of subjugation as a source of philosophical knowledge involves the task of considering it in all its differentiation. In the places from which bourgeois society separates itself, while remaining materially dependent on them, life takes place next to suffering in ways positively dissimilar to bourgeois life.

One counterpart of bourgeois society is Blackness. The social life of the enslaved represents the starting point for the project of Black studies which examines the functioning of Western civilisation on the one hand, and on the other what can only take place outside of it. From a philosophical perspective, Blackness is opposed to the bourgeois. Blackness, writes Laura Harris, means something more and other than 'African descent':

> By blackness, I do not mean to indicate, or to only indicate, African descent. My understanding of blackness here is informed by the writing of many scholars within black studies who have theorised blackness as that which designates irreducible difference, a mode of being that the modern bourgeois subject, conceived in and by European thought – the sovereign subject who is the model for both citizenship and aesthetic authorship – cannot accommodate.[11]

Blackness is a philosophical as well as practical, musical and affective echo chamber for the social and aesthetic legacy of racially enslaved people. Blackness is the antagonism of bourgeois thought and life, an objection beyond demanding improvement or reform. Blackness does not *only* designate Black people, but also has a conceptual existence as ontological condition, aesthetic principle, historical suffering and form of thought.[12] Its definitions are manifold and dependent on context. Blackness plays a role both as a manifestation of difference and identity, and as a revolutionary principle and method of philosophical thought. Writing about Blackness requires keeping the word available for ever new inscriptions and ensuring that its concrete social and political content, the history of violence that it carries, is not neglected at any point. The individual self is deferred, since slaves were dispossessed of themselves. The negation of self-possession which befell the enslaved is perpetuated in the open form of the communal which Blackness denotes. Blackness makes it possible simultaneously to think a critique of Western civilisation as well as a social life which survives in this society. Therefore, in addition to the critique of the bourgeois, the questions will also be: where can an anti-bourgeois subject be found? Can its emergence be a political and cultural goal? Rather than searching for such a subject, it would be wiser to understand the challenge that Blackness poses to thought and to the white self, as an ample opportunity to fundamentally think about the relationship between subject, object and politics. As Fred Moten sees it: 'the animative materiality – the aesthetic, political, sexual, and racial force – of the ensemble of objects that we might call black performances, black history, blackness, is a real problem and a real chance for the philosophy of human being.'[13]

This 'philosophy of human being' entails a fundamental reflection on subjectivity. When Blackness has one day become a mode of the subject, the human will have changed. It is up to philosophy to make the underpinning philosophical negation of the self, under which the enslaved lived, the starting point of a theory of colonial subjectivity, one able to detach itself from the bourgeois logic and ethics criticised by Fanon. Philosophically, it is necessary to find what stands in the way of realising a condition in which 'blackness registers as life and the Negro as human'.[14]

In order to pursue both the social, philosophical and subject-theoretical question of the connection between bourgeois existence, Blackness and human being, two particular traditions of thought will come together here, as the critical theory of the early Frankfurt School meets, in both content and method, the discipline of Black studies. Philosophical bridges between these specific areas of thought often present themselves, but have not been comprehensively worked through. Moten and Saidiya Hartman develop their theoretical projects with occasional reference to Adorno and Walter Benjamin.[15] Fumi Okiji takes Adorno's racist devaluation of jazz as the starting point for her examination of music's critical capacity. Her work undertakes a generous reading, yet against the grain of Adorno the author.[16] Such an appropriation for the better is perhaps the most productive mode of approaching trustworthy theory which has grown old, and I hope to proceed in a similar fashion.

Beyond theoretical connections, there are biographical events which could have forged a link between the Frankfurt School and the Black radical tradition, but which may have been torpedoed by affective differences. The historian Enzo Traverso reports on an encounter between Adorno and the cultural historian and activist C.L.R. James, author among many other works of a theory of the Haitian Revolution,[17] in New York in the 1940s. On the one hand, Traverso attributes the lack of consequences arising from Adorno and James's meeting to Adorno's theoretical focus on catastrophe and James's optimism regarding the possibility of revolution. On the other, he also sees a 'mental, psychological, and existential difference' dividing the two.[18] The gloomy tone that gripped Adorno's thinking, after the Shoah at the very latest, was disconcerting for James as a theorist of anti-colonial revolution. On Adorno's side, it is above all a cultural arrogance which allows him to consider James's position as of little interest.[19] According to Ruth Sonderegger, this encounter can 'therefore be considered a failed one, since it left behind not the slightest trace in the writings of either of the two critical theorists'.[20] It's also well known that Angela Davis studied in Frankfurt, where she attended the seminars of Adorno and Horkheimer. Following Davis's stay in the German city, Adorno gave her an assessment in which he recommended her as a doctoral candidate at the University of California, San Diego.[21] While Adorno did not live to see Davis achieve fame as a communist revolutionary and abolitionist, she established a still little-understood connection between the first generation of the Frankfurt School and the Black Power movement, which resulted, for example, in a conference entitled 'The Example of Angela Davis'. This took place in Frankfurt in 1972 at the time of the decisive hearing on Davis's imprisonment on terrorism charges in connection with the failed prison break of her brother in 1970.[22] In the USA until her arrest, Davis was a doctoral candidate under Herbert Marcuse, on whom she had a significant political and philosophical influence. She wrote a thesis on the connection between German idealism and the Black liberation struggle. In a letter to Angela Davis which Marcuse wrote during her imprisonment, he recounts how working on the publication of Davis's Frederick Douglass lecture reminded him of what he had learned from Davis and Douglass about the concept of freedom: 'Freedom is not only the goal of liberation, it *begins* with liberation; it is there to be "practiced". This, I confess, I learned from you!'[23]

The 'colonial unconscious'[24] involved in the separation between Black and decolonial movements and the Frankfurt School is itself a site of bourgeois coldness. Bourgeois existence articulates itself here as intellectual authority, which wants to protect itself from intellectual contamination – for example from a supposedly naïve belief in revolution. Adorno's disinterest in the Black radical thinking of James or Davis could be interpreted in this light, demonstrating that critical theory itself is prejudiced by the same coldness it theorises and critiques.

Critical theory is in the process of developing towards a theory critical of racism. Somewhat apart from its clear location within Black studies, the socio-political potential of Adorno's negative dialectics is now often put to the test to conceptualise excluded and ignored political actors as radical voices of the non-identical.[25] However, the history of missed encounters between the Frankfurt School and the intellectuals of the Black radical tradition, in the US and elsewhere, may partially answer the question of why European academic critical theory, even at present, offers no meaningful engagement with the colonial structures of Western civilisation and is only slowly beginning to do so.

In philosophical attempts to contribute to a German-language discourse on racialisation up to the present, what stands out is that social philosophy, a theory of the subject and aesthetics remain so distinct from one another that a critical examination of certain assumptions and methods of critical theory has yet to take place. Critique of racism is integrated into existing disciplinary guidelines of academic philosophy as an additional aspect, without changing the perspective of philosophy as a whole.

In contrast, Adorno's work and the canon of Black studies are invitations to consider the totality. To grasp the pathologies of reason must mean to change Western reason in actuality, to take its alternatives seriously, to leave no stone unturned when it comes to fracturing its catastrophic self-preservation. This book positions itself as a methodological intervention. The consequence of a radical critique of all things bourgeois must be to recognise and respond to the unquestionably bourgeois character of academic philosophy. What does critical theory mean under the assumption of this incompleteness, the end of a self-evident universality?

In a world whose social and systemic damage becomes ever clearer, philosophy is confronted with the task of adapting its claim to universality to the fact that the universal can hardly be grasped anymore.[26] Philosophy should begin by examining its own contribution to this damage, for example in the partly systematic racism of idealist philosophy.[27] Even further, however, new theoretical models must be found to describe the constitutive damage caused by Western colonialism and the particular damage of the present.

'We are incomplete.'[28] For philosophy that means, if Adorno has his way, dealing with infinity without claiming to master it.[29] The diagnosis of the incompleteness of human subjects and the challenge it poses are starting points for reflections on philosophical method.

To want to apprehend infinity once and for all means imposing a systematic pressure on thinking, and thus no longer doing justice to the world in which thinking could unfold in its own specific form. How can we hope for that, when we ourselves are not complete? We are incomplete, but some of us are white and others are not. Whiteness usually means that completeness is claimed where incompleteness prevails. The European sciences and the self-understanding of European subjects operate with the traditional assumption of their own ability to objectively describe the world and themselves within it. This means being able to speak in a way that holds equally true for all. The postulate of incompleteness, which initially lies beyond intellectual understanding, breaks with this assumption. An examination of the bourgeois, which is closely linked to whiteness, is thus perhaps only achievable in the negative: the bourgeois self-image – being able to attain complete knowledge of the world – is taken up in contrast to a way of thinking that observes the disintegration of bourgeois forms, concepts and affects. This book confirms the fragility of bourgeois reality.

Fortunately, there are models for such a method. Adorno as well as Hartman practice such a thinking of negativity. This negativity stems from the effort to philosophically come to terms with the incompleteness of human subjects, as demonstrated in the history of violence that people inflict on one another. The shared basic assumption of Adorno and Hartman, that subjects never actually correspond to what we imagine them to be, inspires the encounter here between the theories of subjectivity from these two very different authors. Adorno's preoccupation with the non-identical, when it encounters the 'scenes of subjection' observed by Hartman,[30] gives occasion to a philosophical investigation of concrete negativity. Subjugation through enslavement is the setting for this.

Deconstructive conceptual work is required to do justice to the encounter between incomplete subjects and philosophical thought. Concepts usually develop in immediate proximity to cultural and political materials. In this sense, this book does not merely diagnose a constellation of affects in the European present, as set forth in Part II, 'The Mediterranean', but is based on a subject model that emerges schematically with Homer's *Odyssey* in Part I, 'The Aegean', and develops its full power in the colonial logics of possession in Part III, 'The Atlantic'. This conceptual enrichment across different scenes leans on Adorno and Horkheimer's *Dialectic of Enlightenment*, which allows concepts to constantly shift in connection with their historical references. In some cases, however, I have allowed myself a greater degree of incompleteness in these conceptual explorations, accumulating meanings which are not always mediated with one another. Thus in the case of the central concept of coldness, the end result is not a position for or against this social technique, rather the unsatisfactory conclusion that the benefits and harms of coldness can only be determined in absolutely singular individual cases. For this reason, I dispense with both a conciliatory resolution in the direction of a better solution (at least theoretically), as well as with moral judgement. Conceptual work which wants to discern its own entanglement in a problematic reality can only work towards the disintegration of its problematic parts.

The damage to which concept formation or deconstruction applies can best be grasped through the self-narratives of the bourgeois subjectivity in question. Bourgeois subjects create an ideal of autonomy to which they themselves best correspond. I pursue this self-narrative to be able to name its basic historical motif (Part I, 'The Aegean'), its reproduction techniques (Part II, 'The Mediterranean'), and its effects of power and violence (Part III, 'The Atlantic'). The aim is to recount a history of subjectivity under colonialism, whose starting point is the bourgeois subject and its entanglement with the material and intellectual establishment of the colonial order.

Back to the opening question of this story: what is the self at sea? The Aegean of Odysseus, who knew no distinction between the oceans of the world; the Mediterranean of the present and its domination by the European Union; the Atlantic of the fifteenth to the nineteenth centuries, which became a mass grave for the kidnapped people of Africa: each gives rise to subjects in a particular way. The Aegean – and the gods – are conquered by Odysseus as returning hero; the Mediterranean divides the present world into European subjects, endowed with human rights, and the 'Others of Europe'[31] who are still denied them; the Atlantic covers millions of corpses whose human subjectivity was obliterated from history as cargo. These three scenes reveal how subjects survive. My thesis is that the bourgeois coldness inherent in the European subject characterises an affective subject position that regulates survival and death in the present.

I

The Aegean

In Max Horkheimer and Theodor W. Adorno's *Dialectic of Enlightenment*, the hero Odysseus is the subject of return. In Homer's epic, Odysseus, who wanders the Mediterranean for ten years with his companions, finally makes it home to Ithaca, where his wife Penelope awaits him. Odysseus saves himself. He survives the sea's many dangers and recounts them in the form of a long adventure – books nine to twelve of Homer's *Odyssey*. Odysseus describes the particular threats in his account to the Phaeacian King Alcinous, who welcomes him when he lands alone on the beach of the island Scheria. Although his report is full of suspense, modern readers can be sure from the outset that Odysseus will reach Ithaca alive because the epic begins at its end, with the gods negotiating his homecoming. It hardly makes for a suspenseful narrative. Odysseus' retelling of his experiences at sea in the *Odyssey* does not follow the principle of a sequence of cliffhangers (although it could). The story unfolds as a flashback, which gives it the weight and grandeur of adventure, fed by the knowledge that Odysseus has successfully mastered all the challenges in his narrative.

Adorno and Horkheimer's examination of the epic – which serves as their dialectical paradigm for the formation of the structure of a European subject, as well as the articulation of the historical principles of myth and enlightenment – makes it more than just one of many examples of their theory. Rather, the special position of Odysseus in *Dialectic of Enlightenment* can be seen as a confrontation with a European founding myth. The figure of Odysseus and the way he is conveyed through the *Odyssey* allows for a critical consideration of the apparently natural existence of self-conscious subjects. The conditions of Odysseus becoming a subject, and his self-understanding, manifest in specific orders of control, sensory experience and narrative technique. From a materialist perspective, the many references that point back to Homer's text are reason enough to revisit this work again in the middle of the twentieth century. But Adorno and Horkheimer return to it for a specific, urgent reason: for them, the constellation that unfolds in the twentieth century – the industrial annihilation of the Jewish people, the belief in the ideals of the eighteenth century, and the preparation (*Zurichtung*) of individuals and their perception of the world under capitalism – is already laid out in the *Odyssey*, without the possibility of concluding a linear development of this constellation in the course of world history. Rather, such a reflection on an old text, treasured across the epochs, is an attempt to expose what is revered by involving the underlying relations of exchange in their assessment of it; and to desacralise Odysseus' celebrated actions as concrete human deeds. Adorno and Horkheimer cast a critical glance at Odysseus' strategic approach (cunning), at his characterisation as a hero, and at his relationship to natural necessities. And also at his actions, which seek to govern nature as a force to be subjugated by man – not least of which is his susceptibility to sensual temptation, also considered 'nature'. At the time of the writing of *Dialectic of Enlightenment*, these aspects combined to form a disturbing observation: the subjugation of nature which Odysseus longed for and eventually achieved is not far removed from a technical domination of the world and its peoples, realised in excesses of violence and oppression, and that all of this is connected to the ideals of the European Enlightenment – freedom through autonomy and self-determination. Suddenly, Horkheimer and Adorno's provocative observation makes the unrestricted progress of reason appear first and foremost as a danger. Because these ideals persist to this day within the European tradition and seem to be untouched at their core, it is worth repeating Adorno and Horkheimer's revealing reading. Honouring the heroic achievements of individuals is just as much a symptom of ideologies of progress as is the European isolation from those on the opposite side of the Mediterranean, those deemed 'less civilised than us'.

While there is still an unrestricted validity to Adorno and Horkheimer's analysis and critique of the concepts of myth and enlightenment in service of countering the all too unanimous affirmation of the Enlightenment, this critique has yet to be translated into social practice. Reflection on a specific idea of self-determination – one mostly associated with secularism and material independence through personal capitalist value creation, and called upon as a primary emancipatory means and aim – also indicates that the ideal subject of the Enlightenment still dominates the imagination. Adorno and Horkheimer have critiqued such ideas of the individual and society in many places.[1] Feminist discourse has also contributed important arguments in analysing the entanglements of modern subjectivity and capitalism. The inclusion of reproductive labour in economic critique,[2] as well as the postcolonial critique of universal notions of emancipation,[3] are but two of many aspects demonstrating that Adorno and Horkheimer's points of departure have since been updated and differentiated. This also diminishes the idea of a so-called primary contradiction – exploitation in capitalism as the principal source of social injustice, the elimination of which would also overcome all other relations of oppression. The dialectic of Enlightenment must be analysed multifactorially in the present in order to theoretically accompany the complexity of emancipatory struggles.

A brief glance at some motifs in the *Odyssey* which remain underexposed in Adorno and Horkheimer demonstrates changes in critical discourse directly in the material. This concerns, for example, the position of Odysseus' rowing – thus subservient – companions, as well as the description of sirens as the 'irresistible' force of feminine seduction. Both images call for differentiated analyses of power that cannot be reduced to identifying logics of exchange. What part does the crew play in Odysseus' survival, and what is their relationship to him? How does the description of the siren song as 'irresistible' construct an equation of femininity and nature, thereby drawing on a motif popular for centuries, which denies rationality to women and thereby justifies their oppression?

Re-reading *Dialectic of Enlightenment*, and focusing on how its authors[4] tell the story of Odysseus as a process of subject formation, productively links the epic and Adorno and Horkheimer's reflections with contemporary philosophical questions of subjectivity. In doing so, the fundamental problematic of bourgeois subjectivity is brought up-to-date – or, rather, bourgeois subjectivity is still intelligible *as* a fundamental problem in the present.

1 The Self

The self represents rational universality against the inevitability of fate. —Theodor W. Adorno and Max Horkheimer[1]

Odysseus' Wish

On Odysseus' return from the underworld, the sorceress Circe warns him of the dangers that lie ahead on his journey: the sirens, whose tantalising song no one can resist and on whose island 'great heaps of men, flesh rotting from their bones'[2] suggests the fate of prior sailors; the wandering rocks that were only successfully traversed by the 'famous *Argo*';[3] and Scylla and Charybdis, the monsters living in the rocks, one of whom uses its twelve legs, six heads and three rows of teeth to snatch sailors from their vessels, while the other swallows the water between the rocks, along with the ships sailing upon it, three times a day. Finally, Circe warns Odysseus not to slaughter and eat the cattle of the sun god Helios that graze on the island of Thrinacia. She prophesies that even if Odysseus survives, he will return home 'late and humiliated' and will be responsible for the death of all his men.[4] Circe concludes her instructions as dawn breaks, and, after a sleepless night, Odysseus wakes his crew to set off. As the ship is prepared to journey onwards, he shares Circe's guidance for the isle of the sirens with his crew so that they all can 'die with the truth, or escape'.[5] Circe has advised him to plug the men's ears with wax to evade the allure of song. If he, Odysseus, wishes to hear the song,[6] he should let his men tie him to the mast – and the more he begs them to free him, the tighter they should bind him. As he addresses his crew,

Odysseus makes no mention of his wish to hear the siren song; instead he makes Circe the advocate of this method: 'she says / that I alone should hear their singing.'[7] Their journey begins with a favourable wind, but as the ship approaches the island, they suddenly find themselves in a doldrum. The men take in the sails and sit at their oars. Odysseus prepares the wax, which quickly softens with the help of the sun, and stuffs it into the crew's ears. Finally, the men use ropes to tie their commander to the mast and row towards the island. The singing begins. The sirens claim in their song to 'know / whatever happens anywhere on earth' as they flatter Odysseus and invite him towards them.[8] As Circe has presaged, Odysseus asks his companions to free him with a nod of his head.[9] But they are prepared, and Eurylochos and Perimedes bind him tighter. When he can no longer hear the song, Odysseus gives the all-clear signal.[10] The wax is removed from their ears and the ropes are untied.

Renunciation: The Detached Spirit

For Adorno and Horkheimer, the scene on the isle of the sirens is decisive in recounting 'the history of renunciation', which in their eyes is 'the history of civilisation'. Renunciation corresponds to sacrificing a form of experience: 'All who renounce give away more of their life than is given back to them, more than the life they preserve.'[11] Adorno and Horkheimer explain how Odysseus succeeds in cunningly satisfying the gods through renunciation and nevertheless escaping the mythical destiny of his death. But this 'more' which he renounces will prove to be a successful investment in the end. As a precursor of the bourgeois subject, Odysseus gains surplus value through renunciation, the denial of a certain experience – and even more *in* the act of denial. Through his technique for listening to the siren song without needing to pursue it, Odysseus becomes someone else: he 'throws himself away, so to speak, in order to win himself'.[12]

Renunciation completes the contradiction of the mastery of nature. *Renouncing* the experience of the siren song, rather than undergoing it, takes place in the name of survival. At the same time, this is precisely where Adorno and Horkheimer see a compromised life. Avoiding the experience corresponds to a diminution of life in the name of prolonging it, thereby collapsing the distinction between means and ends. What is sacrificed in favour of what? Life for life?

Perhaps Adorno and Horkheimer are drawing too hasty a conclusion when they conceive of life as a substance that encompasses both self-preservation and sacrifice. In the case of Odysseus, a conceptual differentiation could be made between *survival* as an end and the renunciation of life as a means. The interpretation of the siren scene will make it clear why. Odysseus retells Circe's advice and the instruction of his companions:

> Then with an anxious heart I told the crew,
> 'My friends, the revelations Circe shared
> with me should not be kept a secret, known
> to me alone. I will share them with you,
> and we can die in knowledge of the truth,
> or else escape. She said we must avoid
> the voices of the otherworldly Sirens;
> steer past their flowering meadow. And she says
> that I alone should hear their singing. Bind me,
> to keep me upright at the mast, wound round
> with rope. If I beseech you and command you
> to set me free, you must increase my bonds
> and chain me even tighter.'[13]

His crew, like us, only experiences Circe's advice through Odysseus' account, and therefore cannot be entirely certain that Odysseus isn't passing off his own cunning as Circe's to gain their trust. A decisive and enigmatic point in this strategy is that Odysseus alone should be bound to the mast and listen to the sirens, while his crew manoeuvres the ship past the island with wax in their ears. In his account to his crew Odysseus transforms Circe's advice – that he can choose this path if he *wishes* – into something he *should* do.[14] In this respect, his men must assume that Circe has good reason for thinking Odysseus should be tied to the mast to save himself and the others. Odysseus' part in the actual survival strategy is thus generally passive, aside from the order to adopt this tactic. Once again it becomes clear that physical mastery or willing evasion are not even considered possibilities. The myth leaves no doubt about the impossibility of passing the isle of the sirens. What's more, the commander's capacity to act must be further constrained in order to outsmart the gods or Nature. No other path but the sensory refusal to perceive the siren song would allow the crew to survive. So why may – or must – the protagonist of the story experience the siren song and not, likewise rowing, actively defy the danger with wax in his ears?

In this constellation, Adorno and Horkheimer see the concession, fundamental to cunning, of remaining a slave to nature. Even in his escape, Odysseus conveys such an image to the mythical forces: that they have a hold on him. He 'acknowledges the archaic supremacy of the song by having himself bound' so strongly that through total immobility he protects himself from falling prey to it.[15] To isolate himself from the siren song, not only physically but also sonorously, would predetermine the struggle's outcome and not grant the gods the power to intervene, even theoretically. Odysseus performs a symbolic exchange: *I give this to you all: my suffering, my cry on the mast as a sign of your power to save me and save our ship*. In this way, the gods can be sure of their power on the basis of the hero's obvious difficulty in steering the course.

Odysseus does not escape the sirens by evading their field of force. He 'does not try to steer a different course to the one past the Sirens' island. Nor does he try to insist on the superiority of his knowledge and listen freely to the temptress, believing his freedom protection enough'.[16] He does not avoid the confrontation: in mythical legality, that would be impossible. Instead, he concedes to the mythical forces, i.e. Nature, the power they exert over him. He escapes not by rebelling, but by ducking away: 'He cowers, the ship takes its preordained, fateful course, and he realises that however he may consciously distance himself from nature, as a listener [*Hörender*] he remains under its spell.'[17]

Odysseus minimises his presence to avoid danger and sail past the island 'inconspicuously'. Yet this renunciation of open conflict is revealing. Since Odysseus does not cower out of humility: he 'throws himself away . . . in order to win himself'.[18] He follows all the rules of the mythical order and uses a 'loophole in the agreement'[19] to escape the consequences of this order. However, the contract on human destiny, governed by myth, remains intact *because* Odysseus surrenders to it. The gods get what they want because the myth remains intact. But what does Odysseus gain in the process of simultaneously complying with and subverting the contract? What surplus value does renunciation generate for him?

Experience and Surplus Value

Odysseus divides his self into a part that acknowledges the mythical power acting on him and another that already knows he will escape its coercion. In the middle of this division, which enables a distanced observation of one's own self, a renunciation takes place. Adorno and Horkheimer conceive this as a longing, a desire pressing from afar, but which only preserves as an image the actual danger emanating from the lure: 'the Sirens have a life of their own, but in this bourgeois prehistory it has already been neutralised as the yearning of those who pass it by.'[20] Thus Odysseus can undergo the sensorial experience without perishing.

Adorno and Horkheimer are interested in the proto-economic structure of Odysseus' behaviour. The risks he takes follow a calculation of stake and profit, of risk and surplus value, which no longer appears mythical in modern capitalism, but profane:

> The lone voyager armed with cunning is already *Homo oeconomicus*, whom all reasonable people will one day resemble:

> for this reason the *Odyssey* is already a Robinsonade. Both these prototypical shipwrecked sailors make their weakness – that of the individual who breaks away from the collective – their social strength. Abandoned to the vagaries of the waves, helplessly cut off, they are forced by their isolation into a ruthless pursuit of their atomistic interest. They embody the principle of the capitalist economy even before they make use of any worker; but the salvaged goods they bring with them to the new venture idealise the truth that the entrepreneur has always entered the competition armed with more than the industry of his hands.[21]

The authors explain Odysseus' ruthlessness towards his companions, discussed above, with an entrepreneurial stabilisation of his own survival and profit.

How does Odysseus' entrepreneurial conduct manifest itself, and what affective and aesthetic factors characterise it, apart from the logic of exchange? His actions seem to be driven more by a thirst for adventure than by altruism, exemplified by his sensory surrender to the siren song. For although Odysseus recognises the power of the gods while passing by the sirens and skilfully circumvents it, listening also grants him a desirable climax of experience. Odysseus displays a certain sense of security on the day when he pursues his curiosity at great risk, rather than taking the shortest route to avert danger. Adorno and Horkheimer observe that Odysseus' adventures deflect 'the self from the path of its logic' and that he thus appears 'like a novice incapable of learning – sometimes, indeed, out of foolish curiosity'.[22] After decades of postponing his return home, Odysseus risks a great deal for this extraordinary experience. A glance at the text makes it clear how reckless Odysseus can be.[23] Odysseus is not only risk-seeking when it comes to his own safety, but he is also repeatedly accosted by his crew for endangering them all.

It is the moment of renunciation that makes the risk sensorially worthwhile for Odysseus. This moment opens up a realm of experience that allows him to become intoxicated by danger with the aid of a technically created distance. It is no longer an existential, physical risk that Odysseus takes, rather a skilful bargain with the gods. Bound to the mast, he gains an uncomfortable yet intense aesthetic experience for his efforts.

In order for Odysseus to indulge in the song in safety, certain measures are necessary. Odysseus gives a chain to his crew, who work under him, so that they can bind him to the mast, and uphold his bourgeois ego. He would like to experience the song, to have experienced *everything*, to have gone to the extreme, without having to bear the consequences of this extremity – ruin. Adorno and Horkheimer describe this as a dialectic between self-preservation and daring, which results in a knowing, reckless self:

> 'But where danger threatens / That which saves from it also grows' [Höderlin]: the knowledge which makes up his identity and enables him to survive has its substance in the experience of diversity, distraction, disintegration; the knowing survivor is also the man who exposes himself most daringly to the threat of death, thus gaining the hardness and the strength to live.[24]

Odysseus enters into a calculation that allows him to appear as a hero of renunciation – 'as the implacable judge, avenging the heritage of the very powers he has escaped'.[25] He also secures a surplus value far more private and invisible: his pleasure is his gain, a dividend from the risk, one he 'earns' through his ruse.

But if survival is the goal of the *Odyssey*, nothing requires him to hear the siren song. These two instances of danger are the result of his decision 'to throw himself away in order to gain himself'. His risk here is the surplus value of his adventure: an opportunity presents itself for an experience with himself, one he does not want to miss. But nothing of this hazard is practically conducive to the goal of returning home. Rather, homecoming is delayed, recklessly jeopardised, receding further and further into the distance.

Besides, Odysseus is not travelling alone. A steadily shrinking number of crew members travel with him under his command, performing the physical portion of the effort required to overcome various dangers. They row. They have already been understood as the proletariat of the *Odyssey*, who in 'the primal scene of the division of labour'[26] lay the groundwork for the capitalist Odysseus to maximise profit, and who fall victim to him time and again.[27] Their sensorial experience of odyssey differs essentially from that of Odysseus and suggests a profound division into two subjectivities on the very same ship. Odysseus' rescue is only possible because his shipmates join forces to hold the 'fateful course'[28] that passes by the isle of the sirens. The sensorial orientation of the rowers is sacrificed by the wax in their ears in favour of the survival of all – and it is at the same time exploited by Odysseus, who uses the opportunity to dedicate himself passively to the song. Making use of the crew and their labour power is routinely taken for granted in the *Odyssey*. As will now become clear, this labour power is also the condition of Odysseus' aesthetic experience on the mast.[29] The fact that the crew cannot themselves listen begs the question of the consequences of sensory deprivation, whereas for Odysseus, in contrast, the siren song establishes his identity. His crew members do not have the option of defying the siren song independently, let alone considering themselves safe enough to listen to it.

Excursus: Erfahrung/Erleben

The crew's work and their deafness, as well as Odysseus' elevated position on the mast, allow him to have a bourgeois experience. Odysseus can direct his full attention to the song while his body, temporarily immobilised by ropes, persists in absolute abandon, but at the same time at a safe distance.[30] The constellation described here makes for an aesthetic experience *par excellence*.

This means that aesthetic experiences, as depicted in German aesthetic theory of the twentieth century,[31] are dependent on resources – work – which they do not provide. Aesthetic experience is bourgeois experience, because the capitalist division of labour provides the sensuous foundation for its realisation.

The concept of bourgeois experience is intended to express that the hierarchisation of those who must row and those who get to listen is not limited to subjugation through labour relations. Instead, this 'distribution of the sensible'[32] concerns the differently distributed possibilities of sensorially participating in the world. And it concerns the observation that an undisturbed enjoyment of temptation *without* the threat of death is only available to a single subject in this constellation, namely Odysseus. The consequences of this difference, not treated by Horkheimer and Adorno, can be sharpened with the aid of Walter Benjamin's distinction between two kinds of experience: *Erfahrung* and *Erleben*. *Erfahrung* stands for an essential element of bourgeois subjectivity; *Erleben* for an element of sensuous disorientation. While these terms both mean 'experience' in English, in German, *Erfahren* also means acquiring knowledge, while *Erleben* is focused on the immediate perceptive and affective experience of an event. Benjamin explores the difference even beyond that.

The distinction between *Erfahrung* and *Erleben* illuminates Odysseus' situation in contrast to his crew's, as I will show in what follows. In addition to the class analysis, the concrete position of the people on the ship is of interest: while Odysseus oversees everything while bound to the mast, his crew sits below him and rows. A vase painting from the fifth century BCE represents the moment Odysseus encounters the sirens (see fig. 1). It provides an examination of those sensory aspects of the people on the ship that do not implicitly arise from Odysseus' first-person narrative. The vase shows the ship, the crew and Odysseus in profile, and the sirens as bird-like creatures with human heads flying around the ship or sitting on rocks.

Fig. 1: 'The Siren Vase' (470–430 BCE), British Museum

Here, Odysseus' position on the mast gives him an unobstructed view. Facing backwards, he not only oversees the ship and his working companions, but must also have a clear view as far as the isle of the sirens, provided they pass at an appropriate distance. He is drawn in an unusually exposed position – his gaze is directed upwards and his head is placed higher than any other person's in the image. His sense of sight and hearing are fully focused on the other side of the ship. He seems almost detached from the activity at his feet. His attention hovers over the heads of those who ensure his survival – in this respect, nothing obstructs his enjoyment of the siren song.

His crew, on the other hand, sit much lower and only barely look over the edge of the ship, their view restricted by the rowing shoulders of the person in front. The physical labour of rowing requires the entire upper body to move backwards and forwards, which makes it difficult to deliberately orient oneself in one's surroundings. Furthermore, we know they cannot hear anything. The sensory deprivation in which Odysseus' men ply their oars is significant here. While Odysseus looks, listens and indulges himself at the mast, the oarsmen find themselves in a struggle for survival whose strategy they have not themselves chosen. The crew are relegated to their function and are not able to experience the passage of the isle of the sirens other than as rowing bodies with limited sensory faculties. None of them shares in the journey's decision-making or reflection. Every chance to act as subjects has been taken from them in advance. In this scene of subject-making, a gulf opens between the deaf, rowing crew and Odysseus.

Benjamin's distinction between *Erleben* and *Erfahrung* demonstrates that perception does not automatically constitute meaning. Benjamin describes the mode of *Erleben* as a series of shocks which stand side by side unconnected. They also play a role in Sigmund Freud's trauma theory.[33] On the other hand, *Erfahrung* is closely linked to the ability to narrate and to thus arrange sensations into chains of meaning.

In this context, Benjamin deals with how Henri Bergson's *mémoire involontaire* (involuntary recollection) is constituted: that which has been 'experienced [*erlebt*] explicitly and consciously'[34] can never become part of this involuntary memory. Benjamin refers to Freud to note that that the function of consciousness is to banish memories with harmful content by way of a protective shield. Consciousness forms a barrier to protect the inner circulation of thoughts and feelings from external interruptions or shocks. At the same time, consciousness can be trained to confront these external disturbances. The more often consciousness is exposed to shocks, the more blunted it becomes, and the less susceptible to traumatisation. Benjamin now asks himself about the specific conditionality of shock and the protective shield and mechanisms of defence in the nineteenth century and states, with Paul Valéry, that *Erfahrung* fundamentally takes place in the mode of surprise.[35] Memory is therefore always already the attempt to give these surprises a character, on the basis of which they can subsequently become part of an order. In this way, shocks are absorbed and appear less threatening. However, this process only functions if the event in question is immediately 'incorporated directly in the register of conscious memory',[36] thus putting a stop to its chaotic, energetic unfolding. 'Wakeful consciousness'[37] mitigates the danger that excessive sensory input poses for consciousness. The content of the *Erlebnis* is not rejected, rather its traumatising effect. It is then a question of an event without trauma, of controlling experience through order. Here, the *Erlebnis* can be differentiated from the *Erfahrung*: while an *Erfahrung* remains dependent on the subconscious sedimentation of sensory impressions, an *Erlebnis* is constituted through the conscious control of an influx into consciousness: 'That the shock is thus cushioned, parried by consciousness, would lend the incident that occasions it the character of an isolated experience [*Erlebnis*], in the strict sense.'[38]

Erlebnis is thus a category of experience that never becomes a generic, rich *Erfahrung*, but remains in the stage of a controlled, partly blocked shock and the mere accumulation of sensory impressions. Contrary to intuition, however, this does not then mean that the *Erlebnis* does not come to consciousness. On the contrary, it becomes a part of consciousness in a very specific, sensorially reduced way, so that it can be controlled from the outset.

For Benjamin, this statement raises the question of how lyric poetry, which lives off unconscious deposits of unverbalised events, can exist in this mode of experience, 'for which exposure to shock [*Schockerlebnis*] has become the norm'.[39] For Benjamin, the fact that external events suddenly enter into consciousness in a controlled manner, and reality thus becomes transparent, does not correspond to an enrichment, but rather to an *impoverishment* of experience. Precisely because the sensory apparatus now allows for images which have usually been filtered through the protective shield, it is likely that these images do not entirely reach consciousness – not in complete resolution, so to speak. 'Perhaps the special achievement of shock defense is the way it assigns an incident a precise point in time in consciousness, at the cost of the integrity of the incident's contents.'[40]

The dimension of the moment of shock and the active protective shield determine above all the form in which an event reaches consciousness. Benjamin establishes the following equation: the more that shock occurs and defence is mobilised, the less the event becomes *Erfahrung* and the more it remains *Erlebnis*.[41] In Benjamin's analysis of Charles Baudelaire, *Erfahrung* and *Erlebnis* almost develop into sensory categories of different gradation. While *Erlebnis* denotes the residual event after successful shock defence, *Erfahrung* appears to be a temporally and sensorily multidimensional category which transcends the level of conscious experience.

Benjamin's distinction pertains to Odysseus and his men as subjects of *Erfahrung* vs *Erleben*. The shock defence, which prevents the sedimentation of events on all levels of consciousness, materialises as wax in the crew's ears. In this sense, the isle of the sirens passes them by as *Erlebnis* which they only witness, caught in glimpses between oar strokes. And Odysseus' dangerous yet implicitly aesthetic experience on the mast enables a richness of *Erfahrung*, and therefore, a remarkable experience. The shock defence is forced upon the crew. They are left with a chain of shocks, fragmentary, not poetically usable. Odysseus, on the other hand, takes precautions to ensure that as little as possible escapes him. The tale is spun high up on the mast as proof of the experience from which it draws.

Poverty of Experience

Walter Benjamin thematises the 'atrophy' or 'impoverishment' of experience at various points in his fragmented oeuvre – partly as a social diagnosis of modernity, partly as a theory of media.[42] However, he does not imply cultural pessimism with this impoverishment, but devotes himself to the phenomenon out of interest in the new. Scenes of impoverishment are those aspects of reality which are characterised by industrialisation in the nineteenth century and which change the human capacity for experience. This can be observed in the development of human communication: *information* and *sensation* can be differentiated from *narrative* as the oldest form of communication;

both streamline the communication process and aim to emphasise the essential.[43]

What is Benjamin trying to express with his diagnosis of impoverishment other than his regret about the sensory consequences of industrialisation?

> No, this much is clear: experience has fallen in value, amid a generation which from 1914 to 1918 had to experience some of the most monstrous events in the history of the world. Perhaps this is less remarkable than it appears. Wasn't it noticed at the time how many people returned from the front in silence? Not richer but poorer in communicable experience? And what poured out from the flood of war books ten years later was anything but the experience that passes from mouth to ear. No, there was nothing remarkable about that. For never has experience been contradicted more thoroughly: strategic experience has been contravened by positional warfare; economic experience, by the inflation; physical experience, by hunger; moral experiences, by the ruling powers. A generation that had gone to school in horse-drawn streetcars now stood in the open air, amid a landscape in which nothing was the same except the clouds and, at its center, in a force field of destructive torrents and explosions, the tiny, fragile human body.[44]

Benjamin describes the experiences of alienation which inevitably gripped those made to fight in the First World War. In the discrepancy between the known world of the 'horse-drawn streetcar' and the new and gruesome world of mechanised trench warfare, where a human body – one's own human body – appears absurd and small, *Erfahrung* is impoverished because there is no testimony to be gleaned from it. At this point, it once again becomes clear that Benjamin's concept of experience functions qualitatively. According to Benjamin, *Erfahrung* is not a simple co-presence with events, rather *Erfahrung* describes a particular mode of affective and narrative processing of these events. The First World War marks the point of departure for his diagnosis of impoverishment because the contrast between the event's dimension and an (in)ability to process becomes particularly clear.

Of course, the experiences of Odysseus and his companions 2,800 years after the emergence of the epic can hardly be classified as such. Benjamin's qualitative phenomenology merely provides an element to demarcate Odysseus' rich, bourgeois perspective of *Erfahrung* from the restricted and curtailed one of his companions. All of this follows the intention to better understand the formation of a *Self* – a bourgeois or non-bourgeois self – starting from the sensory experience of both sides. The deafness of the crew connotes a deprivation of their experiential depth, generated not through excessive sensory demand and the protective shield of the psyche, but prophylactically through technical aids (wax in the ears). Odysseus, on the other hand, offers his body so that the experience can sink into all of his pores and seize him with all its might so as to become part of his *mémoire involontaire*. In Odysseus' narrative to Alcinous – books nine to twelve in the *Odyssey* – one can recognise just *how* rich his *Erfahrung* is. After such an experience, Odysseus knows who he has become. He has won himself over.

And what about those who are poor in experience? Benjamin strikes an almost solemn tone, proclaiming the potential of poverty in constantly seeking new beginnings:

> This poverty of experience is not merely poverty on the personal level, but poverty of human experience in general. Hence, a new kind of barbarism.
>
> Barbarism? Yes, indeed. We say this in order to introduce a new, positive concept of barbarism. For what does poverty of experience do for the barbarian? It forces him to start from scratch; to make a new start; to make a little go a long way; to begin with a little and build up further, looking neither left nor right.[45]

The constant fresh start, with a view straight ahead, once again highlights the position of the crew. Their poverty of experience is evident not only in the little they can report from the isle of the sirens – unlike Odysseus. This *Erleben* is not characterised by a coherent sequence, but a *perpetual* new beginning. Benjamin's words also recall the ultimate theme of the *Odyssey*: survival. Barbarism, 'to start from scratch', means that every stroke of the oar is, on the one hand, a new beginning and an existential impulse, and, on the other, is the constant repetition of an unchanging work task – the only possible one. In the case of the crew, the beginning is new only insofar as the sea they encounter is constantly changing. As Benjamin observes, 'This process of continually starting all over again is the regulative idea of gambling, as it is of work for wages'.[46] The social position of the crew is also determined through the mode of their activity and not only through the command structure. If every working day is the same and is necessary to reproduce one's life, which is mediated by wages, then every working day is a fresh start within a logic that refuses change. Nevertheless, Benjamin emphatically stresses the new beginning as a space of possibility: the aforementioned restriction to the bare necessities contains forces that may ultimately be conducive to liberation 'looking neither left nor right'.

2 Homecoming

When the *Odyssey*'s narrative begins, Odysseus is already home. In retrospect, this fictitious circumstance seems like a trick of the narrator's or a betrayal of the reader, who readily lends the rescued man her sympathy. One can perhaps lose sight of the safety in which the narrative unfolds, or completely forget it in favour of the suspense, the thrill. But can it really be forgotten? Doesn't it – as *Erfahrung* – lodge itself deep in the unconscious and congeal into a prerequisite for the narrator to find his voice? The beginning of Homer's epic, quoted above in a different context, refers to this dynamic – struggle for survival, sacrifice, narration and homecoming – in that the narrative voice delivers a concise summary of the twenty-four books that follow.[1]

Escape

Odysseus is introduced as an adventurer, whose goal is to return home with his crew – and whose mission fails due to his crew's stupidity. The Hellenist Douglas Frame defines 'the gradual loss of companions'[2] as the dramaturgical principle of the *Odyssey*, at the end of which Odysseus reaches Ithaca as the lone escapee. For the classicist Emily Wilson likewise, the sacrificial relationship between Odysseus and his crew is central to the heroic story. In it, a categorical separation is manifest between Odysseus, the hero and leader of the journey, and the crew as an accompanying, indeterminate group. If the loss of the crew's lives structures the dramaturgy of the narrative, then Odysseus' survival – his escape – forms its vanishing point. This word expresses a fitting attribute of Odysseus' character. He has *escaped*, which means, he eludes lethal dangers in improbable ways, over and over, and finally eludes responsibility for the loss of his crew members. The word 'escape' (*Entrinnen*) also plays an important role in the work of Max Horkheimer and Theodor W. Adorno. There are indications of what *Dialectic of Enlightenment*'s authors find interesting in Odysseus' tale: 'Homeland is a state of having escaped.'[3] And escape is the verb the authors use to describe surviving the mass murder of the Shoah. In Horkheimer's notes, there is an entry entitled 'The One Who Escapes' (*Der Entronnene*). In this short text, Horkheimer speaks about his Jewishness in the face of the mass murders in concentration and extermination camps, as well as the 'Final Solution', which for all Jews was *intended for them*. Only fortunate circumstances allowed Horkheimer to be spared from the systemically planned annihilation, and out of this narrow, improbable and accidental escape, a survivor's guilt emerged:

> People like me, not just generally speaking, but specifically, i.e. Jews, who looked and thought like Jews, like my father and mother and myself, for no other reason than that they had these characteristics, were slowly tortured to death in concentration camps, thousandfold, after years of unspeakable humiliations, overwhelming fear, injuries, blows and insults . . . I'm supposed to feel satisfaction and peace of mind in my own life, considering that I exist at all, that this life is the consequence of a meaningless and undeserved happenstance, the product of the blindness which life produces, to the point that I feel ashamed to be amongst the living at all?[4]

In *Negative Dialectics*, Adorno speaks similarly – and more drastically – about escaping mass extermination, an escape which, because it is only due to chance, calls into question the right to life in general. Furthermore, survival in the future is not only filled with shame towards the dead, but also with 'drastic guilt'.[5] Under the subheading 'After Auschwitz', Adorno diagnoses an irrevocable consequence for death in general through the incomprehensible profaning of death through mass extermination.[6]

'Their continued existence already necessitates the coldness, of the basic principle of capitalist subjectivity, without which Auschwitz would not have been possible: the drastic guilt of the spared.'[7] Adorno goes to the theoretical extreme here: guilt is no longer a consequence of individual decisions or actions that abet injustice, but the individual's *wrongful* survival of the catastrophe, a charge he also brings upon himself. Auschwitz is a metaphysical intervention in the self-evident nature of life on Earth, because mass extermination has deformed death into the self-evident. Coldness is the means to endure this reality.

The corresponding implication formulates an absurdity, if a theoretically correct one: life itself becomes an offense to the fact that death should have affected everyone. In what is possibly the darkest passage in his oeuvre, Adorno points to the deep structure of the term 'escape'. To escape means to survive in defiance of fate – i.e. myth or the laws of nature, the gods and the sea – and to make it home. In the case of Auschwitz, this is made possible by chance; in the case of Odysseus, by cunning. The one who escapes must grow cold in order to form the horror of his experience into a narrative. This perspective collapses any idealistic conception of history. In his reflection on the extermination of European Jews, Adorno insists that the decisive level of meaning arises from the unpredictable and the unsystematic, and that the improbability of individual escape is the only occasion for hope.

The concept of escape expresses the fact that the threshold between life and death has almost been crossed once, and that life has lost its self-evidence as a result. In this sense, the sentence 'Homeland is a state of having escaped' also contains the hope that after survival something like a homeland will be constituted, which will make bearable the aftershock of the threat. The experience of exile, in which Adorno and Horkheimer found themselves while writing *Dialectic of Enlightenment*, adds a biographical yet already theoretically mediated aspect to their conceptual examination of Odysseus' homecoming. The paradox of escape is the knowledge that it really should have turned out differently.

But escape is not just the survival of certain death. In the spirit of the negative, a utopia – at least structurally – can be derived from the potential of this flight. To be sure, the burden of history is almost impossible to overcome psychologically, is almost impossible to live with affectively, but the fact of having escaped a system and its constraints is good news for Adorno, the thinker of the negative. Escape serves as a hopeful motif. Thus there is 'humaneness having escaped the curse',[8] an escape from 'the constraints of self-preservation'[9] and, finally, a 'Utopia of being escaped'.[10] All of these motifs provide the exception to the systematic, capitalistic course of things: a moment of hope – on which nothing, however, can be built. Only the historical meaning of escape, the sheer fact *that* it happened, maintains the subjective belief in the possibility of the better in Adorno's perspective.[11]

In addition, after this structural definition, a substantive look at the motif of 'being escaped' (*Entronnensein*) is appropriate. Despite the word's negative colouring, no one escapes into nothingness. In other words, the *Homeland* of escape has a distinct form. Odysseus' escape is no mere getaway but an arrival – home, to Ithaca, to Penelope and Telemachus. And Horkheimer and Adorno return in 1949 and 1953 respectively to a destroyed Germany, more precisely to Frankfurt am Main, which remains, in spite of everything, the scene of their happy childhoods and their linguistic and cultural homeland.[12]

Frame demonstrates a connection that philologically inscribes the return home into the thinking with which Odysseus is repeatedly identified in the epic. This connection concerns the two Greek words *nóos* (spirit) and *néomai* (homecoming): Frame displays the common linguistic root of these two expressions. Thus the figure of Odysseus embodies an interplay of homeland and prudence (*Klugheit*), pointing to the close connection of both categories in the world of Homer. Odysseus 'is what he does,' as Wilson puts it: his self *is* the return home. Because Odysseus makes his return *through* his intelligence, Frame assumes that the epic is conceived around the motifs of homecoming and cunning.[13] This philological bridge joins Odysseus' subjectivation at sea with his homecoming: cunning is the means of return. The techniques of cunning and its modes of experience make Odysseus who he is. He throws himself away to gain himself, acts to his own advantage and at the same time in favour of his self-narrative. Adorno and Horkheimer see in him the proto-bourgeois capitalist subject, who makes use of enlightenment as it helps him to conquer nature and appropriate its powers. Meanwhile, Odysseus succeeds in finding sensual pleasure and thus makes his return not only as a victor, but also as a bourgeois.

II

The Mediterranean

We chose with no route the sea and the boats of death, in the middle of the annoyed sea, we stick to hope of dignified life in the north. We thought that when we cross the aggressive waters of the Mediterranean we will land on the 'promised land' which will save everyone's life. We did not know that we would face the monster of the laws, cement and bureaucracy.
—Statement by the Executive Committee of Sudanese Refugees, Ickerweg, 2017[1]

Odysseus could not yet have known that the sea he was travelling on comprised just a very small portion of the world. Today, the Mediterranean divides Europe from Africa and the Middle East. It represents more than ever a kind of moat around Europe, and is tightly bound up with stories of flight. In what follows, the view of the sea shifts to the effect that its position as nature – in and against which a hero, Odysseus, is born – is replaced with the image of a transit zone that harbours and generates suffering. This does not mean, however, that the Mediterranean no longer brings forth heroes. The narrative form of the hero's tale may have changed, but the form in which subjectification takes place in relation to the sea bears similarities to events in the *Odyssey*. Racialisation and class differences separate both the hero of the epic from other actors in the *Odyssey*, as it does modern European subjects from refugees at the mercy of the sea. But twenty-first century heroes of the sea do not fight the power of the gods; they fight the European Union.

The organisation Sea-Watch e.V. has been fighting against the EU's policy of disallowing and criminalising sea rescue for years. Sea-Watch activists, along with those of other NGOs, try to compensate for the state's inaction by increasing their own fleet of rescue boats, crews and reconnaissance aircrafts. They rescue people who fall into distress at sea while trying to cross the Mediterranean to Europe, denied the help which EU law prescribes. The initiative is an extremely difficult undertaking due to docking bans in the ports of Italy, Malta, Greece and Spain. The recurring scenario in which rescue boats are refused permission to dock in the Mediterranean is a testament to Europe's resolute and brutal border policy.

In June 2019, the Sea-Watch captain Carola Rackete created a political stage for this practice by arriving in the port of Lampedusa on the ship *Sea-Watch 3* without permission to dock. At the time, the ship was carrying fifty-three rescued people in need of urgent medical attention. After days of negotiation, and due to the acute deterioration of the condition of several passengers on board, Rackete eventually defied the Italian authorities' ban and steered the ship into port.[2]

The monolithic racism of European political institutions, and the subjects who belong to them, constitutes and secures the borders between Europe, Africa and the Middle East. Following Paul Gilroy, I will refer to this political complex as the 'Black Mediterranean'.[3] At the same time, a closer look at the scene surrounding Rackete reveals the moral outrage at the Italian interior minister Matteo Salvini's cold conduct, which suddenly stood for all to see, impossible to overlook: as a field of bourgeois self-assurance, which the political theorist Ida Danewid sees resting on assumptions of bourgeois innocence.[4] Bourgeois coldness can be understood as an affective dynamic which celebrates moral acts, while leaving intact the logic of subjectivation that co-produces the suffering which was briefly interrupted by Rackete's intervention.

I would like to consider the scenes of failed sea rescue as a starting point to fundamentally illuminate the entanglements between European bourgeois subjectification and the continuities of colonial racism. The Mediterranean and Carola Rackete urge us to answer the question of what it is that allows the European public to endure this suffering, which comes to light on a daily basis, without convincingly attempting to bring about its end. In practices of self-criticism and in the power techniques of bureaucracy, the instrumentalised reason of the Enlightenment emerges as a paradigm of transparency. These techniques and practices operate affectively in that they bind themselves to a specific form of rationality. In my view, the simultaneity of Europe's deadly external borders and the moral complacency of those protected by them is based on a particular formation of reason, realised as coldness. This attachment to rationality creates a mode of existence that I call, after Adorno and Horkheimer, bourgeois coldness. Coldness is the affective enabling condition of administered violence in Europe, and it thrives in contemporary bourgeois subjects' relationship to the world – or, rather, these subjects thrive in the shelter of coldness.

3 Europe

The European Union won the Nobel Peace Prize in 2012. This is perhaps a conspiracy. —Marie Rotkopf[1]

Europe is the site where violence and bourgeois complacency meet. 'Europe' refers to the geopolitical space of the European continent, speaking with one voice, politically and ideologically, through the institution of the European Union. The eastern edges of Europe mark the borderlands of this unity – large parts of the Balkans are still not members of the EU – and the self-assured, identity-forming appropriation of the word 'Europe' is tied to criteria of belonging. This allows for close ties with countries like the UK and Norway, which are not formally part of the union, but often act in alignment with it. That European borders go beyond the purpose of territorial protection is significant for a racial analysis of the failure to provide assistance in the Mediterranean. Now as before, Europe lives as an idea whose former content – being the origin of the colonisation of the world – was replaced, after the Second World War, by the project of positioning itself as an agent of peace. However, critical voices in various fields increasingly confront Europe with the task of examining this political reorientation's plausibility beyond its rhetorical styling.

From the perspective of the history of ideas, a suspicion is solidifying that Europe has the task, among others, of repressing the memory of its colonial violence in favour of a self-narration which emphasises its commitment to Enlightenment ideals.

Ida Danewid emphasises the claim that, due to this history of violence on the continent and the imperial idea of Europe, the ongoing catastrophe in the Mediterranean must be viewed within 'continuities of violence'.[2] It can also be observed that the official discourse in Germany since the 'Summer of Migration' of 2015 has resembled a struggle between the German state and its bourgeois society for interpretive sovereignty over the events in the Mediterranean, such that a humanistic European self-image is secured in spite of these disturbing images and facts.

Carola Rackete: Good Whiteness, Bad Whiteness

On 12 June 2019, 47 nautical miles from the Libyan coast, the crew of the *Sea-Watch 3* saves fifty-three people from a rubber dinghy.[3] Activists of the Sea-Watch NGO patrol the Mediterranean to rescue migrants who fall into distress while crossing the sea. They then bring them ashore to Europe to avoid the Libyan coastguard taking them back to the African coast. The ship now carries people from various countries in Sub-Saharan Africa (Côte d'Ivoire, Ghana, Mali and Guinea), Libya and Egypt. Among them are three small children, nine women, thirty-eight men, and three minors, some of them recent victims of torture and violence.

The events on board after the rescue are well documented, since journalists for the German TV station Norddeutscher Rundfunk's programme *Panorama,* Nadia Kailouli and Jonas Schreijäg, are part of this Sea-Watch mission, which will soon attract a great deal of international attention.[4] As usual, the ship's captain, Carola Rackete, radios for a safe haven to bring people ashore after the rescue. During the night following the rescue, the Libyan coastguard assigns Tripoli as an anchorage to the *Sea-Watch 3* by email. The crew immediately decides that landing in Libya is not an option due to the coastguard's well-known mistreatment of refugees. Civilian sea rescue in the Mediterranean sees itself as dedicated to human rights and considers these rights violated both by the discontinuation of

Europe's 'Mare Nostrum' sea rescue programme in 2014, and by the internment and abuse of sub-Saharan Africa migrants in Libyan camps. Therefore, the crew of the *Sea-Watch 3* makes a promise to those rescued people, many of whom have experienced violence in Libya, that they will not take them back to Libya under any circumstances.[5]

In connection with the Mediterranean route, various journalists have been reporting for years on refugee mobility in Africa, for example from Eritrea, Ghana, Guinea, Cote d'Ivoire, Cameroon and Sudan.[6] Because there are no legal forms of passage to Europe from these countries, many make their way every year through the Sahara in the hope of reaching Europe by sea from Libya. It is not that they are unaware of the journey's dangers. The business of transporting people across the desert for money is now illegal, meaning that refugees are simply abandoned in the desert upon encountering a police checkpoint. And even when the route across the Sahara is successfully traversed, people are often arrested further north in Libya or interned by militias. A CNN report also revealed the existence of slave auctions near Tripoli as early as 2017, where mostly Black people without legal residence status are sold as slaves.[7]

Because Tripoli has been ruled out as a destination for the rescue mission, and the sea rescue headquarters in Italy refuses to assign a port to the *Sea-Watch 3*, Captain Rackete independently contacts the nearest port in Lampedusa. Meanwhile, the ship is now located directly outside Italian territorial waters. Rackete describes the situation on board and the need to bring pregnant women, small children, and those with injuries ashore as quickly as possible. The Italian port workers refer the captain to Malta as potential safe haven, and to the Maritime Rescue Coordination Centre in Rome for further questions.

At the same time, Matteo Salvini, the Italian minister of the interior and declared enemy of civilian as well as state sea rescue, calls the *Sea-Watch 3* situation a 'kidnapping of people for political reasons' and rules out any Italian assistance.[8] On 14 June 2019, he issues a now invalid decree banning civilian rescue vessels from landing in Italy, threatening crews with prison sentences and fines of up to €50,000.[9] On 15 June 2019, some ten extremely vulnerable people – pregnant women, injured people and small children – are picked up from *Sea-Watch 3* and taken ashore by a team of Italian doctors. From this point onwards, the ship remains at sea off Lampedusa, and the NGO issues media appeals and makes legal attempts to take action against the refusal of the Italian authorities. An urgent legal challenge to the European Court of Justice is unsuccessful. Despite the willingness of German municipalities, for example, to take the refugees in, the jurisdiction is shunted between Italy, the European Commission and the ship's country of registration – the Netherlands – while the situation on the ship worsens and those rescued become increasingly desperate and mentally and physically depleted. One of the rescued women explains her frustration: 'It is not that we're not thankful what they did for us. But the problem is we've had enough of being here. We want to understand what you're doing to get us out of here.'[10]

On 25 June 2019, with no political solution in sight, the crew and the rescued have been on the ship for two weeks. The crew fears that the extremely precarious psychological situation could cause people to jump overboard – 'to make a statement or out of actual desperation'[11] – and take action. That same day, Rackete announces to those rescued that she will take it upon herself to steer a passage towards the port of Lampedusa and enter Italian territorial waters without permission. She informs the Italian port of her plan and the expected arrival time. She asks for cooperation, which is refused. Shortly before reaching the coast, the *Sea-Watch 3* is stopped by the Italian coastguard.

The next day, two small boats carrying journalists of different nationalities reach the ship to inform the European public about the situation on board. From this point on, the situation attracts enormous attention; hope for a political solution again revives. The next day, it comes out that Rackete is already under investigation by the Italian judicial authorities for illegally entering Italian waters. Because the breach of law has already been committed, the crew no longer sees any reason to sit idly by off the coast and hope that Italian boats will bring everyone who was rescued ashore sooner or later. The *Sea-Watch 3* finally arrives in the port of Lampedusa under the escort of the Guardia di Finanza, who also protest the rescue. The rescued people disembark after two weeks of uncertainty. Rackete is arrested by the Italian police immediately after docking. In the following days, calls for her release pour in. The media in Germany almost unanimously side with the captain, celebrating her humanist effort and quickly developing a great deal of interest in her as a person.[12] The Italian philosopher Donatella Di Cesare compares Rackete with none other than Antigone and praises her offence as a breach of law in the name of morality.[13]

Through its high level of public interest, the mission of the *Sea-Watch 3* offers an opportunity to consider the role of moral and humanistic frameworks in the context of sea rescue in the Mediterranean. It is revealing that although the German public positioned itself on the side of sea rescue, an ongoing politics of ignorance – leaving people to die in the Mediterranean – can still count on civilian support – despite or precisely through heroising accounts of the figure of Carola Rackete. The apparent contradiction of ignorance towards those imperilled on the one hand, and the moral exaltation of rescue on the other, are expressions of a subjectivity that can integrate both. A similar bourgeois self-image stabilises the racist character of Europe as it simultaneously legitimises it as a moral institution.

What may sound paradoxical is actually the core of a European political self-conception, which calls for an analysis beyond the allocation of individual responsibility. I am accordingly not interested in distinguishing good from bad actors in the current Mediterranean crisis. Instead, I want to find out to what extent European subjectivity is built on a stable, unalterable difference between itself and the other, one it is incapable of dissolving. These reflections aim at the conditions of possibility which sustain violence on the Mediterranean. The embodiment of these historical and social conditions can be understood as colonial subjectivity.

My account of European migration policy thus far is an inventory or diagnosis which emphasises the urgency of identifying the fundamental philosophical problem underlying contemporary violence. The political theorist Jeanette Ehrmann observes this problem in the sense of a 'political theory of the border', thus shifting focus to her own perspective, 'a spectator of the catastrophe of the shipwreck, standing on safe ground, endowed with EU citizenship', which is also mine.[14]

Colonial subjectivity, which is associated with the affect of bourgeois coldness, is most distinctly crystallised in the normative legacy of humanism, which centres individual experience. Institutional forms of humanitarian aid find their moral foundation in this tradition as well. In order to pursue the connection between aggressive migration control and humanistic expressions of compassion, it is necessary to trace both affectively and historically the good intentions that emerge on the aforementioned safe ground. To this end, Ida Danewid analyses how the political discourse around sea rescue in Europe produces the idea of an innocent civilian population.[15] Innocence is the self-conception of European subjects which heroises rescue and obscures violence. Beyond that, the spectacle of rescue, which one could follow to an impressive degree in the case of the *Sea-Watch 3*, is enlisted to actively secure the colonial order of the world through moral self-assurance.[16]

The political scientists Deanna Dadusc and Pierpaolo Mudu speak of a 'humanitarian–industrial complex' to describe the relationship between innocence, power and aid as part of a logic of profit.[17] The entanglement of humanitarian aid with the state management of its deployment leads not infrequently to situations where the causes of the humanitarian catastrophe in question fade into the background, while the supposed saviours garner positive attention. This mechanism plays out particularly perfidiously when, as in the case of sea rescue, the EU begins to apply humanitarian measures to alleviate the effects of the border policy it is itself responsible for, rather than changing the policy.[18] This is interesting background for the *Sea-Watch 3*'s situation, because it adjusts the constellation of actors involved in border violence and sea rescue. After critical consideration of attention economies and their profiteers, it is not possible to make a simple division into 'bad' states and 'good' NGOs. Instead, complicities between white European state representative and white European sea rescuers must be recognised in order to properly understand the structural violence of the situation.

Visibility in the German media organises a simple juxtaposition on the Mediterranean between good, rescuing actors and evil, indifferent ones. Thus simplified, the catastrophe of a person drowning appears beyond those historical continuities that could explain its underlying causes. In the case of the *Sea-Watch 3*, the moral opposition between 'good' and 'evil' is applied to the activists as good actors and the Italian minister of the interior as an evil actor – and both sides fill these roles for publicity.[19] However, instead of this antagonism leading to the increasing visibility of its real object – escape on the Mediterranean and the violence of European borders – it constricts the narrative to ahistorical categories like hospitality, empathy and compassion. Individuals appear as so many outlines, despite the structural and repetitive character of events. The coverage positions Rackete against Salvini and evokes images of David versus Goliath, Joan of Arc or Antigone. The view of the *Sea-Watch 3* lying off Lampedusa, and the focus on its captain, create the impression that it comes down to this one situation, which is crucial for Europe – personified by Carola Rackete – to save its moral face.

Seen from a distance, the duel-like constellation between the captain and the minister of the interior appears as a representation of bourgeois interests and value judgements. Condensed into a single point on the wide sea in June 2019, a struggle is staged between '"good whiteness" (tolerant, multicultural, liberal)' – embodied by Carola Rackete and the Sea-Watch activists – and "bad whiteness" (fascist, white nationalist)' – embodied by Matteo Salvini and the Italian coastguard.[20] This legal battle also appears as a battle of interpretation over the European ideal and its authentic embodiment by heroic individuals. The people rescued, on the other hand, fade into the background. There is no place designated for them in the opposition of good and evil where they might be positioned as actors with their own experiences and perspectives in these events.

The humanitarian moral framework is not only maintained by this juxtaposition of a good and an evil power in Europe. It is additionally and repeatedly fuelled through a long-established affective economy, which individualises structural suffering.[21] In this way, images of suffering appear as invitations to identification through feelings of compassion – and not as expressions of structural injustice, in which empathetic observers are complicit. Danewid sees Judith Butler's ethics of mourning as putting this dynamic under critical pressure, yet not enough to actually overcome it.

Changing orders of visibility is a means of bringing catastrophes under a new interpretation, as in the case of the ongoing catastrophe in the Mediterranean. It is precisely this reformation that Butler calls for in her *Precarious Life* and *Frames of War*, which show how a society's identification and affective awareness of catastrophes imparts on or revokes from affected subjects the status of 'grievability'.[22] Those who are seen as people involved in relationships, and therefore as subjects equal to the observer, are grievable. According to Butler, the affective relationship of recognition is central for rendering ethics possible and for pursuing justice. Such a reference to 'the Others' realises itself through a dialectical interplay between 'I' and 'You', which Butler describes with reference to G.W.F. Hegel's, master–slave dialectic.[23] Butler does not necessarily consider the capacity for recognition as a collective event which is realised at the level of a society, but rather which builds on the dynamic between individuals in a society and their encounters. In this I–You relationship, both sides of a given encounter are put in a position to understand themselves as being equally dependent and vulnerable. Ethics is realised at the level of individuals, according to Butler, who recognise themselves as part of a community and from there develop the willingness to recognise the equal dependency of those who stand outside the community. The central task of Butler's ethics of recognition is to overcome the asymmetries of grievability due to historical and social power relations, and thereby to combat their violent consequences.

Butler has been criticised for locating the core of human ethical possibility in a shared, universal vulnerability.[24] Danewid formulates her critique however with regard to the question of 'the particular kinds of politics it serves to legitimise',[25] and how this politics specifically affects the external borders of the EU.[26] The focus on grievability, and affective commiseration with individual fates, favours a very particular politics of empathy according to Danewid, while other political references to the respective catastrophe are made impossible. The problem with empathy is that due to its constitutive asymmetry,[27] it often invites self-assurance instead of intervention; especially when the situation appears as complex and hopeless as that of Europe's external borders.[28] Talk of grief and concern for others, as a political stance wherein ethics is realised, also reproduces precisely those victim narratives used by the 'bad whites' of the European right (see Salvini calling Rackete a hostage-taker). The result above all is the self-assurance of compassionate Europeans and their 'good whiteness', as well as the denial of the colonial continuity in this racist hierarchy:

> By focusing on abstract – as opposed to historical –humanity, [victim narratives] contribute to an ideological formation that erases history and undoes the 'umbilical cord' that links Europe and the migrants that are trying to enter the continent. This replaces questions of responsibility, guilt, restitution, repentance, and structural reform with matters of empathy, generosity, and hospitality – a move that transforms the responsible colonial agent into an innocent bystander, confirming its status as 'ethical', 'good', and 'humane'.[29]

Not only does abstract humanity in the form of empathy play a role in discourses on politics and affect, but it is an integral part of the normative apparatus of humanism, which representatives of the EU always relate to positively.[30] When there is talk of the situation on the Mediterranean shaking Europe to its core, this refers above all to the crumbling certainty of being able to bury reality under the assertion of humanist values. Danewid's argument elucidates the fact that the apparent duel between 'good whiteness' and 'bad whiteness' helps to push the structural causes of catastrophe out of sight.

This critique may seem excessive in light of how it aggressively questions the motives of the humanitarian aid provided, which initially wants no more than to save lives in acute emergency situations. It is precisely here, however, that a distinction must be made between political and moral critique. It is not a question of denying the necessity and supportive capacity of civilian sea rescue. The point is to recognise that this form of activism neither practically nor discursively addresses the historical grounds of the catastrophe it tries to mitigate. This fact is obscured through the affective social categorisation of humanitarian aid as innocent and universal, which additionally renders its ability to exercise power invisible.[31] The moral exaltation of Rackete as a person is an apt illustration of this problematic.

Despite all this, both Dadusc and Mudu, as well as the Italian philosopher Sandro Mezzadra, categorise the events surrounding Rackete as a successful intervention in the usual discussions about border protection and aid. Mezzadra emphasises the different motives of humanitarian activism, which range from the cosmetic alleviation of acute suffering to demands for 'no border'. He insists that Rackete precipitated a 'radicalisation of humanitarianism', which newly challenged the EU and its border patrol practices.[32] Dadusc and Mudu see this case as an opportunity to render the EU's criminalisation of sea rescue visible, concluding their argument with a reflection on 'autonomous solidarity'.[33] Countless recent laws in Italy and Greece have hampered independent support for refugees, by the civil population or among refugees themselves, or made it totally impossible, in order to uphold the working order of the humanitarian–industrial complex.[34] More promising forms of resistance against this regime would therefore lie in practices deviating from the kind of humanitarian aid the state desires, instead supporting forms of 'autonomous solidarity'. The fact that precisely these forms of action are criminalised and prosecuted attests to this strategy's success: the actions have shown to be dangerous to a given policy.[35]

This book is not the place to evaluate activist work or assess its prospects. Here, it is more important to face the European self-conception and its erosion to understand the moral system behind the continued efficacy of migration control. It is obvious that the conditions in Germany's so-called anchor centres (in fact, practically detention camps) and other European camps like Moria in Greece are untenable, and that every person who drowns in the Mediterranean due to a lack of rescue does not tragically do so by accident, but is a victim of deadly violence. Nevertheless, the EU's closed-door policy continues without much civil resistance because it is equipped with an affective source of justification. Bourgeois coldness represents the European bourgeoisie's relationship to the world, in that it cultivates a moral self-image, as well as a disposition towards individualised sympathy. Europeans view the death of Black people on the Mediterranean through the self-image of innocence. Innocence prepares the affective ground to allow for coldness to prevail unhindered, in the form of ahistorical compassion.

4 Critique

The events in the Mediterranean, and the discourse surrounding them, have illustrated the emergence of an affective position which will be further theorised as bourgeois coldness. In the context of European border control, individualised compassion, constant affirmations of humanist values and narratives of development aid fulfil the function of reconciling a European self-conception with the unsustainable situation at its external borders.

The deep entrenchment of racial difference in European perception, as well as the hubris of humanitarian morality, come to light particularly in the attention paid to sea rescue. The ability to adopt such a selective yet morally justifiable view can be examined on the basis of bourgeois discourse in contemporary Germany. There is a tendency for the good intentions of reasonable citizens to accumulate, which, through their permanent mutual confirmation, results in the collective affect of bourgeois coldness.

In what follows, the aim is to shed light on the bourgeois consent to racism and its affective and ideological conditions. Bourgeois self-attributions in particular – virtues of the Enlightenment that enjoy the highest social legitimacy – should lose their innocence. In addition to critical analysis of this normative framework, the affective binding forces that it unfolds will here be brought into focus. Bourgeois subjectivity in the present settles into self-created, well-insulated institutions that enable a cooling towards the rest of the world.

Bourgeois ethics and politics are closely linked with the idea of universal, progressive reason. Historically, the bourgeoisie found its fundamental paradigms in eighteenth-century Europe with the emergence of a social class which raised a claim to political co-creation, but which belonged neither to the nobility nor the proletariat. My aim then is to describe the intellectual, moral, political and subsequently emerging affective paradigm of the bourgeois way of life as the problematic spirit of the present.

The bourgeois is the carrier subject and the intellectual author of a colonial order, and is thus constantly capable of refreshing this order. The examination of European institutions plays a decisive role here because these institutions, conceived with bourgeois values, allow colonial practices to survive in more or less sublimated forms. The genealogy of bourgeois subjectivity beginning with Odysseus pursues the goal of placing the bourgeois subject model of the present in continuity with a will to dominate (nature). This will has been broken many times over throughout history, and now it seeks, in various practices of self-criticism, protection from its own reflection.

With the help of a critique of affect extended from a critique of reason – which finds its starting point in early critical theory and is sharpened anew by the Enlightenment-critical positions of Black studies – bourgeois identity is revealed as a lived ideology of intelligibility. This ideology aims at a successful democratic discourse to be sure, but it creates a rigorous subject ideal that presupposes certain forms of legibility. Bourgeois attempts to make the boundaries of subject formation less violent through inclusion and participation only relocate the boundaries, but do not tear them down.

The acceptability of the situation at Europe's external borders – the bourgeois coldness and the accompanying policy of isolation – is promoted by a colonial form of reason. In this context, the Frankfurt School's critique of reason is of use; 'instrumental reason' describes the pathology of the twentieth century[1] and, as an analytical concept, can also help to identify the establishment of colonial relations of subjugation in progress-oriented ideals of reason. Colonial reason is not synonymous with the practices of coldness described above; rather, it forms the preconditions for their unhindered exercise and constant reproduction in the field of rationality. In order to understand how reason and coldness collude, the coagulation of colonial ideas and myths must be understood in the affective constellations of the present.

Critique of Reason

In his *Critique of Instrumental Reason*, Max Horkheimer attempts to trace and differentiate the philosophical, scientific and everyday use of the concept of reason from the Enlightenment to the present. Ultimately, he diagnoses a close connection between reason, use and the profit motive, as set forth already in *Dialectic of Enlightenment*. Horkheimer formulates an immanent critique. This means that reason is reflected upon and criticised in the face of its crises in the twentieth century – and not measured against external ideals. Frankfurt School thinkers always concern themselves with concrete social formations in order to ascertain the negativity of reason. The use of technology and the positivistic sciences represent fields of practice for instrumental reason. On top of that, the bourgeois way of life, which is fully reconciled with reason according to its self-conception, is a venue for studying the material effects of the ideal of reason.

Theodor W. Adorno and Horkheimer's critique of alienation has been relativised as a provincial and nostalgic longing, if not an entirely romanticising one, for a comprehensible and less complex world, especially due to its obvious rejection of technological innovation and mass pleasures under the punitive label of the 'culture industry'.[2] All too prevalent in their depictions of the entertainment industry is the image of two ageing professors, increasingly overwhelmed by the present, whose horizon is formed by their sheltered, carefree childhoods near Frankfurt and Stuttgart – but this contrast does not render their analysis irrelevant.[3]

Dated as Adorno and Horkheimer's observations may seem, I would like to persist methodically in a critique of reason's unreconciled, negativistic basic impulse. This allows me to take thought itself into account as an enabling condition for violence. To renounce reconciliation, but not the harsh critique of the given, means for thought to bear responsibility for the negativity which it has itself brought forth. This operation yields an undermining critique, which does not heroically confront its groundlessness, nor allows itself to be daunted by it either. In this renunciation of secure ground, the critique of reason's claim differs from ritualised bourgeois self-criticism, which will be discussed at the end of this chapter.

The structurally radical confrontation that initiates an undermining critique takes place with regards to subject matter which Adorno and Horkheimer left out, and which nonetheless partly informs their work.[4] Examining the present colonial present should make it possible not to reduce the global problematic of Western reason to principles of value creation, but to better understand it through categories of coloniality and racialisation.

This recalibration of the critique of reason has direct consequences for a theory of the subject. Frantz Fanon was one of first thinkers of the colonial form of reason's psycho-social consequences, in that he made the dynamics of recognition and subjugation in colonial encounters comprehensible as affective, subjectivising forces.[5] These were primarily established and tested in the history of colonialism through capitalistic and nation-state dynamics, which Cedric Robinson describes[6] and which have been expressed using the term 'racial capitalism'.[7] Achille Mbembe's concept of 'Black reason' refers above all to those practices inside of which white knowledge is established as an objective source of reference, thus creating an effective instrument for the maintenance of colonial regimes up to the present day.[8] According to Denise Ferreira da Silva, the primacy of transparency is a central instrument of colonial reason in constantly redrawing the line between white universality and non-white others.[9] Sylvia Wynter meanwhile has recognised in the humanist idea of reason a production mechanism for a severely curtailed form of personhood.[10]

To describe colonial reason from the perspective available to me means making my own thinking the subject of analysis. To do this, I draw on Adorno and Horkheimer's method of the critique of reason, because it enables an open-ended self-questioning. The determination of the object to be critiqued is just as important here as reflecting on one's own horizon. Accordingly, the object of my critique is bourgeois reconciliation with problematic reason and the multiple relations of violence it reproduces. I leave open what form of life or reason could replace this reconciliation, when the elements it is based upon have shown their propensity towards violence. My analysis is limited to critique.

For Adorno and Horkheimer, to expose structures of violence in reason requires the work of mediation, which eventually leads back to the logic of exchange as original sin and primary contradiction. To diagnose alienation in the tradition of critical theory would fall short and run the risk of falling back on subject ideals of immediacy that take the wind out of the sails of a radical subject critique. In this sense, the aspects on the basis of which I critically approach reason should, on the one hand, have clearer material references in order to avoid the danger of drawing from the arsenal of transcendental categories; on the other hand, they should be locatable historically as well as in the present, so as not to awaken the semblance of a universality of critical concepts. Bourgeois existence is thus to be understood as a special mode of colonial reason which affords me critical access from the present. Differentiating its modes of operation makes it possible to recognise genealogies within the colonial order, and thereby to point critically beyond the current moment.

Bureaucracy

There is an almost intuitive connection between coldness and bureaucracy. As an instrument of administration, bureaucracy cuts informal affective ties and replaces them with formalised affects that conform to abstract rules. The task of bureaucracy is initially nothing more than to be the administrative executive of the law. It gains autonomy only through the unplanned independence of its apparatuses. Hannah Arendt sees in bureaucracy a 'rule by Nobody'[11] that in the last instance endangers democracy, while at the same time it may be considered 'the most social form of government' because of its independence from individual factors.[12] The problematic process of bureaucratic 'ordinances' (*Verordnungen*) becoming independent, which Arendt contrasts with 'laws', becomes particularly evident when these ordinances affect unprotected people and deny them the possibility of resistance against administrative treatment.[13] People without European citizenship who apply for a settlement permit in Germany, for example, experience bureaucratic contingency. Lack of protection is especially severe in cases of deferral of European asylum procedures. The reasons why asylum seekers cannot be given an answer and protected quickly can be sought and found in bureaucracy: the so-called case-by-case review, which ensures that asylum seekers are examined on the basis of individual criteria – and not just the basis of one criterion, for example the person's nationality – requires a considerable amount of personnel, as well as the standardisation of judgement criteria and procedures that the German Federal Office for Migration and Refugees must carry out. If for no other reason than the limited personnel capacities of this agency due to underfunding and an unexpected increase in applications, asylum procedures should more and more be processed digitally in the coming years: a bureaucrat would then only have to cast a 'final glance' at the proposed result.[14] The intensive assessment of asylum seekers by a case worker would thus be broadly eliminated.

This example demonstrates the fundamental contradiction of bureaucratic practices: the pragmatic organisation of highly delicate legal processes increasingly obscures their delicateness. Through a set of criteria, bureaucracy relieves people of the ethical burden of judgement. These criteria are mostly guidelines, which are in turn derived from laws in a more or less direct way. The law forms the backdrop for bureaucracy in this respect: clearly its condition of possibility as well as its basis of legitimation. The hope that bureaucracy will enable an implementation of the law without human interference led the sociologist Max Weber to see bureaucracy as an indispensable component of successful forms of government. An administrative apparatus, according to Weber, ensures the best possible implementation of the constitution and helps provide civil democracy with a secure foundation.[15]

Bureaucracy is not external to active civil and public servants, rather it represents a mode of subjectification that closely binds corresponding figures to the state. So bureaucracy appears at first glance to be diametrically opposed to the bourgeois as the domain of liberal discourse, so central to the thought of Jürgen Habermas.[16] However, a fundamentally positive attitude towards the state, shared by the citizen (*Bürger*) and the bureaucrat, reveals a shared investment in bureaucracy. Its stabilising power for state structure, and its exonerating power for the individual, are conducive to the Western ideal of the state. Even if the citizen may detest the dry taste of bureaucratic procedure, he remains deeply enmeshed in the state model which depends on it.

Bureaucracy's relationship to contemporary bourgeois society must be gauged by looking at the ideals and fears associated with bureaucracy. This includes searching for structural racism's enabling conditions in bureaucratic procedures, as well as for the lines connecting the bureaucratic sphere to direct state violence. Bureaucracy has the ability to conceal such violence and thus enable unaffected citizens, who are not racially marked, to accept it in an affectively cooled-off form. The European bourgeoisie and modern statehood prove to be co-original and well disposed towards each other.

Bureaucracy and administration are closely related practices. In his essay 'Culture and Administration', Adorno looks at the state's organisation of reality, which provides him with an occasion to identify an irreconcilable task. Adorno illuminates the paradoxes of *every* attempt to administer culture – as a sphere of all activities not subordinated to a reproductive purpose. This attempt always appears 'askew' and 'irreconcilable' and already begins with the intention of narrowing the scope of the term 'culture'.[17] Adorno speaks of the 'administered world' to diagnose the 'the extension of conditions of exchange' into all branches of society.[18] According to Adorno, the fundamental problem of this tendency is that it impoverishes the mind in the course of its instrumentally rational integration, which he repeatedly problematises.[19] This impoverishment also forges ahead in administration, since technical administration 'is an external affair by which it is subsumed rather than comprehended'.[20]

Culture is a particularly exemplary case for making bureaucracy intelligible as a form linked to bourgeois subjectivity. If the bourgeois subject wants to reconcile statehood with a liberated way of life, it aims precisely at the balance between culture and administration. Thus a region emerges in which inherently bourgeois concerns and conflicts can be represented and heard.

At the intersection of culture and administration, battles are fought over cultural budgets and urban development measures, which are expensive but culturally valuable from a bourgeois perspective – the controversial Elbphilharmonie in Hamburg, the controversial Humboldt Forum in Berlin.* It is

* The Elbphilharmonie is a classical concert hall in Hamburg which opened in 2017. Designed as an architectural landmark, the use of €789 million of public funds to complete it – an escalation of costs and the result of poor planning – caused controversy. The Humboldt Forum is the reconstructed city palace in Berlin, which opened in 2021 as a museum of colonial collections, amongst other things. This historically accurate reconstruction of the early eighteenth-century Baroque *Berliner Stadtschloss*, demolished by the GDR government in 1950, was built on the site of the Palast der Republik, the governmental building of the GDR, which was torn down in order to make space for the reinstated Prussian palace. It was not only this decision to replace an important building of recent German history with one calling back to German imperial monarchy that sparked public debate. The fact that several right-wing donors had enabled the reconstruction of the castle, and the initial intention to exhibit colonial confiscated art instead of restituting it to its original locations, was strongly criticised. €572 million of public funds were used to co-finance the project.

at this point that the bourgeois negotiates his own identity between *Homo oeconomicus* and culturally interested cosmopolitan. Adorno is interested in the connection between culture and administration and the question of how to understand the constitutive entanglement of these two realms in bourgeois life. To what extent has culture always been a bargaining chip or a state educational programme? Adorno scoffs: 'Culture long ago evolved into its own contradiction, the congealed content of educational privilege.'[21] The institutionalisation of culture robs it of the freedom it made possible in other contexts. The bourgeois can be understood in Adorno's text as the willingness to recklessly permit the administration of supposedly highly valued cultural artefacts, thereby enclosing them and ultimately destroying them.

Adorno's critique reminds us that administration affectively structures the world, rather than merely providing access to the given world. For Adorno, administration represents a given attitude that is difficult to abandon. It implies the 'expansion of administrative competence into a region, the idea of which contradicts every kind of average generality inherent to the concept of administrative norms'.[22] It could be interpreted as an ethics of the domain of responsibility. In a broader historical and geopolitical sense, it must be clarified how European administration justifies and organises itself through colonial legislation, in areas of the world for which it simply claims responsibility. Ultimately, the relational coldness adopted by bureaucracy proves to be not just an executive calculation, but a condition of the modern state.

The 'authority' (*Behörde*) is the organ of bureaucracy according to Weber.[23] It is a unit of the state that is not endowed with legislative power, but with a purely executive power which usually entails little authority to make individual decisions. The authority implements rules derived from laws. As a result, 'individual arbitrariness' is ruled out and prevented 'in favour of an objectively regulated procedure'.[24] The authority regulates property relations, rights of residence, family status and permits according to procedures and decision-making templates created for this purpose. The cliché of the uber-officious German civil servant is due above all to the official task of disappearing behind the state and only appearing as its executive hand. Arendt senses the problem here that bureaucracy always conceals from people 'what or whom it actually governs' through its appearance as a series of ordinances.[25] The possibility of those under rule gaining insight into the rationale and intentions of decrees is made impossible by 'the carefully organised ignorance of specific circumstances . . . in which all administrators keep their subjects'.[26]

The consistent split between the concrete subject and his role in the state points to the affective intervention implied by a bureaucratic order. In the gap between the state and the individual, an 'intermediate zone' of 'paperwork' arises, according to the anthropologist David Graeber: it is 'ostensibly private, but in fact entirely shaped by a government'.[27] This is the reason bureaucracy's consequences must be borne individually for the most part, and often in isolation. This applies to the burdensome administrative procedures that relatives usually have to devote themselves to while grieving a death. It was likewise impressively on display in Germany in the distribution of vaccines during the coronavirus pandemic, overseen and meticulously regulated by the Ethics Council – and yet the distribution contradicted the individual and social feeling of efficiency and justice.

In his book *The Utopia of Rules*, Graeber supports the thesis that bureaucracy is a form of government which expresses the structural violence inherent in the state. This means that the affective impression of bureaucracy as 'fundamentally nonsensical', which emerges in the moments when citizens are confronted with it, belies the fact that bureaucracy can be fundamentally helpful – only not in an unjust state.[28] Ultimately, what is obscured in the superficial, sensory-affective resistance to forms, and the experience of the subject filling them out, is the actual depth of bureaucratic violence. Graeber underpins this relationship by describing police officers, who, just like other civil servants, are obliged to protect state sovereignty, as 'bureaucrats with weapons'.[29] According to Graeber, the police contribute to the solution of administrative problems by using or threatening violence.[30]

The focus on the police brings the relationship between law, bureaucracy and violence, as problematised by Arendt, back to the fore. Bureaucracy can be described as a mediation technique that technically diffuses responsibilities from the start, thus exonerating the conscience of the individual subject. This applies to police officers, who know they are protected, on the one hand by the sovereignty of state authority, and on the other via the legitimation of violence through slow official channels. And this point holds for Adolf Eichmann, the *SS-Obersturmbannführer* responsible for the organisation of the 'Final Solution', whom Arendt observed at his trial, always acting in a law-abiding and dutiful manner, yet showing initiative and 'not just obeying orders'.[31]

As 'the purest form of rational and legal rule',[32] bureaucracy implies the de-individualisation of decision-making processes. Thus it has also become the target of criticism by market-liberal positions. The civil service, which is supposed to put the brakes on the dynamics of a largely uncontrolled capitalism, is plainly seen from the position of market liberalism as an agent for obstructing progress. This juxtaposition is historically incorrect, however, as Graeber demonstrates: in reality, the development of free markets already entailed enlarging the bureaucracy to support them; yet the most aggressive affects directed against bureaucracy are sustained by the notion of self-regulating markets.[33] Graeber complains that the critique of bureaucracy has been so effectively established by the pro-capitalist side that it is hard to reformulate it as a left critique of the technical outsourcing of state authority. Such a critique would always run the risk of uncritically appropriating the generally right-wing aggression against state representatives.[34] The disparaging view of civil servants in the critique of bureaucracy[35] gains its 'legitimacy' on the right by way of the notion of the free market as universal solution; or, alternatively, through the aristocratic idea that only rule by individuals can function in the long term.[36]

For Arendt and the critics of the bureaucratic optimisation of the asylum process, it is not the actual ability of bureaucrats to act that is at the forefront; rather it is the character of bureaucracy itself that thwarts empathetic relationships and obscures the humanity of those subject to its administration. Bureaucracy is thus a practice that replaces the individual and direct confrontation with 'the Other' to whom the law is applied. It is precisely in this suspension of situational judgements that Weber sees the most rational and highest form of legal rule.[37]

It remains problematic that bureaucracy can hardly adequately weigh and consider every aspect of a specific situation, let alone its methods. Its primary task consists in formalising rational principles to make them practically applicable. The question of who authors this rationality goes unanswered: 'The question is always: who controls the existing bureaucratic apparatus?'[38] For Weber, this is a practical question that arises sooner or later in every form of the state in order to ensure the established form of rule's continuity. Arendt, however, fears that the 'apparatus', precisely through the openness of the question, will grow independent and turn into a 'rule by Nobody'.

The self-evident existence of bureaucracy in modern states, which Weber boils down to the formula 'Rule in *everyday life* is primarily: *Administration*',[39] requires a reflection on its modes of existence: administration is probably less ideal than Weber wishes, and less demonic than Arendt stylises it. Rather than ascribing neutrality to bureaucracy as an isolated technique of exercising power, it is more helpful to ask what the long-term affective consequences of its practice are. Taking a relational view of bureaucracy in its interplay with other social forces is useful for describing its concretising and reinforcing function, for example regarding racism and white ignorance. Bureaucracy holds a formative capacity for each institution that realises it – and an exonerating effect for those who rely on its implementation.

Lone Wolves and Co-creators

For years, the police, the judiciary and state security refused to even consider racism as a motive for the series of murders committed by the right-wing terrorist organisation National Socialist Underground (NSU), although this suspicion proved true in the end.[40] The narrative of the 'lone wolf', which attributes right-wing extremist murders to isolated accounts of radicalisation, remains part of the official classification of right-wing criminal acts, without questioning how people could acquire radical ideas without a social network in the first place. This narrative minimises the ongoing danger of right-wing extremism, especially for migrant parts of the population, and it absolves the social milieu in immediate proximity. When the racist motive behind the murders was considered for the first time in the NSU trial of 2006, it was also on the basis of a '"lone-wolf hypothesis", which painted a picture of a "mission-driven perpetrator" with a right-wing background'.[41]

This lone-wolf narrative serves here and elsewhere to disavow a structural, historical view of right-wing extremism in Germany since 1945. It is a means of self-appeasement for the white, German-speaking population, who know themselves to fall outside of the target of Nazi attacks and therefore have little interest in investigating their true scope and danger. Engagement with the history of right-wing extremist violence in Germany[42] would quickly cast doubt on narratives of successful denazification. Furthermore, the neutrality of government bodies is increasingly called into question through successive exposure to right-wing radical organisations within the police and the judiciary.[43] Here and in other cases, the authorities are pursuing strategies of reconnaissance that position the perpetrators far outside the allegedly shared liberal political system, coldly shrugging off the evidence provided by victims' relatives and activists about broad support structures for right-wing ideologies. In the NSU trial, this disregard went so far that family members of the victims were accused by the responsible authorities in order to dodge fundamental questions about right-wing ideologies within the security services.[44]

The lone-wolf narrative and the NSU trial as a whole seem to exemplify the implementation of bourgeois interests through bureaucratic power. One goal of bourgeois politics is to ensure that the state's ideas and representations of justice are in line with its own. The democratic ideal provides that the state only acts in the interests of the morality of its population – or vice versa. Bourgeois citizens feel obliged to shape the state as an organ to which power can be transferred without concern. Bureaucracy can thus be read as a sphere in which the concordance of state and subject is arranged through the embodiment of the former through the latter. Civil servants adopt state principles into their self-conception and thus represent the possibility of unifying person and state. Citizens rely on this model. If this trust in the state proves to be misplaced – as in the case of the NSU trial – it threatens not only a crisis of legitimacy in the relevant institutions, but also the bourgeois subject and the public sphere they shape. Therefore, ties between state and subject must not be under-estimated when it comes to explaining the persistence of those lone-wolf and drug-gang narratives which exonerate the bourgeois public.[45] Coldness towards witness reports given by the victims' family members is bourgeois self-preservation in the courtroom.

Agreement with the state, which also entails its co-creation, is not fundamentally problematic. A different state and other institutions could very well prevent right-wing extremist violence and, through sanctions, contribute to the establishment of justice. By contrast, bourgeois trust in the administration as portrayed leads to a bureaucratic form of thought and judgement that does not do justice to the form of right-wing extremist violence. This was clear in the NSU trial, where the racist motive was repeatedly pushed into the background and relativised until the NSU exposed itself through the suicide of its key players.[46] Within the frame of what is called 'legitimate state criticism', certain interventions remain impossible and certain realities unheard.[47] Bureaucracy is often the entity that obstructs justice by mechanising decision-making processes, reluctantly reacting to new developments, and shaping subjects. One reason to deny right-wing extremism – not of course the only one – is fear for the stability of the bourgeois state.

The racist veil which caused the NSU investigations to fail so catastrophically from the start is a striking example of the existence of such structures in German institutions – and for a bourgeois public's inability to recognise and name them and to take effective action against them.[48] The trial observers reported that the federal prosecutor's office strategically acted 'to minimise the NSU Complex and reduce it to an admittedly monstrous but manageable criminal case'.[49] The official agreement on the trivialising narrative served the 'public good' – that is, to secure the unfettered public legitimacy of authorities and government bodies.[50] The fact that the Turkish background of some of the victims was reason enough to investigate drug-related offences should sufficiently depict the extent to which racist assumptions are inscribed in state institutional practices. The case is situated in historical continuity with the self-conception of colonially active state formations, whose understanding of justice is often not in contradiction to their violent practices. Here too bureaucracy acts as a conciliatory mediator between the state and reality. Bureaucracy then means – consciously or unconsciously, whether through obeying or optimising – orienting processes of action and thought towards a state in order to constantly enhance its stability. In case of doubt, bureaucratic activity positions 'the executive above parliamentary control under certain circumstances' in the interest of the 'public good'.[51] The bourgeois consent promoted by these processes becomes a problem if profound changes in state structure are needed to pursue justice, which then requires historical reflection on exclusions, racist devaluation and the bourgeois self-image.

Bureaucracy serves to stabilise power by transferring its exercise to individuals who do not have to feel responsible for its consequences, since they can always point to the welfare and mandate of the state. In connection with bourgeois morality, this stance can endow a sense of identity and thus strengthen affective ties to the state. This can be seen, for example, when the state is perceived as a vulnerable individual in need of protection: as 'wounded by unfair criticism'.[52] Bureaucracy contributes its part to developing coldness by giving an affective charge to the state and its welfare, as well as internalising the assumption that state institutions act legitimately *per se*.

The law and its administration are never legitimised solely by their capacity for successful social organisation, rather they also transport values and feelings that inscribe themselves as 'affective citizenship'[53] in the normative sensibility of citizens. Thus a pathos can arise which stylises the state as a venerable object worthy of protection. Ashis Nandy's book *The Romance of the State* refers to the romanticism associated with the founding of nation-states.[54] In the colonial world, the modern nation-state is invested with the hope of guaranteeing progress through secularity and capitalist production, thereby acquiring the status of a thoroughly positive idea.[55] Romantic feelings for the state foster the faithful execution of bureaucratic tasks and may even help bureaucrats to serve the state.

Giorgio Agamben is interested in the religiously sanctioned character of bureaucracy, which also reveals an impassioned relationship between bureaucrats and the state. In his study of Thomas Aquinas's angelology – the study of angels – he notes: 'Not only are celestial messengers organised according to offices and ministries, but worldly functionaries in turn assume angelic qualities and, in the same way as angels, become capable of cleansing, enlightening, and perfecting.'[56] This parallel manifests itself in the adoption of the terrestrial – or more precisely state-administrative – vocabulary from angelology. Long before its modern bureaucratic usage, 'hierarchy' can be found in Aquinas as 'sacred rule',[57] and the 'ministry' – derived from the Latin verb *ministrare* (to administer) – refers to the task of angels to serve God as His stewards.[58]

The status of the state as divine or exalted, as a result of romanticism, implies that citizens and bureaucrats have a certain readiness to sacrifice in exchange for the promise of security.[59] Besides, the romantic relationship strengthens the sense of legitimacy in the bureaucratic exercise of power. Analogues to angels' sovereign tasks as being 'capable of curing, enlightening, and perfecting',[60] civil servants of the constitutional state make consequential decisions about societal belonging, public and private property and the provision of aid. They are therefore only partly individual – but always structural – holders of a power entrusted to them by state authority. This power's high degree of structuring in authoritative bodies and responsibilities – we recall Weber's description – makes its execution seem self-evident.

Hannah Arendt's fear of 'rule by Nobody' is particularly easy to understand when the real danger proves to be the unspectacular way in which the exercise of power manifests through authorities. In contrast to laws, ordinances and procedural adjustments seem as if they are not worthy of exceptional resistance because they arouse little public interest and only concern very particular social realms, which in turn do not exceed the jurisdiction of the regulatory authority. When an agency under the Italian Ministry of the Interior unilaterally issues guideline for docking permits that make sea rescue difficult or impossible, the path to challenging these rules takes longer, paradoxically, than if they were the result of the parliamentary legislative process. Similarly, it takes a while for anchor-centre conditions initiated by the Ministry of the Interior to become well known enough to be the subject of controversy. Bureaucracy fosters affective habituation to the existence of state power.

Having engaged with bureaucracy as the mediator of nation-state power, I question this power's structure and legitimacy. My interest remains the position of bourgeois subjects within this power structure. Bourgeois citizens base their affirmative understanding of the state on the law. The law represents both the foundation of bureaucratic legitimacy and the state's anchoring of bourgeois morality. Walter Benjamin's 'Towards the Critique of Violence' formulates a critique of liberal law that shakes these two foundations.

Law and Violence

Walter Benjamin deals with the mediation of violence by law as a whole.[61] Benjamin examines the establishment of law by demonstrating the principle of natural law's effectiveness in modern, positive-legal state structures, and by overturning the supposed opposition of law and violence into a dialectical relationship. According to Benjamin, the common ground of natural law and positive legal traditions consists in their shared conviction that justice can be measured in the relationship between means and ends: 'Natural law attempts, by the justness of the ends, to "justify" the means, positive law to "guarantee" the justness of the ends through the justification of the means.'[62] Benjamin's essay draws the connecting lines between democratic institutions and their histories shaped by violence, which can neither be eliminated nor ultimately legitimated. 'Towards the Critique of Violence' reveals those manifestations in which violence is distinguished as a founding moment or a destructive force. Benjamin helps to provide us with a deep understanding of the constitutive violence without which constitutions could claim no validity.

In the text, 'critique' is to be understood as a differentiation of various forms of violence. On the basis of a distinction between violence in natural law, which sees violence as a means towards just ends, and violence in positive law, which seeks to 'to "guarantee" the justness of the ends through the justification of the means', Benjamin shows that the respective use of violence is merely a matter of different levels of mediation.[63] Benjamin contradicts the modern sense of justice: in positive law, violence is not eliminated by pacification, but survives in it. The distinction between law-establishing and law-preserving violence helps to critique the concept of positive law as such. And admittedly this is because, as Benjamin explains, 'violence does not abdicate' in the establishment of positive law. Instead, lawmaking functions in such a way that legitimacy lies in the end with the content of the law. This must be established through an ultimately arbitrary (*willkürlich*) violent act.

Positive law acts as if non-violent because, once the law is established, it ensures the continuity of order from this alone. It is this representation which Benjamin problematises because it obscures the bonding of law to that act of violence without which the law would not exist at all. In this sense of a critique of violence, it is essential to constantly remember that 'Lawmaking is powermaking, assumption of power, and to that extent an immediate manifestation of violence.'[64]

It is thus the establishment of justice's ends through a speech act that gives the state the authority to vanquish contingent power relations through the law. What Benjamin presents to his readers here is in complete opposition to the bourgeois conception of the self and the state. Benjamin's critique, however, is not an objection in the sense of a clear solution – he is not concerned with abolishing positive law outright – but with a genealogy of law's condition of possibility and, at the same time, with a survey of its natural limits. This means that Benjamin does not set out ethically to resolve the relationship between law and violence which satisfies the claim of legitimation. The philosopher Daniel Loick summarises the text and its consequences as 'exposing the consubstantiality of law and violence' and thereby 'the lack of a priori legitimation in every violent execution of the law'.[65] The 'critique of violence' thus reveals a groundlessness of ethical justifications in the context of the bourgeois state, for whose limitation Benjamin takes no responsibility, if only because it is exactly this sovereign responsibility in the face of the problematic at hand – of ultimate justification – which has grown suspect. Instead, the text leaves the reader in a dizzying space of ethical uncertainty, not even reassuring her by calling for general non-violence.[66]

Benjamin's text gains political plasticity through examples. His treatise is by no means an extravagant reflection on the nature of the state, but it can also be read – with emphasis on the relevant passages – as a model for the justification of anarchism and abolitionism. He discusses the general strike, the police and the demarcation of borders as institutional moments of positive law's realisation, which cannot disguise their violent content without difficulty. The general strike shows the extent to which the state can guarantee freedoms without having to openly and violently restrict them. And the police – whose 'power is formless' and whose form of regulation remains unclear, especially in a democracy – are reminiscent of the monarchy's exercise of power.[67] Benjamin's observation that the drawing of national borders in the wake of a post-war peace treaty is a manifestation of a 'mythic lawmaking', as opposed to divine justice, is noteworthy with an eye to the division of land by colonial powers. Colonies are a space for testing bureaucratic techniques – especially with respect to establishing and defending secure property relations. Benjamin's distinction between mythic and divine violence is a theological line of flight in his theoretical work which is central to the tradition of reception around its Jewish-messianic aspects. The question of how divine violence behaves in relation to mythic violence is one I will neglect, instead limiting myself to deconstructing the existing order, which Benjamin's text makes possible.

Mythical lawmaking, as Adorno and Horkheimer also show, has no legal or moral justification at its command.[68] It is fate and not punishment – a document of the existence of the gods and not their reaction.[69] In this sense, mythic violence establishes justice and thus ultimately acts in free-floating contingency. This contingency, however, is precisely what is overturned through the act of its establishment through violence, because from this point on it must be administered, even treated legally, in order to preserve life. This establishment can also consist of acts of colonial land acquisition that anticipate the struggle for land and establish a legal system in this violent act of primitive accumulation, one still in effect today. The struggle of Indigenous movements for reparations in the United States, in South America and in other colonised areas is proof of established law's contentiousness. Eve Tuck and K. Wayne Yang's assertion that decolonisation is first and foremost a material issue of land and resources finds support in Benjamin's critique of law.[70] For Benjamin, the act of territorial lawmaking consists in drawing boundaries after war: 'An application of the latter' – power as the principle of all mythic lawmaking – 'that has immense consequences is found in constitutional law. For in this sphere the establishing of frontiers, the task of "peace" after all the wars of the mythic age, is the primal phenomenon of all lawmaking violence'.[71] The establishing of frontiers which peace brings in its wake puts an end to violent conflict. That it is carried out by the victor, however, remains an expression of the violence that decided the conflict in the end.

Benjamin's assessment of the presence of violence in modern state structures can be read as a call for revolution, or as an unfortunate inevitability. In the text's much-discussed final sentences, he describes lawmaking and law-preserving violence as reprehensible, ending in an aporia: ultimately, only divine violence is legitimate.[72] This passage is by no means a flight towards the metaphysical, or an attempt to assign responsibility for ethical questions to a god of some kind. Rather, deferring judgement to an instance whose order we mortals cannot know measures up to an insistent conviction that justice exists. This conviction alone, combined with the question of how one can do justice to it, may bring about historical change for the better.[73]

The tolerable mediation of violence through positive law in state constitutions gives occasion to the bourgeois conviction that one lives and acts within systematised justice. The modern state is based on the trust of bourgeois subjects who rely on its realisation of justice. Against the background of Benjamin's study, bureaucracy proves to be the last step in numerous mediations of violence – with the goal of making this violence appear as invisible as possible, and the state as legitimate as possible. The violence which Benjamin's essay brings out of its hiding place, guarded by the liberal bourgeoisie, and brings to light anew, breaks with bureaucratic self-evidence.

In contrast, a counter-violence threatens to break out which will no longer accept this self-evidence as soon as insight into its conditions has been gained. Jacques Derrida writes about the openness of this foundational violence: 'The state is afraid of fundamental, founding violence . . . violence able to justify, to legitimate . . . legal relationships, and so to prevent itself as having a right to the law.'[74]

If bureaucracy is able to transform the exercise of violence into a matter of course, then the stability of the state it serves depends on its existence. Questioning or even omitting this sediment of mediation lays bare the 'right to the law' that Derrida speaks about here, and which would expose the violence intervening in bureaucracy and the legal relationships it administers. The paradigm of such violence is revolution.

Bureaucracy separates practical and state-regulated communal life from the act of violence that establishes this order, and it does so sensorily. Therefore, it touches on both what Benjamin calls 'lawmaking' and what he calls 'law-preserving' violence. Benjamin cites the aforementioned example of the police as a state entity in which both forms of violence fatally mix: 'True, this [the police] is violence for legal ends (it includes the right of disposition), but with the simultaneous authority to decide these ends itself within wide limits (it includes the right of decree). The ignominy of such an authority . . . lies in the fact that in this authority the separation of lawmaking and law-preserving violence is suspended.'[75] The idiosyncrasy of lawmaking itself where 'no clear legal situation exists',[76] and at the same time implementing existing law, could be transferred to the sphere of bureaucracy more generally. Although the theoretical incorporation of the police into the bureaucratic state apparatus seems to downplay and misrepresent its devastating self-empowerment and overt violence from the start – as someone like David Graeber suggests – Benjamin's structural analysis of violence in sites of its relative invisibility still demands a closer look. Like the police, desk clerks are also tasked with directly enforcing the legal system and thus inevitably encounter ambiguities that force them to apply their own judgements. The NSU trial revealed the extensive possibilities for covering up the misconduct of colleagues and profiting from this misconduct.

Bureaucracy is at the end of the state administrative chain. It is the executive organ that is supposed to carry out, in its most harmless form, the violence inscribed in the state – and it is precisely this task that betrays its coldness. The mediated connection between violence, both the kind which establishes and that which preserves, is the condition for the cold bureaucracy of the so-called desk criminal of the Nazi regime, now a historical cliché, and for the deadly management of human beings at Europe's external borders. That the current forms of articulation for direct violence do not involve armed conflict, but rather scenes in which state sovereignty is delicately attacked, explains how the supposed threat to the entity of the state legitimises extreme brutality. Here the bureaucratic apparatus extends its techniques for exercising power in order to do justice to what Max Weber proclaims as 'rational rule', or what civil servants understand by it.[77] The Greek coastguard's push-backs of refugees are ultimately the operations of an extended arm of administrative activities; initially they were only discussed as breaches of law through the utmost effort of activists, until they were gradually registered by the European Court of Justice. The fact that push-backs have taken place many times, and presumably continue to occur, and that the conditions of their legality are being discussed, reveals the violent potential in the administrative power to act.

The relative continuity of liberal statehood in Europe finds expression in the attitudes of subjects who are shaped and surrounded by bureaucracy. It is only through their willing adaptation that bureaucracy and state-thinking coagulate into bourgeois coldness. Loick diagnoses an 'appalling righteousness' of European subjectivity, 'which straightforwardly hides a meaningful exercise of the legally guaranteed freedom of individuals'.[78] According to his critical theory of law, forms of sociality in Western societies would have to first be discovered and tested beyond their legal-normative character in order to truly correspond to prospective freedom.[79] This is because the fixation on liberal rule of law, which Loick calls 'Juridicism', 'in reality constitutes and privileges a very specific subjectivity – namely that of white, European and male possessive individualists'.[80] Preliminary decisions about the domain and the 'target group' of laws entail a particular affective organisation of a state and its society, which helps to determine who can live well there. Normalising these preliminary decisions as generally shared results in the affective security of bourgeois coldness, which protects European subjects from the shock which would otherwise seize them in the face of the damage they have done to the world. 'Juridicism' denotes the relationship between state violence and bourgeois society, as well as the subjectivity in which it operates.

This society can hardly remain unproblematic when Benjamin's open-ended critique of violence is made to confront the fact that constitutional ordinances solidify themselves in the subjectivity of people who live under them, and that after some time the insight into the contingency of constitutional ordinances fades. Examining bureaucracy shows how bourgeois consent to violence is organised. Once again, the question arises as to what constitutes the intersection between civil society and the ambiguous, 'disgraceful' moments of the legal system. In other words, even the existence of the police is subjectivising, and bourgeois consent to the law as such entails consent to police – and bureaucratic – practices. This does not primarily take place through the rational agreement of bourgeois subjects with the legal norm, but rather primarily on the basis of an affective synchronisation with the world, which is structured by this legal norm. Examining institutions from the perspective of affect theory can provide insights into the subject-forming moments of the bourgeois order.

Police Supremacy

The racist institutional structure of the police cannot simply be understood as a supplement to Benjamin's analysis, adding a contemporary relevance that Benjamin could not yet have anticipated. No – the racial structuring of society is not a by-product of police activity, but its goal. How else could the obvious discrepancy between police activity and liberal-democratic values be explained, other than by the fact that a monopoly on the use of force is directed in practice at what this order seeks to keep at bay? What is this order if not a declaration of loyalty to white supremacy, which supports and protects the uniform unconditionally? Benjamin's leap into the complete void of ethical justifications for state violence is only useful if racialisation is understood as the paradigm of this void. White supremacy is the repetition of unfounded structural and singular acts of violence against non-white people.[81]

Any other position on police violence can only frame its effects on Black people and other people of colour as essentially secondary and legitimate side effects. This perspective, which simply accepts given violence in order not to recognise the depth and continuity of its contingency on racism, is the essence of white supremacy according to Steve Martinot and Jared Sexton.[82] It is ontologically sustained through its flatness, its fully free-floating existence, the blunt repetition of violence: 'It is the same passive apparatus of whiteness that in its mainstream guise actively forgets that it owes its existence to the killing and terrorising of those it racialises for that purpose, expelling them from the human fold in the same gesture of forgetting . . . The truth is that the truth is on the surface, flat and repetitive, just as the law is made by the uniform.'[83]

Violence is thus still flat when it has been transformed into liberal law. Law too must manifest itself over and over to endure, and it would simply disintegrate without its updating. It is not only civil servants and state representatives, whose lives are directly linked to the state, who now have the greatest share and use in covering up the void through a liberal state legal order. All those who profit from white supremacy – from financial advantages to the recognition they experience or the harmony it promises – are still dependent on the 'Avant-Garde of White Supremacy'.[84] They maintain the state by accepting its allocations of violence. They live as bourgeois citizens, turned away from such scenes.

To conclude this examination of bureaucracy and law, a historical review reveals a founding paradigm of bureaucratic violence and the bourgeois avoidance of it. For the coldness of bureaucracy has yet another prehistory besides that of the colonial land grab, which anticipates the third part of this work. Administrative violence culminates in the dehumanisation of abducted and enslaved Africans as 'cargo' on the Middle Passage. This is particularly evident in the insurance calculations that covered the death of such people during the crossing, which were intended to subsequently compensate slave traders and trade organisations for the loss of their 'goods'. Here, murder and indifference are not veiled by rituals of liberal compassion, but recorded as a factor in the financial administration of the slave trade. The social death of the millions thrown overboard and drowned in the Atlantic occurred long before their organic death. The Middle Passage lends this ideology without depth its initial gruesome evidence, simply through the sheer mass of its victims. The insurance calculations register the dead before the ship even sets sail.

Self-Criticism

When will we finally shatter the power of words by the moving of skins? —Christian Maurel[85]

In the act of self-criticism, the bourgeois returns to itself. The bourgeois way of life seeks to promote the reproducibility of rational forms of life and thus to uphold the belief that these can always be altered if they should prove false. This takes place in an inner space of pre-emptive negotiation that the bourgeoisie created over the course of the eighteenth century, in the form of the proverbial coffee-houses and other spaces of discourse.[86] Jürgen Habermas's examination of this formation process differentiates between concepts of the public sphere. Central to this is the difference between a more institutional understanding, meaning statehood in its various manifestations, and a civil one, which denotes the processes of 'public opinion'.[87] The latter is of interest in its specific form of 'the bourgeois public sphere', parallel to the developments of humanism and capitalism.[88] The history of the bourgeois public sphere's emergence is enmeshed in the bourgeois ideal of the subject who seeks to overcome the challenges of modernity by simultaneously shaping and internalising its conditions. This is achieved in negotiation processes between bourgeois citizens, in spaces designed specifically for this purpose in the nineteenth century and that enable a 'critical public' through the state and its projects.[89] Habermas finds the ideal form of this public in the coffee-houses and salons frequented by men during the eighteenth and nineteenth centuries, before the decline of this form in the twentieth century, according to his diagnosis. This ideal consists in the constant refining of discussion dynamics and opinion-forming, depositing these abilities in ever deeper layers of bourgeois consciousness.[90] The moments of this social class's self-criticism take place between hot and cold drinks, representative and conspiratorial conversations, between reasonable judgements and discerning taste.[91] The restricted access to these spaces makes it possible to develop 'reason, which through public use of the rational faculty was to be realised in the rational communication of a public consisting of cultivated human beings'.[92] Finally, protected from the direct influence of sovereign rule, the self thus formed can be constructively questioned with the help of morals acquired through reasoning.[93]

The subject form of the bourgeois citizen lives up to these demands: self-critical bourgeois citizens have shifted the negotiation process into the interior of their bodies and minds.[94] According to the historian Reinhart Koselleck, inner dialogue makes the citizen a critic: 'It is precisely by virtue of his double function, being both accuser and defendant all in one, that the critic rises to the level of a non-partisan entity, becoming the advocate of reason.'[95] In this way, bourgeois critics see themselves capable of wielding an autonomously judging gaze towards their reality and the affects and objects which surround them – even of 'understanding themselves as the living process of enlightenment'[96] and 'knowing themselves, on the basis of [their] enlightened status, to put everything on trial, everything that contradicts heteronomous determinations of [their] moral autonomy'.[97] Critique of the self is an articulation of the claim that one indeed embodies the Enlightenment and does not exclude oneself from the process of judgement. It is immanent to the critical-emancipatory view of the world.

According to the historical epoch analysed by Habermas and Koselleck, the self-critical faculty is no longer reserved for the collective of the bourgeois class, clearly defined in economic and social terms. Self-criticism has long since crossed the boundaries of the institutional spaces located by Habermas – mass media and bourgeois meeting places like theatres and cafés.

Consistent self-criticism, for example, found a radical but politically hopeless articulation in the communist groups of the 1968 generation.[98] It is understood as the practice of identifying the ideological damage to oneself and, on the basis of these insights, enabling oneself to fight for the systemic change which puts an end to that ideology's constant reproduction.

An understanding of critique as work on the self, without the horizon of systemic change, finds expression in the entrepreneurial logic of the present. Neoliberalism's ideology of optimisation demands that the self constantly *get better* by relentlessly evaluating one's own performance.[99] Of course, a fundamental difference arises between the stated objectives of neoliberal and left self-criticism – the maximisation of profit for the former, and political change for the latter. Self-criticism is also credited with realising identity political demands for participation, as well as recognition in democratic and institutional public spheres. Diversity and equity programs are equivalent to the internalisation of self-criticism within institutions in the bourgeois era. Here, self-criticism behaves like a democratic instrument to pursue the establishment of just conditions without the use of violence. In this context, self-criticism steers socially relevant questions into the interior of the self in the hope of a non-violent, affective intervention in its depths.

Insisting on morality against practical considerations is a deeply bourgeois tendency – such morality makes the subject a bourgeois subject.[100] The bourgeois class has exercised authority since the eighteenth century in this way, preventing radical interventions with a politics of sound judgement and, not infrequently, silencing voices other than its own. In this way, bourgeois media's reference to the supposedly moral character of certain criticisms – prepared as they are to put up a fight against critical discussions of institutional racism, patriarchal structures and economic disadvantage – suggests the defensiveness of the bourgeois position.[101] The relish in disqualifying new intellectual actors on the political stage is, formally, a betrayal of bourgeois morality and its fidelity to the better argument, but at the same time it reveals how the bourgeois discursive space has clear borders that its members are ready to defend at any time. These struggles can be read much more meaningfully as struggles over interpretive power within existing institutions rather than struggles against these institutions, and they express, once again, that liberal forms of critique have always operated with self-limitation. Robyn Marasco notes that, 'Habermas treats critical philosophy as a rescue operation – most of all, critique must be saved from itself'.[102]

The demands of various actors for participation in institutional power do not in principle contradict bourgeois democracy and its self-conception, acquired from the Enlightenment and the ethics of discourse. And in Germany, a learning process can indeed be observed: everywhere, one can find simple strategies such as the diversification of editorial boards and panels, as well as the ready assurance that people want to learn about racism in order to overcome it.

Yet the transformation of bourgeois order does not succeed by improving the existing one, even though intervention in the existing order makes visible distribution criteria and can concretely improve living conditions. The more radical political question regarding the bourgeois order is whether it suffices to critique problematic institutions in the form of inclusion and democratisation – and whether these institutions can be effectively transformed.[103]

What might be observed in German public discourse in the coming years is of interest to me at the level of the individual bourgeois subject. Self-criticism can be considered the minimal degree of reform, taking place in the self's very interior. In its ideal form, self-criticism is always able to arrest the self in terms of its rational, moral insight, so that it can continually provide information about right and wrong and behave accordingly. Despite Adorno and Horkheimer's mistrust of bourgeois reason, self-criticism proves to be something of a political fall-back option. The intact subject remains for them the linchpin of change. In this regard, I will argue the extent to which the insistence on self-criticism marks a limit to Adorno's readiness to take political risks.

To understand the extent to which self-criticism conserves the existing order instead of overcoming it, critique itself must be targeted as a subject-constituting practice. How the practice of critique begets the self, how it additionally stabilises the individual and holds it in its social place, is an essential mode of bourgeois reproduction. I am interested in the soothing effect of self-criticism, its sedative characteristic, which sustains the bourgeoisie in a society which is formally democratic but actually divided along the lines of 'race', class and gender. It can make the individual subject aware of bad conditions and their own participation in them, but it can hardly change these conditions in actuality. I want to problematise the unquestioned position of self-critique as the *ultima ratio* of bourgeois morality. As a philosophical legacy, self-criticism pervades the white European, bourgeois and perhaps especially German self-conception. Subjects who see themselves as self-critical are by no means safe from the pitfalls of heroic self-representation – on the contrary. Self-criticism, as an activity reserved for autonomous subjects, can be a source of social recognition. Adorno even sees the danger that the 'German conceptions in which autonomy for its own sake is so extravagantly glorified' extends to 'the deification of the state'.[104] What is meant is that autonomy reconciles the relationship between individuals and the state, rather than formulating an objection to it. Based on Friedrich Nietzsche's critique of bourgeois morality, a consideration of self-criticism in myth, and, finally, on account of self-criticism's ambivalent position in Adorno and Horkheimer, it becomes clear to what extent it preserves bourgeois society: self-criticism is when those in power make time for themselves, as Elsa Dorlin puts it.[105]

The expression 'virtue signalling' has taken hold to describe practices in which self-criticism is used as a commodity.[106] In digital and commercial communication, self-criticism is a dominant form of courting consumers, utilising the political awareness of various actors as market value. For companies and public figures alike, exhibiting a willingness to morally scrutinise one's own actions is crucial for popularity on the liberal and affluent political spectrum. For companies, the demand to correct their visual appearance in favour of plausibly diverse representations is an everyday marketing measure. For public and political figures, demonstrating political sympathies with the less privileged is an important way to signal approachability to all manner of concerns, regardless of responsibility and material change. Here, self-criticism is reduced to representative acts, in many cases with no material equivalents.

Self-criticism in the consumer world can be understood with the help of Adorno and Horkheimer's dialectic of myth and enlightenment and analysis of the culture industry. The commodification of critique causes enlightenment to fold back into myth, integrating it into the logic of exchange without resistance. In the market, critique sometimes presents itself as an ennobling substance that lends products an aura of political consciousness. Critique withers away to a representation – it becomes non-performative and ultimately ineffective.[107]

Roland Barthes's theory of everyday myths thematises the signs of wear that weaken political concepts over time. This also applies to critical interventions at the moment when they are appropriated by capitalism. Barthes sees myth as an element of deformation. Myth changes the relationship between word and reality. For example, discussions under the once clear political mandate of climate protection now predominantly concern optional technological innovations or individual and fairly ineffective micro-measures – but not the global reduction of CO2 emissions by ending the use of fossil fuels. Myth does not necessarily conceal the truth;[108] but it deforms a relationship to it and changes the concept's concrete implications.[109] The practice of self-criticism signals a readiness towards fundamental change, bringing it about in a sense. However, it shirks its responsibility if it is satisfied with the representation of change – for example, a change in personnel, rather than questioning objectives and procedures beyond one's own person. As myth, self-criticism is ineffective, and thus does not help to achieve lasting change in the world. When self-criticism turns into humiliating gestures or minor adjustments, an irreversible deformation and diminishment takes place. The insight that self-criticism has now taken on a mythical structure means that something else must take its place to fulfil the political task it no longer can. Self-criticism has suffered a loss in power through attrition, through inflationary usage and capitalist deformation. When self-criticism no longer succeeds in always holding out the prospect of the end of the institutions and forms it critiques, it betrays its original purpose.

It is difficult to practice critique in such a way that it develops the power to overcome. If critique constitutes the subject, it is especially questionable how the subject which critique produces can wish to overcome itself and the practice of self-criticism. Because the bourgeois subject internalises critique, is even 'formed through such a process of critique',[110] the perpetuation of critique always entails the perpetuation of the subject.[111]

The conviction that the best answer to critique should always be found in the subject is a misconception. This realisation can be utilised towards capitalistic ends, since it results in endless opportunities for optimisation. Perhaps this is why it is so persistent. The myth of critique contributes to the valorisation of institutions and companies when they undergo this self-referential, self-critical cycle, and in doing so generate the broadest possible visibility. Even the mere claim of a willingness to respond to social demands for change is enough to allow continued operation in this society, and to be supported in doing so.

Barthes describes how 'myth is speech *stolen* and *restored*. Only, speech which is restored is no longer quite that which was stolen: when it was brought back, it was not put exactly in its place'.[112] The logic of exchange adopts self-criticism to create surplus value out of it. Whether the called-for changes actually take place is ultimately irrelevant in terms of profit – the gesture of assimilation is enough to restore legitimacy. Having been misappropriated in this way is problematic for self-criticism: it ossifies and loses its political credibility.

What is sometimes dismissively called 'cancel culture', referring to the boycott of people and institutions after moral hubris or other transgressions come to light, is a desperate reaction to this feeling of a lack of political credibility. The reassuring tone in which self-critical intentions are often expressed is the antithesis to the anger that occasionally breaks out when parts of civil society try to weaken the influence of morally dubious individuals in line with their own sense of justice. Self-criticism is a means by which bourgeois subjects impose an accepted hiatus from political responsibility in which they can be protected from the emotions of others, until they feel ready to respond. In short, self-criticism is an aid – in the political as well as the personal sense – for not having to deal with the feelings of others. 'As reason posits no substantial goals, all affects are equally remote to it.'[113]

Through its integration into value creation and mythical reproduction of the status quo, self-criticism thus appears as a sustaining rather than an intervening force. It serves the self-soothing of subjects and institutions. It allows for the preservation or the restoration of a legitimate, moral self-image in a variety of ways – not through a confrontation with the world and the material and affective consequences of one's actions, but through introspection, the adaptation of self-representation, and a damage control which in the end is purely conceptual.

Self-criticism is the bourgeois subject's cunning in remaining what it is – an entity enabling the state and its order – while credibly conveying what it willingly wants to become: a better human being according to its own image. But to use extensive resources on such self-engagement inevitably comes at the cost of changing the conditions which maintain stability, materially and epistemologically, for bourgeois society. The bourgeois subject pushes for adaptation.[114] Wanting to effect political change with respect to the individual self cannot work, it only leads to the kind of compulsive self-reflection characteristic of all rulers: 'By making themselves the exclusive object of attention and concern, they lend themselves meaning, weight and space, and thus reproduce the material preconditions for ensuring the continuation of their rule.'[115]

Nietzsche's Rage

The same puzzle picture that Odysseus made use of – between thinking and being, name and existence – is at play in the question of the performativity of self-criticism. The bourgeois subject is the carrier of a self-assurance which extends its capacity for reflection to infinity in order to maintain its own form of life.[116] Self-criticism is the refusal of a more painful and profound close examination of the self, one which ends with overcoming the self.

As Peter Sloterdijk writes: 'It is not infrequently necessary for the pure interest in surviving to be able to be Nobody.'[117] He is referring to Odysseus in his fight with the Cyclops Polyphemus. The well-known warrior's cunning in introducing himself as 'Outis' (Nobody) saves him from the Cyclops's revenge. But does Odysseus really overcome himself by becoming nobody, or does he merely display the cunning which allows him to emerge from the battle as a hero, not just a survivor? We know that a pure interest in survival would have been better served by escaping the Cyclops sooner. So what would it mean to truly overcome the self and become nobody for the purposes of survival? If the self opens up further courses of action through self-criticism, instead of limiting itself through humility, then the circumstances that provide its means of life will be expanded in the process. What would the rupture have to look like for it to inhibit the self-preservation of bourgeois subjectivity and its self-perpetuation?

Critique, in the eternal paths of reflection and self-improvement, leads down a long road to a dead end, with no possibility of turning back. Overcoming the self is not a linear or purely intellectual process. This is why it is not easy to write about self-criticism without performatively getting trapped in the contradiction of using self-questioning to maintain one's own power. Certainly, philosophy itself represents an obsessive form of self-reflection as activity – and in particular the attempt to critically examine its premises. Philosophy always runs the risk of getting stuck in a habitualised, ineffective self-reflection, building 'bridges-of-lies to ancient ideals'.[118]

Friedrich Nietzsche in the nineteenth century pursued the project of undermining 'our *faith* in morality'.[119] In so doing, he posed a challenge to Western philosophy that continues to this day. With its attempt to articulate 'the inexpressible of philosophy', Nietzsche's critique aims at neither a natural end nor a tangible solution.[120] Nietzsche imagines an existence which leaves the bourgeois-Christian ideals of his present behind in favour of an unbridled freedom, which only a new type of man could realise in his eyes.[121] Regardless of the concrete political realisation of this idea, its implicit philosophical task – not to conceive of freedom in unquestioned harmony with the morality of the Enlightenment – was accepted by many. German and French philosophy of the twentieth century formulated approaches – often with reference to Nietzsche's philosophy – to give more material credibility to the Kantian practical reason which arises from the subject capable of morality. By theoretically taking up political catastrophes and everyday realities, this subject's relationship to the world becomes more tangible and complex. However, Adorno's objection to 'system thinking', Martin Heidegger's philosophy of being, and Derrida's thinking of alterity all ultimately still rest upon the specific faculties of the subject.

Nietzsche's intervention in Enlightenment thought is not a mere correction to a misunderstood ethics of conscience. It is worthwhile to offer an affective reading of his philosophy in order to understand rage as an elementary resource of his position. Nietzsche's wrath, partly aggressive and partly cynical, produces a surplus. Nietzsche rejects the bourgeois, self-reflective mode of existence, not only because of its social consequences and moral hubris, but also for aesthetic reasons. He dislikes the type of person who is guided by morals because this person is witless, ambitious, and therefore deeply uninteresting. He is furious at self-satisfaction, which has no motive other than docile inclusion in the existing order. The reproduction of the existing order can be traced back to this visionless, boring ambition. Rage is an important engine for the critique of bourgeois society, seeking to break its self-perpetuating dynamic. It faces the proper, assimilated life, embodied by the bourgeois, with a fundamental aversion to self-assurance and the will to adapt. Rage unleashes a sensorium in Nietzsche's text in order to root out bourgeois tendencies towards containment in social interactions and cultural phenomena, to ridicule them or otherwise declare enmity.[122]

In the process, argumentative mistakes appear and nuances are lost – Horkheimer finds *On the Genealogy of Morals* 'too crude despite its subtleties', and Habermas, who completely misunderstands the vehemence of Nietzsche's statements, accuses him of a 'pathos of his judgements and his prejudices'.[123] However, one mistake is avoided without fail when rage trumps the fear of overshooting the mark: the mistake of protecting bourgeois society out of reverence. The assessment in favour of a paranoid,[124] maximally critical approach, at the expense of a cautious one that strives for accuracy, is reflected in a statement by Nietzsche on the function of knowledge: 'Thus the *strength* of knowledge does not depend on its degree of truth but its age, on the degree to which it has been incorporated, on its character as a condition of life. Where life and knowledge seemed to be at odds there was never any real fight, but denial and doubt were simply considered madness.'[125] For knowledge to acquire this character, for it to become lived knowledge, it must be put on a level with an affective repertoire in order to meaningfully articulate it. Habermas reproaches Nietzsche with subordinating knowledge to an 'interest' and refusing self-reflection by means of this displacement. This leads to a 'psychologisation' and eventual 'dissolution' of knowledge altogether.[126] The philosopher Jutta Georg counters that Nietzsche is indeed concerned with the qualities of honesty and integrity affirmed by Habermas when he exercises maximum severity against himself and the social conventions surrounding him.[127] Contrary to Georg's appraisal that this mode of knowledge is not affective, I think that Nietzsche's mercilessness towards himself and the surrounding world can hardly take shape without a vocabulary of affective motivations which inform the cognitive process. Revulsion against feigned harmony and rage at the blindness of his contemporaries are without a doubt two guiding principles in Nietzsche's thinking. His work manifests the felt truth that critique of bourgeois society has had an affective component since its inception. It is hardly possible to formulate an objection to bourgeois society in a 'neutral' way, because precisely this insistence on such disinterestedness, and the associated disqualification of emotion-informed statements, is an intellectual pillar of the bourgeois society that Habermas upholds like no other. Habermas's theoretical conviction according to his *The Theory of Communicative Action*, that every conflict can be resolved through linguistic practice, and that no affective resources are needed to express a position, thus stands in contrast to Nietzsche's philosophy of life.

Nietzsche does not remain mired in the gesture of angry rejection. He sketches out a freedom he envisions beyond bourgeois conditions. And there are concrete transgressions of bourgeois morality that he precisely analyses. Both are important impulses for examining the practices of self-criticism. For Nietzsche's search for the 'free spirit' in *Beyond Good and Evil*, bourgeois Christian morality, which readily claims responsibility for itself at all times and seeks to grow through its tasks, is a clear obstacle. As a result of this observation, he casts doubt on the altruistic character of good deeds, with an eye towards the feelings of the good Samaritan – and thus on the very possibility of genuinely moral acts:

> There is no way around it: our feelings of devotion, of sacrifice for our neighbour, and the whole morality of self-renunciation must be mercilessly called to account and taken to court; and likewise the aesthetics of 'disinterested contemplation' under which the emasculation of art today seductively tries to create a good conscience for itself. There is much too much allure and sugar in those feelings of 'for others', of '*not* for me', for us not to need to be doubly suspicious here and to ask: 'are these not perhaps – *seductions*?' That they are *pleasing* – to someone who has them and to someone who enjoys their fruits, even to the mere spectator – still does not serve as an argument *for* them, but demands caution instead. So let's be cautious![128]

Nietzsche addresses the moral foundation of bourgeois subjectivity and morality, which constitutes the basis for self-enlightenment and self-criticism. Admitting one's own moral misjudgement to correct it in the future, however, is not a selfless act in Nietzsche's eyes. Moral feelings, experienced by the subject willing to change and its observers, are an essential part of why moral actions are attractive. The bourgeois good conscience is the clearest expression of this dynamic – Nietzsche's image of the enemy is of Christian origin. The idea of conscience inscribes morality into each individual subject and bestows its activation with a feeling of reward. Working on the self becomes attractive. What's more, Nietzsche traces the religious foundation of modern subjectivity, which only appears to have dissolved. Nietzsche's rage targets the self-conscious bourgeois who no longer needs religion according to himself, but who orients himself autonomously in life. Religion is considered '"uncleanliness" of the spirit' by the bourgeois order. Secular morality, on the other hand, is declared a principle, and self-criticism the means of self-perfection.[129] The bourgeois citizens who turn away from religion are 'good people', whose need for meaning must now be satisfied in a different form.[130]

Nietzsche reminds us that self-criticism can be read through the history of the subject as resulting from of a process in which ecclesiastical authority was replaced by the moral integrity of the individual subject. The Enlightenment shifted the judgement of good and evil to the realm of autonomous persons. Nietzsche's energy is directed on the one hand at identifying the particular failures of this transfer, and on the other at naming the substitutions which the supposedly autonomous subject carries out in its 'industriousness', since it lacks the orienting point of the Church.[131] He has the educated bourgeois classes in mind in particular, who not only look down on the Church as an outdated institution, but also entirely overestimate their own ability to make moral judgements and live freely. In this model, 'modern ideas' serve as an indicator of freedom, which Nietzsche dismisses as naïve, probably because they are so ignorant of history.[132] So an image emerges in which all the simple-mindedness of the enlightened person is destroyed and self-criticism has lost its noble character. Bourgeois practice appears as the opposite of a caring and productive participation in society. Instead, seemingly selfless actions are recognisable as the result of an agonising void to be filled with excessive reflections on oneself. Nietzsche does not trust enlightened subjectivity one inch.

Various thinkers have philosophically taken up Nietzsche's vehement rejection of bourgeois critique and morality. Gilles Deleuze notes, however, 'perhaps not in the way he [Nietzsche] would have wished'.[133] Nietzsche had indeed formulated an alternative proposal for how critique might avoid exhausting itself in the empty gestures with which Christian thought repeatedly assures itself. Critique is only promising if it enables shifting focus away from the self and towards values – since values are indeed worthy of critique, contrary to the Christian position. Nietzsche suggests genealogical work for this task. Deleuze describes it as such: 'The problem of critique is that of the value of values, of the evaluation from which their value arises, thus the problem of their *creation*.'[134]

Nietzsche's call for a critique of values instead of self-critique was taken up in the philosophy of Deleuze and Michel Foucault, through a commitment to genealogical work and a theoretical renunciation of the unity of the subject – but still nowhere near as social practice.[135] In this sense, it remains the task of a critical theory of society to register the endurance of the bourgeois moral order and value systems in the present, and to attend to the very conditions of its reproduction, which remain undisturbed by Deleuze's and Foucault's philosophical interventions. They are tenacious systems, ultimately rooted in the history of bourgeois society's formation, which goes hand in hand with capitalism and the demarcation of racialised others. The latter was ignored by the French genealogists. And there is still more to be said on the question of critique's form. Why can the bourgeois subject be understood as critical and yet repeatedly fail in the acceptance of less rigorous forms of subjectivity than its own, and fail in the implementation of material justice?

In the sense of its idealism, the bourgeois self wants to constantly improve but can no longer see that it would help the world more if it abandoned itself. Bourgeois self-preservation on the basis of self-criticism means understanding the bourgeois way of life not primarily as a commitment to certain values historically linked to class. Instead, the bourgeoisie tends to insist on one method: the gesture of understanding itself as an adequate medium for all interests, and trusting itself to express them. The bourgeoisie survives through the conviction that it has always been a part of the solution, rather than part of the problem. I would therefore like to achieve a perspective on bourgeois subjectivity that prefers its overcoming to its optimisation – a perspective that recognises and precisely names the strategies with which bourgeois subjects and societies constantly renew and maintain themselves. Only in this way can we begin to think about what another society might look like. What would it be like to be primarily concerned with the world and no longer with ourselves?

A Home in the Mind

Theodor W. Adorno and Max Horkheimer are critics of bourgeois reason. In the first part of this book, I reconstructed *Dialectic of Enlightenment* as a critique of the proto-bourgeois genesis of Odysseus and pointed out problems in the idealisation of personhood. When it comes specifically to self-criticism, however, the judgement of bourgeois subjectivity becomes more colourful. The way the authors of *Dialectic of Enlightenment* forge a connection between Enlightenment reason and fascism, and the fact that the text makes make no political offer, can sometimes plunge the reader into an abyss. When consulting later writings to get to the bottom of their political positions, it becomes clear that, for both authors, self-criticism represents a positive feature of bourgeois society. For Adorno and Horkheimer, self-criticism is a kind of intersection where the bourgeois use of reason meets a reason cleansed of its instrumental deformation. For even if the critique of reason remains the ultimate goal of their work, it hardly produces political directives.

Both see in the self-critical capacity an essential moment of hope for political praxis – perhaps the only moment of hope that philosophy has to offer. Horkheimer partly relativises the decisively exposed transgressions of bourgeois reason, because even this reason teaches 'critique, even that of ourselves'. He calls for us to 'not be ungrateful to the bourgeois order'. He seems hopeful about reason on account of its ability to reject fear:

> We must not be ungrateful to the bourgeois order. Its greatest shortcoming is not the misery it contains, for it could overcome that, but rather that it is liquidating itself through the operation of immanent laws. The most important intellectual debt is that our thinking carries the signature of freedom, that – however great our fear of the end – there is a sense in which we do not feel it, for our reason has not been intimidated. If we want something higher than this bourgeois order it is only because, even as it was just beginning to gather strength under feudalism, it taught us

> to be critical, and also critical of ourselves. We want something better but we must be careful that its arrival not stifle that will.[136]

Overcoming the fear of ruin caused Odysseus to act with cunning – and cost his companions their lives. But Horkheimer wants it to be taken into account that – apart from Odysseus' heroism – reason is a source of freedom when the subject is in distress. Horkheimer thanks the bourgeois order for its practical utility since it frees one from fear, even in catastrophe. He urges restraint in the hasty and total rejection of critique based in reason, because it sets free the ability to reject immediate threats and is ultimately the condition for everything 'higher' that might follow. Such is a confession of Horkheimer's on the basis of his and Adorno's critique of reason: both owe the bourgeois order their intellectual existence – and their resilience. They remain in its thrall. They derive the urgency of their thinking and their secure footing from a *bourgeois* spirit of freedom. I am not so much concerned in this context with making a philosophical assessment of this constellation. However, in order to understand the self-preservation of the bourgeois subject, it is crucial to observe that Horkheimer and Adorno profess reason above all in moments of concrete political questioning. They entrust to reason the genuine political function of protecting the self from catastrophe and opening up spaces for action, even when circumstances are overwhelming.

In the mind, Horkheimer sees a place to reside – like a bedroom in a bourgeois home. There, the bourgeois self and all the intimate aspects of its life are protected. One can always come inside, even when catastrophe looms beyond the door. The mind can repel fear because it is conscious of its temporality and its overwhelming force, classifying and relativising it, putting it in its place – and because reason offers the philosopher, a bourgeois by profession, an immaterial home in his own mind.

But can the mind really offer reliable protection against the paralysis of fear? Elsa Dorlin writes about 'self-defence and the politics of rage' in order to understand the connection between actively reacting to threat and the affective register of rage.[137] The subject overwhelmed by fear in Dorlin's work is the Black American poet June Jordan, who survived rape and who sought to envision her own self-defence strategy. Dorlin comments on Jordan's portrayal of defending herself against a white man:

> In a fraction of a second, her fear evaporated – she would rather die than obey this white man. Race reanimated her paralysed body. It was racism rather than sexism that served as the pivot point here, raising her power of action to a 'do or die' level. Jordan's rage expressed itself through self-defence and in reference to the existence of a community in struggle. She managed to strike him in the head and escape.[138]

In contrast to Horkheimer's crisis strategy, Jordan's defence against fear in the immediate presence of threat can hardly be perceived as a rational act. Certainly one can understand internalised rage at white men, whose victim she in no case wants to be, as the result of discursive processes which have shaped her awareness of living in a racist society. Yet it would be inadequate to view reason itself here as a resource for self-defence. Unlike Horkheimer, Jordan has no room to retreat to. To have been raped is characterised by the destruction of any possibility of practically distancing oneself, except for the experience of escaping one's body, which many survivors report. The threat is too close to imagine a second, safe room, and can thus only be rejected through an active reaction. One cannot, while being raped, have the knowledge that there is no reason to fear. To overcome fear's paralysis can only mean trying to interrupt the catastrophe in the act itself – by physically defending oneself, or leaving one's own body. Jordan's rage is the condition of preparing herself for such an activity and to be able to escape. Those in fear resort to the resources closest at hand. While Horkheimer trusts reason to relieve him of fear's immediacy, Jordan has developed an affective self-defence that goes beyond a purely psychological distancing from events. She unleashes bodily capacities. Of course, Horkheimer and Jordan – or Dorlin – are talking about different forms of fear. Nevertheless, their respective portrayals might allow us to deduce how they understand a politics whose general task is replacing fear with agency. While Horkheimer would like to contain his experience of fear through rational relativisation and classification, Jordan primarily wants to establish the capacity for immediate action – for self-defence.[139] Jordan does not react against reason. Rather, her politics as enacted here show that her history as a Black woman is more adequately articulated in the informed rage towards her rapist than in a retreat into a reason cleansed of affect. In this way she too can defend herself against the intimidation Horkheimer invoked.

The bourgeois subject was 'trained through a process of critique', writes the artist Hito Steyerl.[140] Critical reason is the home of the bourgeois subject and thus has an interest in the continued existence of conditions which enable it to appear as possible, correct. If we imagine Adorno and Horkheimer as the bourgeois citizens they were, then it is no wonder they turned to reason against fear.[141] Independent of pushing their thinking to the limit, on the basis of which both rigorously examined possibilities of thought in the face of the Shoah, reason remains as the object and operator of philosophical questions, as the philosopher's trusted mode of existence. This is not necessarily a contradiction, certainly not a failure of their philosophy. The existential function of reason, critique and self-criticism plainly reveals the interest in self-preservation that underlies reason and the citizen who embodies it, even in the form of self-criticism. Critique, and the subject it nourishes, remain dependent on each other – and thus they maintain the bourgeois order.

According to Steyerl, critique even becomes an 'independent institution' within this function, entangled in a contradiction. It then becomes 'a means of government that produces adjusted subjects'.[142] Therein lies a political problem, especially when reason, in the form of self-criticism, is seen as a knight in shining armour – as in Adorno and Horkheimer. As a result, critique cannot be construed as a resistance to governability, as is commonly understood. More often it looks to an independent institutional existence.[143] This existence is formed in such a way that bourgeois subjects are born, and preserved, when they speak of change. It also shows how self-critical reason is sufficient legitimation for claiming positions of power. Such an institutionalisation is an important resource for enshrining self-criticism, and thus bourgeois identity, in the state's domain. Steyerl observes this process through museums, which, in her view, attain legitimacy precisely through the fact that they repeatedly legitimise and optimise nation-state narratives through their critical questioning, so that ultimately it is a morally motivated self-criticism which directly benefits the preservation of the state.[144] Contemporary art as a whole tends to position critique as a central aesthetic quality, becoming more institutionally stable rather than porous in the process.[145] Since the 1970s, when certain artists opened the field of institutional critique, in theories as well as practice, they themselves have become institutions of critique over the last fifty years.[146] The consequences of such a position within the commercial and high-value art market continue to prompt different evaluations and controversial discussions. Commodification of critical positions is clear to see here regardless.

It would be rash to politically categorise the various spheres of (self-)critique that assist in bourgeois self-preservation, or to unambiguously define their consequences. Self-criticism does not automatically lead to positions which clearly oppose revolutionary projects. The examples above of left-wing practices which aim at individual transformation are, like Adorno and Horkheimer's political statements and the commodification of critical practices in the field of art, signs of the fact that bourgeois practice endures across camps. These are individualised forms of self-critique. It is important to speak here of 'bourgeois practice' instead of 'bourgeois identity', since it operates independently of identifications and can only be overcome in practice.

Christian Maurel makes this explicit when, in the 1970s, he rages against the bourgeoisification of the French gay movement in his writing: 'Leftists are never overwhelmed; they just save themselves for another time.'[147] For Maurel, this 'leftist' becomes bourgeois when he makes a claim to stable forms of living and desiring and becomes increasingly preoccupied with himself. This self-reflexive stasis affects the entire leftist movement when it institutionalises itself. Maurel sees this as precisely what makes it powerless: 'everything this left touches dries up.'[148] When 'the Left' can no longer dedicate itself to any impulse from the outside world, but instead pursues the mere goal of penetrating everything reflexively, and only then changing it, this leads to a drying-up of all the life for whose sake the movement began. With regards to the gay movement to which he feels he belongs, Maurel finds it especially incomprehensible that the homosexual capacity to desire in resistance does not ultimately lead to rejecting bourgeois forms of life. He is angry about the willingness of his homosexual comrades to be ensnared again and again: 'They are homosexuality's damaged. They have been reterritorialised in the apparatus that their desire could have dissolved.'[149] Here, desire is an instance of intervention that makes something else more important than the affirmative self-reference of bourgeois subjects.

How can the conviction of being at once the medium and object of change be ruptured in favour of a willingness to follow transformative forces that elude one's own intellectual control? Where can bourgeois morality and its myth of self-criticism be disrupted? 'When does the force of words break the power of the body?'[150]

Self-criticism is a potent feature of the bourgeois, which reproduces itself unremittingly. My aim is not to discard self-criticism outright, but to make transparent its preconditions – the autonomous subject – and its political consequences – a stabilising rather than transformative practice – in order to measure its political limits. This allows us to say something about the bourgeois laws of motion in general: the bourgeois avails itself of reason's ability to be institutionalised, as well as its affective binding force – for example in the form of self-criticism. It rests on a mutual dependence of person and institution. As a result, it establishes families, schools, neighbourhoods – and keeps nation-states stable. The bourgeois seeks to promote the reproducibility of rational forms of life through the means of critique. By prioritising the reproduction and optimisation of its forms of life, it becomes increasingly unlikely to overcome and abolish the inequality on which these forms of life are based. Bourgeois life can thus be understood primarily as the affective substance of modernity, binding people to institutions and thereby relegating the founding moments of these institutions to the background, as well as the possibility of overcoming them. What follows will affectively consider the persistence of this process. The rhetorical focus of bourgeois forms of life on the concepts 'reason' and 'critique' can easily conceal the fact that the establishment of these forms is based on affective bonds at least as much as on rational principles. It is only through these bonds that critique becomes a way of life, and reason a stance.[151] At the same time, critique and reason become intellectually opaque in this affective form of existence; they begin to take on a life of their own which may undermine their underlying system of values – or articulate their own value system that implicitly carves out a shadow existence of modernity.[152] Habitualised self-criticism has always tolerated a shadow existence of modernity – self-criticism allows the bourgeois spirit to see distressing conditions as bearable when it cannot independently change them. When it loses access to the progressive power of its proclaimed ideals, the bourgeois becomes bourgeois coldness.

5 Coldness

Bourgeois coldness is an affective social technique. It is deployed at various levels, guiding and controlling affective dynamics to ensure the continued existence of given social conditions. Coldness can pacify interpersonal relationships or expand into a social programme. Coldness is an affective instrument for relating to a challenging or even unbearable reality. In this function, it provides help. Bourgeois coldness goes further, denoting the social convention that no other reference to the present is possible or necessary other than a cold one. In this form, coldness is a resource for promoting affective stasis in the particular interest of a bourgeois class.[1]

Coldness is a technique in that it is learned, practiced and deployed. The micro-level of its application can be illustrated by the painful end of a romantic relationship, where potential suffering is limited by deliberately cooling the relationship.[2] Coldness also proves to be a subversive strategy when it erects an affective wall against institutional attempts to appropriate political positions for their own self-preservation. This coldness outside the bourgeois makes it possible to maintain differences where they are politically important.[3]

To consider the full range of coldness and to ultimately understand its bourgeois appropriation, this chapter moves through various levels of its sedimentation. The starting point is Theodor W. Adorno's diagnosis that Auschwitz would not have been possible without coldness.[4] This leads him to an anthropological concept of coldness which stands in opposition to the pragmatist, behavioural understanding in cultural historian Helmut Lethen's 'theories of conduct'.[5] Ultimately, both positions are based on the problematic notion that a distanced coldness is opposed to unmediated warmth, often additionally associated with femininity. This notion is rectified by Audre Lorde's feminist affect theory.[6]

Coldness and Auschwitz

> As I said, those people [absorbed by technique] are cold in a specific way. Surely a few words about coldness in general are permitted. If coldness were not a fundamental trait of anthropology, that is, the constitution of people as they in fact exist in our society, if people were not profoundly indifferent toward whatever happens to everyone else except for a few to whom they are closely bound and, if possible, by tangible interests, then Auschwitz would not have been possible, people would not have accepted it. Society in its present form – and no doubt as it has been for centuries already – is based not, as was ideologically assumed since Aristotle, on appeal, on attraction, but rather on the pursuit of one's own interests against the interests of everyone else. This has settled into the character of people to their innermost center. What contradicts my observation, the herd drive of the so-called *lonely crowd* is a reaction to this process, a banding together of people completely cold who cannot endure their own coldness and yet cannot change it.[7]

In both Theodor W. Adorno's own texts and in his duet with Max Horkheimer, coldness is the affective term for social indifference as the result of an interest-based social order. In his radio lecture 'Education after Auschwitz', Adorno even describes it as an enabling condition for the Shoah – at the same time, it is said to be a 'fundamental trait of anthropology' and thus to have been effective without interruption at least up until his own time. Adorno cites three exemplary symptoms of this anthropological constellation which show how coldness finds manifest forms in the culture industry and, what's more, is ideologised as an attitude of strength. It can be understood as a mode of reified consciousness – that state of mind which experiences itself as unalterable.[8] It is an individual stance of hardness, sport and technology, that for Adorno exemplifies the cooling of human relationships. He presents hardness as a socially honoured, masculine personality principle.[9] Sport has both a community-building and a socially threatening effect – especially for the spectators – when it promotes aggression.[10] And technology contributes to the general alienation of social suffering by obscuring the potentially cruel consequences of one's own actions through technological mediation.[11]

All of these articulations of coldness can be mitigated through social change. Patriarchal ideology would have to be ruptured, sport democratised, and alienated labour abolished in order to counteract coldness at the level of society as a whole. For Adorno, however, Auschwitz is proof that coldness itself is sooner capable of producing a horrific order before the social conditions under which it was able to gain strength can change. Its anthropological development has to do with the fact that it resonates in subjective dispositions. How can we counter the genesis of bourgeois coldness before it coagulates into the anthropological component that made Auschwitz possible?

In his lecture, Adorno dedicates himself to the concrete in an astonishing way, seeing it as the first task of education 'that Auschwitz not happen again'.[12] Through education, children as well as adults must be prevented from falling prey to coldness. Adorno does not consider himself qualified to develop pedagogical concepts, but nevertheless reveals his idea of 'educational groups' to facilitate education in rural areas.[13]

On the conceptual level, education signifies a 'turn to the subject'. According to Adorno, the subject must be competent in self-reflection in order to resist the fascist masses. When it comes to concrete steps against social indifference, he ultimately regards engaging with the genesis of cold subjectivity as the most promising theoretical means to understand socially accepted suffering and to create a basis for self-enlightenment:[14] 'The only education that has any sense at all is an education toward critical self-reflection.'[15]

The critical self-reflection of rational beings, which in the best case renders education possible, finds its starting point in Immanuel Kant. Despite his numerous critiques of the principle of autonomy, Adorno believes it is the solution to what I above call 'a political relapse': 'The single genuine power standing against the principle of Auschwitz is autonomy, if I might use the Kantian expression: the power of reflection, of self-determination, of not cooperating.'[16]

Individual autonomy, acquired through critical self-reflection, promotes the individual's powers of resistance, so that in the moment of burgeoning fascism, critique can also be outwardly exercised and democracy protected. Adorno comes to this conclusion, at any rate, after his reflections on 'Education after Auschwitz'. Similar to Horkheimer's use of reason as a defence against fear, Adorno argues that the anti-fascist political mobilisation of individuals can only be conceived as the result of their self-reflection. But the gap between Adorno's consensus with Kant's autonomous subject model as well as Horkheimer's critique of this ideal in other parts of their work raises questions.[17] How does Adorno suddenly come to approve of the very subject of Enlightenment which he problematised in *Dialectic of Enlightenment*? It may have something to do with the fact that the reification of political questions into philosophical considerations often puts them fundamentally at odds. This friction was already articulated in Horkheimer's defence against anxiety, where he justifies the bourgeois order, and the reason on which it is based, as a refuge from intimidation.

When the authors of *Dialectic of Enlightenment* discuss reason as such, it is exactly this notion of an autonomous, disinterested reason that they critique, yet which is rehabilitated as a model in 'Education after Auschwitz'. Taking Kant as their starting point, reason is understood as a higher principle that is independent of social interests in its jurisdiction. In fact, it is only a formalisation of bourgeois interests that can claim philosophical legitimacy. Regarding Kantian reason, Adorno and Horkheimer write that it is 'the usual endeavour of bourgeois thought to ground the respect without which civilisation cannot exist on something other than material interest'.[18] Thus it is not true that reason enables anything higher than the shrewd and veiled pursuit of one's own interests. In this form, it is not entitled to embody 'moral forces as facts'.[19]

The critique of autonomy in *Dialectic of Enlightenment* is expressed as an affective analysis of bourgeois attitudes. In *Dialectic of Enlightenment*, which unlike 'Education after Auschwitz' does not strive towards a practical, action-oriented perspective, coldness is declared 'bourgeois'. Here, Adorno and Horkheimer speak of a solidification of the 'general' in the self under the sign of autonomy, and they connect this attitude to stoic apathy. In Stoic philosophy, apathy denotes a state free from suffering, attainable through a particular way of life which promotes self-distancing through mental exercises, thereby entirely renouncing positive as well as negative passions, bit by bit.[20] Adorno and Horkheimer present the relationship of stoic apathy to bourgeois coldness in such a way that the latter takes the former as an example: 'Just as the Stoic indifference on which bourgeois coldness, the counterpart of pity, has modelled itself was more loyal, however wretchedly, to the universal it had rejected than the compassionate baseness which adapted itself to the world, so it was those who unmasked pity who, however negatively, espoused the Revolution.'[21]

In this extremely convoluted sentence, the relationship of the bourgeois positions to two ethical forms is made clear. On the one hand there is pity, on the other the universal. Pity realises moral behaviour through sympathy; the universal achieves morality through moral laws. Stoic apathy's relationship to the universal is ambivalent: although it withdraws from it by confronting the world with fundamental acceptance, at the same time this attitude still adheres to a universal rather than to 'the commonality all participate in' ['the compassionate baseness' in the standard translation].[22] With this expression, Adorno and Horkheimer refer to the majority society, which has 'adapted itself to the world' they observe.

It is neither easy nor important to fathom all the layers of meaning in this play on words. The message of the statement lies in contrasting stoic apathy / bourgeois coldness on the one hand, and on the other the commonality all participate in. Besides, the indication that apathy and coldness adhere to a moral universal is an important one. To understand the second part of the sentence, we need recourse to the preceding text. With reference to Nietzsche, Adorno and Horkheimer write about pity as a moral principle that is 'always too little'. Instead of insisting on universal justice, he who pities perceives injustice as an exception and thus does not touch the 'rule of inhumanity' which he believes he opposes. Pity is therefore the individualisation of regular suffering. So it makes sense that the espousal of this moral principles implies an 'espousal of Revolution', even if only a negative one. The critique of pity sees right through the structure of pity as unsatisfactory and weak.

Bourgeois coldness neither upholds law-abiding morality, nor does it open space for empathy. It musters 'wretched loyalty' to the universal; perhaps it is ready to betray the universal. That coldness finds its model in the Stoics suggests its ability to distance itself from reality – not only by simply 'adapting itself to the world', but also by firmly anchoring its position. In this, it expresses its capacity for autonomy. But the actual change seems to come only from those who focus their power on identifying what is false, on identifying pity.

For Adorno and Horkheimer, the concept of bourgeois coldness captures the bourgeoisie's ethical form of existence – not really capable of pity and attached to the universal primarily in the sense of their own interests. This coldness thus reveals the affective consequences of bourgeois society. Its continued existence is due above all to its ability to conceal. Because bourgeois citizens, as the living embodiment of the Enlightenment, can always trace their actions back to autonomy and morality, they achieve success as entrepreneurs and administrators. Once the profane foundation of reason and its function of self-preservation has been unmasked, the bourgeois becomes highly suspicious in his seemingly harmonising social function. The ideals of the Enlightenment are not superior to the struggle of social forces for material survival, rather they perpetuate it by other means:

> The system which enlightenment aims for is the form of knowledge which most ably deals with the facts, most effectively assists the subject in mastering nature. The system's principles are those of self-preservation. Immaturity amounts to the inability to survive. The bourgeois in the successive forms of the slave-owner, the free entrepreneur, and the administrator is the logical subject of enlightenment.[23]

The question of how to practically overcome the connection between the Enlightenment and violence is different from that of its origin. The conceivable answer when considering political and social circumstances is not often satisfying in philosophical terms, because it always confronts questions of resources and availability. Reason may be highly questionable in this respective form, and yet it is an instrument Adorno and Horkheimer are familiar with and seek refuge in – despite the danger of reason stagnating into bourgeois coldness. Adorno is more likely to admit the inevitability of participating in this coldness.[24] Perhaps only the strict distinction between politics and philosophy can meaningfully order the contradiction between critical deconstruction of reason and its use despite all this.

If for June Jordan only a politics of rage can repel the concrete threat, as opposed to Horkheimer's claim of the mind's immunity to intimidation, then here is a further indication that thinking does not constitute a politics alone – and that Adorno and Horkheimer's political relapse has more to do with an affective proximity to reason than a genuinely political potential. In any case, it suggests that analysing this problem requires a language of its own for the affective constellations that attend it. The critique of reason alone can neither elucidate how bourgeois coldness is constituted, nor offer strategies for overcoming it.

In 'Education after Auschwitz', Adorno discusses love as a principle that stands in opposition to coldness. It is, particularly in childhood, the prerequisite for forming a subjectivity that can face its own fears without directly transforming them into aggression. Adorno emphasises that he is not interested in 'preach[ing] love', because a sermon, that is, a verbal injunction, would contradict the principle of love itself.[25] It should not be forgotten that 'the people whom one should love are themselves such that they cannot love, and therefore in turn are not at all that lovable'.[26] The lack of love is just as much a part of social reproduction as capitalist conditions and cannot be compensated for by mere wishful thinking: 'The exhortation to give more warmth to children amounts to pumping out warmth artificially, thereby negating it.'[27] With this negative insight and the call to analyse coldness instead of wishing for warmth, Adorno leaves the theme of love behind. But the very fact that love becomes a concern in 'Education after Auschwitz' expresses Adorno's tenuous hope that promoting immediate human connection can achieve something politically at the individual level.

And even if this hope sounds naïve, one can in fact observe the interpersonal effects of coldness in love. The reversal of generosity and warmth into decisiveness and coldness characterises the end of romantic relationships. This change is not so much determined by overwhelming emotional states, but is brought about by the participants, formerly lovers, in an interplay of emotional competencies. A new order arises to replace the close relationship that used to prevail, with something that can offer temporary orientation. Coldness does not present as an affective steel cage[28] and a repertoire of entrenched behaviours here. Coldness is a technique for dealing with reality when reality becomes uncertain. It helps to organise feelings in such a way that the feeling individual remains protected – and sometimes their counterpart as well. This is helpful when generosity as a mode of interaction has lost its naturalness after the end of a relationship. Coldness suspends articulations of the desire to maintain the affective signs and forms that characterise a relationship, and it represents a way to overcome habitualised love. Coldness does not primarily function as an imposed social order but is also applied in the politics of intimacy.

Helmut Lethen describes coldness as the basis of 'theories of conduct' which 'in moments of social disorganisation . . . help to distinguish between self and other, inside and outside'.[29] Coldness is not an affective microstructure that merely accumulates in interpersonal relationships.[30] Coldness is avoided, and in it we find a tool to counteract social destabilisation. It supports individuals and groups by making socially and affectively complex situations manageable by 'cooling' them down. It supports individuals as a resource for self-protection and is on call when individuals, for whatever reason, no longer feel capable of participating in expansive emotional states, or participating at all. Nevertheless, it is not enough to assume a psychological retreat reflex here. Coldness exists as a form that is chosen and shaped. Thus it offers a framework for injured people to protect themselves from their anger towards others. Coldness is mobilised on the assumption that such an outburst can no longer accomplish anything, that it is powerless in the face of reality. One opts for coldness when the disclosure of emotional states must be prevented in order to avoid injury or to control fear.

In this sense, Adorno's pessimistic diagnosis, which opposes Aristotle's image of attraction among members of society on the one hand with their respective self-interest and the ruthless pursuit of it on the other, is not quite as rigid and dark as it might appear in the context of Auschwitz. Coldness by no means reduces human behaviour to self-interest. Rather, it is an affective instrument for mediating the discrepancies between particular, individual or collective feelings and shared realities. Perhaps even an essential one for survival. And for each reflection on political options, it is more helpful to turn to the emergence of coldness, its function and its potential than to declare it an anthropological constant. Otherwise, how are we to identify the moments when cooling down seems to be more promising than holding on to charged relations with reality? Coldness also seems to be a bridge affect which provides the subject who still loves with protocols to avoid being torn apart by ever new attempts to surrender to closeness despite everything. Coldness then is certainly a bridge affect when it protects bourgeois subjects from confronting the full extent of violence which structures their reality.

Theories of Conduct: Cold and Warm

Helmut Lethen writes of a social 'alienation as an art of living', 'learnable techniques' to 'get close without violating each other, and to separate without injury'.[31] With this, he captures, among other things, the delicate character of separation without rupture, or rupture without separation. The counterfactual spectacle of coldness enables the person who was just recently in close proximity to simulate a decision, and then gradually to make it. Coldness is a way to interrupt relational arrangements of closeness by offering an alternative form of reference.[32] This also applies to social relations and agreements, which can be replaced by coldness or preserved with its help, in order to counter a changing world with stability.

Simulated decisions that serve to maintain stability are not only relevant for relationship conflict and the preservation of societal norms. Taking Helmuth Plessner's 1924 essay collection *The Limits of Community*[33] as a starting point, Lethen develops a historical theory of behavioural theories in the Weimar Republic that focuses on an ideal of personality, one which largely dispenses with authenticity. The art and literature of *Neue Sachlichkeit* (New Objectivity) serve as a model, conveying the idea that individual emotional expressions must give way to a strictly regulated form of social interaction in order to make civilisation and democracy possible. This idea bears distinctly misogynistic traits, not only in Plessner's work, but also in Lethen's interpretation.[34] Organising social interaction through theories of conduct instead of affective agreements is reserved for male subjects: 'Woman herself is excluded from the fencing hall of subject constitution.'[35] Women appear to Plessner as originators of feeling, primarily responsible for every form of closeness.[36]

In this context, coldness as a social technique needs to be framed more precisely so as not to be understood as a simple form of affect control with positive connotations in patriarchy, and one which is opposed to the 'cult of authenticity' criticised by Plessner and Lethen. The example of a romantic relationship makes clear that coldness, as the conscious elimination of loving gestures, is just as much a malleable affective mode as warmth – a provisional counter-concept – as the cultivation and profusion of these gestures. Analogously, Lethen sees coldness in the social as a tool 'when the horizons of orientation collapse in a historical situation and the space of human movement is under extreme agonal tension'.[37] Coldness can restore stability in an uncertain reality.

Only a naïve patriarchal logic could, however, come up with the idea that warmth and affection are 'natural' forms of interaction, while coldness is what makes self-regulation necessary in the first place.[38] On the contrary, as I explained with regard to the space-creating function of self-criticism, coldness provides a place for subjects to rest their emotions by making themselves less receptive to the affective demands of their counterpart or environment. On the other hand, in the example of generosity, warmth requires the willingness and ability to receive and read those requests – and to answer them by expending one's own emotional resources. Coldness enables inner emigration, while warmth seeks to hold on to shared affective structures. Both are shaped modes of social relation. Lethen's theory of conduct explores the malleability of social relations, but remains one-sidedly fixated on the idea that feelings can be limited, instead of also considering their production and learnability.

In spite of all this, coldness and warmth – just like the dynamics of self-criticism – are not easy to categorise on the moral and political spectrum. Coldness is not always bad, and warmth is not its resolution. It may not even be possible to clearly position warmth as the opposite of coldness, because its participation in bourgeois coldness, for example in the form of pity, would need to be demonstrated first. Coldness faces an initial all-encompassing affective overload and seeks to overcome it through transparency and structure.

Lethen also shows how the cult of authenticity and interiority entails a politically counterproductive cult of the (bourgeois) subject. To that effect, coldness is a reaction to the overemphasis on subjective inner life. Adorno sees the problem of coldness most clearly expressed in fascist complicity. Neither Adorno nor Lethen develop an idea of coldness's opposite that goes beyond the projection of immediate, emotion-oriented and naturalised femininity. Both lack a complex understanding of affective techniques, which do not necessarily merge with the subject models that produce them, but merely inform aspects of these subjectivities. Accordingly, my aim is to understand that subjects are partly responsible for the adoption and reproduction of affective techniques because they can shape them. These shaping processes are then articulated in social roles and expectations until they attain structural dimensions.

Adorno and Lethen ultimately lack a feminist perspective on feeling and affect as essential resources for shaping social life. Such a perspective challenges the notion that coldness alone denotes the prevention of affect articulation and also rejects the idea that behind the barriers of alienation, there is a natural space of shared warmth.[39] In order to deal with this complexity, it is promising to consider the perspective of those who have always been dependent on their affective resources to navigate social conditions.

Feelings and Emancipation

In a conversation with the poet Adrienne Rich, Audre Lorde describes which childhood experiences – positive and negative – imparted emotional competence to her. She talks about her relationship with her mother, which always rested on Lorde's nonverbal grasp of expectations and moods: 'One of the reasons I had so much trouble growing up was that my parents, my mother in particular, always expected me to know what she was feeling and what she expected me to do without telling me. And I thought this was natural. My mother would expect me to know things, whether or not she spoke them.'[40] Lorde's memory forms a background to her position, developed as an adult, on the relevance of feelings to political action. The ability to read and assess her affective environment was essential for her survival as a child and provides a reason to develop a social theory of feelings. In close historical proximity to the conversation between Rich and Lorde, Silvia Federici writes an essay for the 'Wages for Housework' campaign where she addresses the emotional labour of housewives, which consists of reading male feelings and transforming them for the better: 'The more blows the man gets at work, the more his wife must be trained to absorb them, the more he is allowed to recover his ego at her expense.'[41] Especially under capitalism, the patriarchal division of labour has been and continues to be re-enforced by the fact that women's uncompensated emotional, sexual and reproductive labour is seen as their 'natural' role, and any deviation from it is sanctioned.[42] An emotionally informed orientation in the world is essential for women in patriarchy because it helps them to escape violence. Reading moods is a basic skill that people threatened by violence acquire in order to be prepared for it or to escape it. Beyond that, women in particular are often recognised only in their roles as wives, mothers and caregivers if they demonstrate emotional fluency. Federici and others, especially white feminists of the 1970s, vehemently criticise the identification of femininity with emotional capacity and want to see it dissolved and overcome to achieve gender justice. The claim of women to be able to socially develop beyond a caring role is key for individual emancipation. Yet it is rash to reject all the skills acquired by living in the restrictions of this role due to their patriarchal devaluation, rather than making them the starting point for a new social order: an order that does not separate emotions from rationality, but fundamentally recognises the affective constitution of human beings. This, at least, is how Lorde develops her idea of liberation, and the sentence 'The master's tools will never dismantle the master's house' is to be understood in this sense as a critique of domination applied to the rationalist-structural principles of patriarchal societies.[43] Lorde summarises the genesis of a world polarised into emotions and ideas on the basis of roles that embody this separation in the social imaginary: 'The white fathers told us: I think, therefore I am. The Black mother within each of us – the poet – whispers in our dreams: I feel, therefore I can be free.'[44]

Other feminists have criticised Lorde for reproducing precisely those images that have always justified the oppression of women. But that is not what she advocates in her political programme and her philosophy of Black feminist justice. Her aim is not to exclude feelings, but to understand their function within the dynamics of racist and misogynistic oppression and any attempt to overcome it. Feelings not only contain information about social points of view and experiences, but can likewise protect subjects as barriers and safe havens, strengthen them or slow them down. On no account, however, is the negation of feelings a promising path. Lorde says of herself: 'I kept myself through feeling. I lived through it.'[45]

According to Federici and Lorde, feelings cannot be reduced to mere side effects of life or colourations of everyday existence, but they are tactics with which people negotiate their survival. Elsa Dorlin understands the existential function of feelings, particularly in the realm of care, as 'dirty care' or 'negative care'.[46] She uses this term to describe the ability to read others affectively in order to coexist with them without being harmed. This ability is used by victims of domestic violence, who adjust their behaviour based on the affective signals of the perpetrator in order to escape aggression, as well as by those Jewish people, for example, who do not display religious symbols in public to protect themselves from assault.

As a particular 'relationship to the world',[47] care is misunderstood when it is conceptualised as purely altruistic, selfless and dedicated to the other. Dorlin foregrounds the connection between care and the oppressed subjects who practice and depend on it: 'Concern for others arises within and by means of violence, and it generates an ethical position quite different from affective proximity, love, or abnegation in the most demanding forms of care.'[48] Care in a world structured by patriarchy, racism and class hierarchy is a direct response to the violence that these conditions produce. The caring subject is therefore, first, not an unscathed person who has a lot to give, and second, not someone who is inexperienced, because through their care work they constantly learn more about the violence that confronts them and those they care for on a daily basis. Care ultimately means to study violence the better to protect against it: 'rather, we are concerned for others in order to anticipate what they want, will, or can do to us – which might devalue, exhaust, insult, isolate, injure, worry, deny, frighten, or de-realise us.'[49]

Feminist affect theory is interested in the malleability of social relationships and the role feelings assume in them. Negative dimensions of the world's establishment are instructive in this regard. Violence, neglect, lack of resources, protection and perspectives have always been silently registered by women, children, people who live outside of gender norms and others to whom care work has been assigned without them being asked, in order to avoid being held responsible for precisely these deficiencies. The oppressed have always repaired the damage that surrounds them through their own invisible labour, thereby supporting themselves and others. At the same time, people in this position are moulded into subjects capable – or perceived to be capable – of tolerating it. Recognising this part of the social world characterised by deficiency reveals the coldness that this deficiency helps to produce. Coldness is not the absence of emotional attachment. Coldness binds subjects to institutional and affective forms that make the ethical neglect of others possible – even powerful, even appropriate.

Not infrequently, such attitudes, which legitimise state violence and justify racism by denying it, are the result of self-reflection or have at least evolved in the course of self-reflection.

Often, these cold forms promise security: the failure to rescue people at sea as 'securing Europe's borders', the criminalisation of the Hanau victims of the National Socialist Underground in the context of so-called clan crime and the internment of refugees in 'anchor centres', not for their own sake but to protect German cities. As Dorlin shows, security is a need that marks a claim of participation in bourgeois society.[50] Coldness longs for security in one's own living conditions and itself becomes the norm. Coldness keeps the actual affective dynamics to which it formulates a response – insecurity, political unimaginativeness, material fear of loss – concealed under the surface; it appears cool and convinced of the correctness of its ties to the bourgeois value system.

Coldness is the affective consequence of the self-preservation of bourgeois society, which in turn draws strength from members trained in self-reflection. Both intertwine in such a way that the lofty aspiration to achieve transparency through constant self-questioning, and the affective security that this self-questioning provides for bourgeois subjects, combine to form a *perpetuum mobile*: denying suffering while propagating enlightenment. Bourgeois coldness means clinging to self-criticism and investing all one's ethical energy in it, instead of moving beyond it and above oneself, guided by other feelings.

In contrast to the theories of coldness with which Adorno and Lethen emphasise the orienting function of the supposedly anti-affective mind, Lorde tells the story of an orienting world of feeling. It was precisely the perception of affective registers and her turn towards her own feelings that enabled Lorde to understand the world and its institutions. For Lorde, this affective process of understanding is always tied to expanding the space for feelings in language. It is only through expression that feelings become social and can thus be recognised in the shaping of communal life.[51]

Lorde works with a theory of feelings that does not position them as an intrusion, exception, opposite or surprising immediacy, but which emphasises their ubiquity. In a patriarchal society, whose stability is based on the naturalisation and feminisation of emotional expression, people typically have to undergo a learning process to refamiliarise themselves with reading affects or to learn how to read them in the first place. And even if feelings are recognised as elements of the social, they continue to exist as tools of racialisation and remain subject to complex dynamics of readability.[52] But the affective comprehension of power and the fundamental malleability of affective dispositions[53] has always been an enormously important resource for the survival and advancement of those who do not meet the norms of European subjectivity, which is modelled on white masculinity. This fact affords a new look at the discourse of coldness. Instead of seeking coldness in the idea of an even more static anthropologisation, one confronted by a vague, affective 'addendum',[54] the moments that activate coldness should be understood as active conservation efforts. Coldness distances to secure something that has begun to teeter. The chance that it may still fall remains.

Coldness has proven to be an individual and social technique that, on the one hand, functionally organises interpersonal relationships in the form of micrological theories of conduct and, on the other hand, stabilises bourgeois social conventions – subsequently elevating them to a norm. The malleability of both levels of coldness entails the insight that social emancipation has an irreducibly affective aspect. Critiquing conditions of violence also means recognising the affective structures shaped by them and reading the depth of violence within them. The aim of feminist affect theory outlined with Lorde would be to not react to affective overload with the cold fixation of an order, but to seriously address the complexity of emotional processes.

In July 2020, in a conversation about the university and its relationship to the Black Lives Matter movement, Biko Mandela Gray talks with Fred Moten and Stefano Harney about Syracuse University's decision to establish so-called social justice hiring clusters to signal support for anti-racist social movements.[55] According to Gray's observations, however, the primary effect of these 'clusters' is to undermine the legitimacy of other, already existing radical protest movements on campus. Instead of actually engaging with local protests, the university appropriates the message of the country-wide Black Lives Matters protests to its own comfortable ends, without going beyond the efforts of self-sustaining critique. The conversation's starting point is Moten and Harney's text 'the university: last words'. Moten responds to these observations and analyses the affective pressure to act that the protests have transferred to institutions. Universities, according to Harney and Moten, respond to the demands of their students and a growing public with affective strategies so they can continue to appear as legitimate actors in light of political and social events:

> The righteous uprising and insurgency and expression of feeling in the face of the ongoing brutality produces then the necessity for the institutions, in order to try to maintain the illusion of their legitimacy. They have to express a sentiment. And we've seen that over the last couple of months. And then the further expression of their sentiment manifests in, what do you call it, 'social justice cluster hire'? 'Imagination grants' – we have 'imagination grants'.[56]

The protest against white supremacy demands not only the specific changes that this protest names, but also affective participation in the intensity of the moment. Institutions like the university respond with sentiments to demonstrate a will to change, while avoiding actual change itself. These strategies are acts of coldness, because their horizon consists in securing the severely damaged status quo. Affective ties to this state of affairs must be renewed and reformulated. This happens in diversity programs, the re-establishment of social justice initiatives and rhetorical expressions of solidarity as good publicity. Moten agrees with Gray, who is 'disgusted' by the actions of his institution: 'You recognise it and it's disgusting but you can't let it be so disgusting to you that it stops you from doing what you was gonna do anyway.'[57] Instead of investing energy in the struggle against all these false initiatives, one's energy must be reserved for the real thing, even when the disgust is directed at an institution that one belongs to. Even interwoven with deficient, illegitimate institutions, one can still do what one was going to do anyway. There is no protest strategy, no matter how sophisticated, which can cleanly free the individual from the entanglements of a world established in the bad without getting caught up in them. 'There is no right life in the wrong one',[58] as well as no institution that allows subjects to represent exclusively pure motives. Yet it can drive one crazy not to shrink from contact with this problematic institution, while at the same time fighting its catastrophic consequences and recognising all the relations one maintains with it. Such an existence requires incessant affective demarcation from the wrong, while at the same time consciously exploiting the resources on hand. This struggle against the malign institution's cold adaptation to ever new conditions thus requires an affective strategy to avoid being torn apart by this dual operation. Cold institutions must be met with coldness. According to Moten, anyone in this position must choose between two options: to be crazy or cold. 'You can drive yourself crazy by trying to free yourself from the complicity, of that feeling. But it's almost better to just be cold to that shit.'[59]

Here this bridge affect, which I have earlier called coldness, has a political function. It creates a temporary island for existence, saving subjects from the whirlpool of bad affective dynamics. Instead of involving oneself in the theatre of institutional sentimentalities and searching for one's position within it, coldness freezes the gaze and differentiates between right and wrong, liberating and commodified feelings. It becomes a protective mantle for what one is 'gonna do anyway', a political barricade in these affective events to separate those who are fighting for the whole from those who only want to pacify the fight. Here, the institution proves itself a boot camp for coldness. Recognising this, and simultaneously using coldness as a defence strategy against institutions, explicates the paradoxical dynamics of affective politics. The bourgeois institution cultivates coldness for its own preservation, but it does not retain control over the competence for coldness that it thereby creates, nor how this competence is employed.

Against the background of this appropriation, there has always been coldness that does not remain within the bourgeois framework. Outside institutional walls, coldness finds expressions that are aesthetically legible – as coolness. This is not bourgeois coldness; it does not emerge in institutions. Instead, this coldness is 'Nothing, Everything', is 'Nowhere, Everywhere', and belongs to 'Nobody, Everybody'.[60] It has its own place. Outside the bourgeois world, outside institutions, equipped with no stable boundaries, offering no security. It arises in the waiting of those who can no longer wait:

> We who can't wait keep waiting on this ongoing advent of texture. We who are nothing, we who have no one, can't wait for you to learn how to wait for it. We who have nothing hold it in reserve. We're at your service. We can't wait for this impatience to repair. Our look is cold, so cold it's cool and bears no judgement. So cold it burns and won't belong, no word is bond, we're all so close, we're all right here, outside your jurisdiction, criminal in the work and out of phase, at prayer, in preparation, of repair.[61]

Moten makes it clear that coldness does not belong to the bourgeoisie, because its aesthetic dimension, for example, does not come into its own there. Coldness is sometimes coolness, like jazz and the calm of waiting and the renunciation of explanations.

And, finally, coldness is necessary for survival. Not only in the fight against the institution's affective appropriation attempts, but also for the 'question of whether it is even permissible for someone who accidentally escaped and by all rights ought to have been murdered, to go on living after Auschwitz'.[62] The 'ones who escaped' need coldness in the face of death, only averted by chance. There is no other way to live in the twentieth century than through this affective reorganisation of a world in which the annihilation of six million Jews took place. Adorno inevitably speaks of himself in this context, as a Jew who escaped extermination. Coldness is both Auschwitz's condition of possibility as well as the precondition for life in a world after Auschwitz: 'Their continued existence already necessitates the coldness of the basic principle of capitalist subjectivity, without which Auschwitz would not have been possible: the drastic guilt of the spared.'[63]

This deep and darkest point of *Negative Dialectics* closes the circle of coldness. As a social practice, coldness is prerequisite condition for Auschwitz, and at the same time the strategy for living with its consequences.[64] Coldness appears in Adorno's work when the only alternative left is bottomless sorrow. It thus proves to be an instrument for the psychic, social and affective regulation of the individual, his relationships and the social world. However, in order not to fall into an anthropologisation that describes coldness as stagnation and progressive social damnation, it is necessary to understand the moments of its activation and repudiation in the present. In diagnosing coldness, it is possible and even necessary to be precise, because coldness takes various forms. Only with a clear, aesthetically informed gaze can its play of coolness and bridging be recognised. Bourgeois coldness may represent a configuration of relative historical continuity, but its actualisations must be revisited again and again to observe their efficacy. Affects cannot be understood other than through their recurring presence. That also means always feeling out the centres of pain that become living realities through coldness. At these sites of fractures and hinges between diffusion and regulation, affects prove to be moments of social malleability. And for this reason, coldness is never the only means of relating to the world.

Bourgeois coldness has affective grounds, but no justifications. As a protection of the status quo, it protects subjects from uncertainty. As self-criticism, it disguises self-protection as progress. As a mode of action, coldness represents a resource for being able to react to affective dynamics and ruptures in a targeted and result-oriented manner. At the same time, it makes it possible to deal with structures of violence without becoming too entangled in their complicity. Therefore, coldness must be understood as something deployed reactively and which is not normatively determined. Coldness is a means, a social diagnosis and a survival technique. Coldness as a corrective to impending collapse is self-protection. Coldness as a way of life is consent to violence. The passage between the two is constantly being redefined.

III

The Atlantic

I needed to see the Atlantic, which was where I reckoned with the dead, the men and women and children who were all but invisible in most of the history written about the slave trade; academics had continued to quarrel about how many slaves packed per ton constituted 'tight packing' and a deliberate policy of accepting high mortality, estimate rates of cargo productivity in the slave trade versus the other kinds of commodity trade, and quantify the gains and losses of the slave trade with algebraic formulas that obscured the disaster: Deck Area = Constant × (Tonnage) 2/3. The ocean never failed to remind me of the losses, and its roar echoed the anguish of the dead. —Saidiya Hartman[1]

Odysseus, as has been seen, troubled various islands and their inhabitants with his presence in the Aegean, Ionian and Tyrrhenian seas; Christopher Columbus crossed the Atlantic to continue the history of European colonialism on the Caribbean island of Guanahaní. In *Omeros*, his adaptation of the Homeric epics, Derek Walcott sketches out a direct comparison between the Caribbean archipelago and the islands of the Mediterranean.[2] Both island groups denote hubs of historical and cultural memory. Their visibility in European historiography is the result of seafaring expansion projects.[3] Odysseus' journey follows the innocent leitmotif of homecoming after the long and brutal Trojan War. This journey is sustained by Odysseus' heroism and unfolds its colonial character along the way, with deadly consequences. Columbus's departure follows an idea of the world, as well as the human species, which culminates, as the literary theorist Sylvia Wynter puts it, in a 'brutal invasion and conquest that led to a degree of genocidal extinction and still ongoing ecological disaster unprecedented in human history'.[4] The motif of conquest and appropriation guides modern colonialism and initiates the destruction of human societies as well as the entire planet.

The reported perspective of these voyages decides its meaning and effect. In the last lines of Walcott's epic poem, in an image of Achilles retreating from the beach and returning home, the sea, left on its own, takes over the narrative in its eternal motion: 'When he left the beach, the sea was still going on.'[5] The sea is history, and it writes incessantly in its mostly illegible script.[6]

Saidiya Hartman seeks out the Atlantic to learn from the ocean's depths – from its roar and from its movement – what the archives do not want to reveal about the transatlantic slave trade: catastrophe. The ocean not only harbours twelve and a half million nameless dead bodies; the circumstances of their deaths are inscribed in the particular injury to these bodies. An enslaved girl, only mentioned in a court case because the captain who was supposed to bring her across the Atlantic killed her, bears the provisional name 'Venus', serving as a ubiquitous placeholder for the designation of Black women. Hartman tries to follow the tenuous trace of life that Venus left behind and struggles with the limited possibilities of her research. Faced with an archive, written by the victors, with only violence to report, she is guided by the desire to oppose this archive with other histories, ones which tell of murdered subjects rather than the anonymous dead. We know nothing of Venus, find no 'pathway to her thoughts, no glimpse of the vulnerability of her face or of what looking at such a face might demand'.[7] We don't even know her name. Such work 'against the limits of the archive'[8] can only succeed as narrative; as a narrative that begins to fill the gaps through speculation, thereby going against a supposedly reliable body of knowledge. 'I intended both to tell an impossible story and to amplify the impossibility of its telling.'[9] To push against history requires a motive that runs deeper than the will to set things right. The Atlantic provokes a longing for a historical reconciliation that has yet to occur. Hartman admits her desire to end the story of the murdered Venus with a consoling thought: 'But in the end I was forced to admit that I wanted to console myself and to escape the slave hold with a vision of something other than the bodies of two girls settling on the floor of the Atlantic.'[10]

Subject histories uprooted by the transatlantic slave trade, unavailable to memory, are like a negative of the bourgeois self. The people abducted via the Middle Passage either died during the crossing or, sold as slaves, were robbed of their biography – their kinship relations, their cultural heritage. This self was able to articulate itself in a few ‘slave narratives’ in the context of abolitionism, but this literary form was shaped by white, colonial values and interests as well.[11]

Hartman travelled along the West African coast in the 1990s to visit slave trade sites. She describes a Black identity marked by the slave trade as an ‘identity produced by negation’ for generations to come.[12] The third part of this book explores negation. What exactly does it mean that identity, and consequently the self and the subjectivity which carry this identity, are produced by negation? This negation is made concrete by the racist dehumanisation and destruction of the self through its objectification in the slave trade and the order founded on it. But the point here is not to reconstruct personal experiences of deportation and enslavement, but rather to consider the theoretical consequences for the subject as a result of the transatlantic slave trade, which shaped the colonial endeavour through the subjugation and commodification of human beings from the sixteenth century onwards. Which criteria did Europeans use to distinguish themselves from the enslaved self? And is there a responsibility to remember the enslaved, degraded to objects, as subjects in spite of everything, to wrest them somewhat from all-encompassing historical violence?

The contours of the subject model of Odysseus, and those of bourgeois identity, follow from the same colonial dynamics which give rise to this objectification.[13] The ‘afterlife of slavery’[14] is perpetuated in contemporary institutions as anti-Blackness. The abject status of Black life,[15] which anti-Blackness names in the USA in particular, has consequences for thinking the subject in general.[16] Blackness, as it denotes enslaved peoples, forms a concept of the negative of human being.[17] Humanistic thinking, which theoretically manifests in the dehumanisation of slaves, is thus a residuum of anti-Blackness.[18]

Any examination of the history of colonialism and racism must take into account the extraordinary violence which has penetrated the self to such an extent that Blackness has taken on the meaning of absolute plasticity, associated with the 'subhuman' and the 'superhuman' alike.[19] This meaning of Blackness appears to partially or completely dissolve the category of 'subject'. How can theoretical considerations for the subject still be made on the basis of such a spurious conception of people? The question leads back to Theodor W. Adorno's programmatic sentence: 'It is to be achieved only negatively.'[20]

It is precisely the subjectivity that, as Hartman shows by reference to Venus, *must* have existed – but whose traces have been erased except for a few remnants,[21] and which provides an occasion to approach the history of the subject from the point of view of the violence that shaped it.[22] An 'identity produced by negation'[23] refers to someone whose life can hardly be distinguished from violence and the impossibility of individual freedom, who therefore hardly meets the criteria of subjectivity. In this sense, the enslaved undergo negative subjectification. The method that seeks theoretically to trace this subjectification must proceed accordingly. To search for enslaved subjects – if they exist at all – means to follow the lines of their erasure. Once again, this happens through the strict formations of European, bourgeois and autonomy-centred subjectivity. To trace how and where the autonomous subject is theoretically installed is also to reveal its absence. Furthermore, moments appear when the line drawn between autonomous white subjects and subjugated Black objects breaks down.

The following chapters are devoted to scenes of impossible autonomy. At the same time, they critique ways of thinking and concepts that want to maintain autonomy as a standard. This part deals first with the category of property as the foundational condition for modern subjects, and with the expropriation of the self, which defines slavery as a social (non-)relationship. With this expropriation, an absolute power relationship arises that ultimately makes it possible to reinterpret Black suffering as pleasure – and thereby to inscribe violence so deeply into the body that it almost evades recognition.

This form of racial subjugation continues to permeate the history of the Americas even after the formal end of slavery. The discord between Hannah Arendt and Fred Moten in their observations, from different times, on the notorious school segregation case in Little Rock, Arkansas in the 1950s raises the question of which political subjectivities this relationship of subjugation produces. Political action goes hand in hand with ideas of visibility and transparency, notions which stand in opposition to a practice directed towards invisibility and fleeting tactics. The latter is the basis for answering Hartman's question about the possibility of 'slave agency',[24] that is, action under conditions of absolute subjugation. It also allows us to reflect on freedom without obsessively calling on its bourgeois form. The autonomous self is no longer the self-evident medium of individual liberation once its limits have been traced. It loses its integrity; but there begins to emerge an answer to Paul Gilroy's question: 'What understanding of self is it to supply the subjectivity that can focus the subject of black politics?'[25]

6 Property of Self

Property can be understood as one of the concepts that separate the bourgeois subject from the racialised subject. The idea that individuals possess themselves, especially as developed in John Locke's social contract theory,[1] assigns 'justly captured' Indigenous people[2] and enslaved Africans to a fundamentally different category of existence.[3] Their status as 'chattel', over whose lives someone else holds power, positions them outside of humanity by converting their status into that of a commodity. 'Possessive individuality'[4] is a crucial feature of the European colonial self-understanding, shaping the logic of possession in slavery as well as the subjectivity of the enslaved. Property is an important structural element of the colonised world and its racist practices. The political theorist Brenna Bhandar paradigmatically illustrates this fact in her study *Colonial Lives of Property* by contrasting the Lockean form of selfhood with the legal form of 'Indian status', which was created in Canada in 1886 for members of the First Nations.[5] The special characteristics of this status provide a negative foil to the idea that individuals belong to themselves.[6] Furthermore, Iris Därmann's deconstruction of Locke's political philosophy, and Cheryl Harris's examination of the history of whiteness as property, help to interpret property as a central category of the colonial order.

Colonial Abstraction

Brenna Bhandar shows that the legal status question, like the original appropriation of land, belongs to a genealogy of property that can be used to understand colonial power relations. She initially pursues the concept of property in its concrete function of colonial land grab and examines the practices by which colonial powers established ownership and transferred land inhabited and cultivated by Indigenous people into their own ownership. This approach explicitly challenges the assumption that property is a 'natural' category merely designating existing practices and legally securing them.[7] The aim is to understand the contingent character of the principles which make colonialism appear equitable in Locke's account, as well as the interests behind them. Bhandar's aim is to historically demonstrate the co-originality of property, in the modern sense, and colonial subjectivity. She notes that property and racialisation rest on a similar logic of abstraction.[8] In Bhandar's work, the Marxist concept of property undergoes various historical contextualisations to illustrate the development of its power. At the same time, it is placed in relation to contemporary conditions and political struggles. Bureaucratic processes of land registration are particularly decisive in this regard. In an interview, Bhandar mentions that 'in many colonial contexts, Indigenous people were either not entitled to register property . . . or there were too many bureaucratic and practical hurdles' to allow them to do so.[9] In this respect, such registration systems served above all to directly expropriate people whose relationship to the land was primarily characterised by use.[10] In acts of abstraction, European colonial investors ensured that it was the property relationship recorded on paper which determined the disposition of colonial landscapes, and not the relationships and practices in which the land was embedded.[11]

This fact is reminiscent of the effects of bureaucracy in the bourgeois state, which I have analysed above. In both cases, the modern rationalisation of human–world relationships[12] described by Max Weber helps bourgeois subjects establish an order that holds them in place. Bhandar's thesis of a racialisation co-original with the property system reveals the extent to which both processes follow the logic of abstraction. The purpose of the 'formalisation of land ownership' was to effect capitalist progress and to provide investment-happy colonial rulers with a sense of security.[13] In many cases, this abstraction is reflected in the land itself through 'singularisation'.[14] Monocultures are a means of increasing profit: 'In early modern England, establishing title to land by making it more productive meant eliminating biodiversity and isolating and breeding a species – barley or rye or pigs. Localised ecosystems were aggressively transformed so that monocultural productivity smothers anacultural generativity.'[15] Increase in production through monocultures is one way racialisation is inscribed into land use. Thus only those individuals who apply the principle of 'ownership through improvement', to both themselves and the earth, are capable of using the land appropriately.[16] According to Locke's conception of the connection between labour and ownership, Europeans were concerned with improving their own persons, and proper land use was measured by English agricultural methods.

As a result, the emerging racial order made it possible to justify the appropriation of land by claiming that the 'savages' showed 'a lack of respect for property laws'. For the Europeans, it was clear: those who – in their eyes – did not 'improve themselves' could not own land. The land had to be protected from the incorrigible.[17]

According to Bhandar, abstraction thus determines the process for the colonial appropriation of the world: in the case of land, through commodification; in the case of 'race', through 'scientific' hierarchisation.[18] By exploring the beginnings of the capitalist mode of production, Bhandar promotes an understanding of 'how capitalist forms of appropriation, exploitation and production produce the worlds we live in' – and how these worlds acquired and maintain their colonial character.[19] The debate about the restitution of objects looted in colonial wars is just one current arena that testifies to the contemporary relevance of pre-capitalist property relations and acquisition practices.[20] Yet the concrete subjectifying effects of property logic are even clearer when they operate in institutional contexts.

Just Appropriation

John Locke authored the theoretical initial position that establishes ownership of the self as a prerequisite for personhood and participating in the state order. The philosopher Eva von Redecker calls this stance 'phantom possession' and locates it as a central element within the liberal fantasy of sovereignty which aims at the domination and exploitation of all life.[21] Brenna Bhandar and Iris Därmann devote themselves to the historical and biographical circumstances surrounding Locke's philosophy in order to understand the material conditions and interests within which it is embedded. This includes the fact that this canonical theory of the Enlightenment cannot be separated from the figure of Locke as co-author of the colonial laws in Carolina and as the author of a 'theory of race'.[22] Locke was not only a shareholder in the Royal African Company, and thus a successful investor in the transatlantic slave trade, but was also involved as secretary of the Lords Proprietors of Carolina in the conception and transcription of the 'Fundamental Constitutions of Carolina' (1669).[23] His relationship to the colonies was thus by no means neutral, but rather supported by large investments – material as well as intellectual. Alongside these material aspects, Locke's understanding of the self at the philosophical level participates in the fundamental distinction between a bourgeois interior and a racialised exterior.[24] Locke's contribution to the colonial project consists, at the very least, in having provided a philosophical justification for land expropriation and slavery – and what's more, in a moral system which determines property's central position in fundamental political issues to this day.[25]

In the context of Locke's prominent idea of the self-ownership of persons, it is interesting to see how Därmann reclassifies human labour, which occupies a central and seemingly innocent position in Locke's work. Contrary to what might be expected from Locke's manifold involvement in the colonial enterprise, he is by no means an advocate of the mere straightforward appropriation of land and goods as it has mostly occurred. Rather, he insists on practices that give these acts their legitimacy: 'For Locke, it is not discovery and symbolic seizure, conquest and military subjugation, land grabs and mere enclosure, treaties with natives or European competitors that originally establish the law, but labor alone.'[26] Thus natural law initially provides for the equality of the colonists and the colonised when it comes to the distribution of goods. Everyone is entitled to what the land provides through their own work: 'This law of reason makes the deer that Indian's who hath killed it.'[27] According to Locke, no external legal order is needed to implement this simple rule – it is natural law. Determining ownership by how much land a person can plough, plant, cultivate and utilise does not seem so controversial.[28] The egalitarian nature of this principle begins to falter only when the concept of labour is more narrowly defined by the colonists, and in due course criteria set for what land has already been worked over, and what land is available for use and appropriation as 'wasteland' or as 'commodity without owners'.[29] An ideology of 'improvement'[30] ensures that Indigenous land use is characterised as 'helpless' or even accused of 'letting divine creation rot'.[31] 'Nothing was made by God for Man to spoil or destroy,' Locke states.[32]

This argument goes along with the conviction that English agriculture is vastly superior to Native American land use. For Locke and other colonists, it follows that the land itself is practically thirsting for the efficient labour and expert control of white men.[33] This principle was then reflected in the colonial economy as well, because the sale price of land was measured primarily by the labour previously invested in it.[34] Thus, in moral terms, Locke starts from a structure of necessity that justifies colonisation, but which was ultimately constructed by the colonists themselves. It is exactly this structure that provided a perfect justification for the 'planter aristocracy' and the plantation system in the South of the United States.[35] The ownership of one's own person is closely intertwined with this idea of property through labour. Just as labour appropriates land for the individual, so a person's thinking and 'self-recognition of one's memory of past and present thoughts'[36] makes them belong to themselves.[37] 'Self-knowledge is self-possession and self-positioning in Locke.'[38] This self-possession is not so much the precondition for freedom as its realisation.[39] According to Locke, however, a relationship to oneself that demonstrates and asserts this mindset of being a free, self-possessing person is the precondition for building a bourgeois state based on property. The models of selfhood and economic activity as practices based on property relations are by no means relevant only as historical genealogies. They continue to form the basis of the individual's engagement with the world and with the self.

'The Enlightenment is the universalisation/globalisation of the imperative to possess and its corollary, the imperative to improve', Fred Moten and Stefano Harney write in 2021.[40] To improve oneself and the world is the utmost imperative of Western institutions, and a principle that subjects of capitalism have gradually internalised and applied to themselves. Locke's theory of the subject has not only been used to justify settler colonialism and its practices, but also finds ever new sources to unfold its effects in the omnipresent, neoliberal 'commitment[s] to continuous improvement', embodied by all who participate in institutions.[41]

An engagement with Locke's theory of the state based on his writings does not yet reveal the full story of his involvement in the colonial enterprise. Därmann is interested in the temporal concurrence of Locke's theoretical work and historical events in the 'New World'. The land-acquisition process in Carolina, the area to which Locke refers, was by no means always peaceful. There were wars between the English who settled in the area and Indigenous people who defended themselves against them. Thus, the category of 'conquest' and 'just war' found its way into Locke's *Two Treatises of Government*, giving rise to the moral apparatus of justification for colonial violence.[42] The defence, sabotage and 'refusal to work' of the Indigenous peoples served as a pretext and sufficient cause for the English to enslave them. This brutal task was initially outsourced to the Westo tribe, however, with whom the English had formed an alliance.[43]

Within Locke's philosophical system, enslavement is a consequence of property's pivotal position. His argument goes thus: *Because* Indigenous people have destroyed property in the form of colonised and cultivated land, they evidently want to harm other people, and so disqualify themselves from participating in bourgeois society. But Locke justified the ultimate termination of peace by equating the attackers with wild animals: as Därmann puts it, 'To practice "justice" in the warlike state of nature means for Locke to "destroy" the attacker "like any other wild animal or harmful creature" or to enslave them in a "state of perpetual war", in order to rob them of their self-possession and all that belongs to them.'[44] Through the state of war, the supposedly inalienable possession of one's self can be snatched through the use of force. Locke justifies enslavement with the authority over land use that the Lords and Proprietors, supported by Locke's political philosophy, have established in the New World.

Whiteness as Property

The 'right to exclude' which characterises property belongs to the white colonial subject. While self-defence on the part of the Indigenous population is interpreted as a war of aggression and an animalistic will to destroy, the brutal response of the English appears as a mere reaction to restore (colonial) order.[45]

Whiteness was enshrined in the US legal system as a social identity and legal category that determines standards of justice – to this day, it unfolds a structure of privilege and precarity. In her article 'Whiteness as Property', Cheryl Harris is interested in the symbolic and implicit values that whiteness has accumulated in the course of colonial history, but ultimately she is concerned with the material and explicit manifestation of whiteness *as* property, bound up with value and exchange relations.[46] This includes whiteness as a basic perquisite for acquiring and enforcing property rights,[47] whiteness as an institutional, legal privilege, for example in the form of citizenship, and whiteness as an exclusive identity marker that gains its attractiveness from scarcity. All these examples suggest that being white is both an object which can be possessed and at the same time that it founded the social structure in which private property develops. Engaging with whiteness as a social structure of dominance thus requires questioning the conditions which produced it, parallel to the analysis of its structures. As a result, it concerns not only the illegitimacy of white privilege, but also the fact that it is hard to conceive of these institutional and capitalist privileges without whiteness. To describe whiteness *as* property raises the question of its condition of possibility, whether in terms of possession of oneself or the land on which one lives.

Brenna Bhandar builds on Harris's analysis in her book, referring to the form of ownership that characterises whiteness as 'social and cultural forms of capital'.[48] The two authors emphasise different points, however. While Bhandar essentially examines the logic of ownership in terms of colonial land ownership and the question of who could possess land, Harris focuses on the dispossession of the self which enslaved Africans experienced, and whose consequences extend to the present.[49] In the caesura brought about by the transatlantic slave trade, Harris locates the demarcation that equates whiteness with autonomous personhood and excludes Blackness from it. Upon their arrival in the New World, Black slaves represented that devalued form of life, that 'object on the ground',[50] from which whites distinguished themselves, while at the same time understanding their whiteness as an achievement of civilisation and ability: 'Slavery as a system of property facilitated the merger of white identity and property. Because the system of slavery was contingent on and conflated with racial identity, it became crucial to be "white", to be identified as white, to have the property of being white. Whiteness was the characteristic, the attribute, the property of free human beings.'[51] Being white was valorised primarily through contrast, based both on visual characteristics and social situation. When freedom is exclusively granted to white people, it coagulates into a racialised trait, an inalienable property of white people. Racialisation's violence becomes apparent when whiteness is regarded as a 'necessary resource for being a person'.[52] Personhood itself is thus elevated to a special status.

In order not to jeopardise the discriminatory power established by the institution of slavery, criteria were laid on the basis of blood ties to supposedly provide 'objective' and legally binding information about a subject's racial status. Lineage is always more decisive than a body's visual appearance when it comes to 'proving' whiteness; lineage has always formed the residuum of pseudo-scientifically legitimised racism.[53] The fiction of 'race' is preserved by a diffuse historicity: 'As there is no way to actually measure blood, as Hartman notes, the tangled lines of genealogy and association . . . determine racial identity.'[54]

Harris's primary goal is to reveal the enduring material reality of legally enshrined structures of discrimination. National doctrines such as 'separate but equal' effectively contributed to the concealment of these structures and continue to do so today. 'Whiteness as Property' is not just an analysis of the past, rather it lives on in various forms of structural disadvantage – especially in institutions whose founding histories are inscribed with white supremacy. The sense of entitlement that distinguishes whiteness is also transferred to streets, linguistic conventions and interactions. Moten and Harney describe logistics – technology for the movement of property – as a paradigmatic white science. Logistical processes reveal a way of dealing with space in which white subjects constantly manifest and renew their entitlement: logistics 'is what many white people . . . are doing when you see them walk straight past a queue of people and take a seat, or move to the center of a crowded room, or speak more loudly than those around them, or block a sidewalk while discussing "choices" with their toddler'.[55]

Harris notes that, particularly where so-called affirmative action programmes, for example, are intended to disrupt histories of injustice, the claims of whiteness are actualised without interruption when such programs are ahistorically declared unjust.[56] She sees a 'white expectation of admission' at work, an expectation to be admitted everywhere – and the uninterrupted willingness of white people to understand themselves as victims when they are denied access to space or institutions.[57] Harris analyses these dynamics by reference to a racist logic of expectations that elevates white satisfaction to a universal standard. Equality remains subordinated to this in that the expectations of white people structure the discussion about equality and continue to misrecognise inequality.[58]

White people's sense of security that their expectations will remain the benchmark for justice makes whiteness a property in the form of normativity. The endlessness with which white people pass these privileges on, the matter of course with which they – I – accept access to institutions, is a profound aspect of bourgeois coldness. The colonial property order makes it clear how the cold and white-articulated claim to ownership and universal access is part of bourgeois identity. Harris emphasises that even if 'whiteness as property' does not mean always winning, white people will at least never lose.[59] Their position within the colonial state order has always been intertwined with property, which is itself a possession.

7 Expropriation of the Self

Ownership of the self is an essential element in the history of racialised subjectivity. The possession of oneself is attributed to subjects identified as white, and it is materially manifested through their position in the world. This equips white people with an interpretive authority which they can legally assert and which enables them to define the conditions of the social in their favour for the long term.

Fred Moten and Stefano Harney describe the social model of self-possession as the '(anti)social contract', since the dispossessed stand on the other side of white advantage: 'Thus, the social contract between the improving and accumulating ones, is inscribed upon the flesh of those who cannot be, and in any case refuse to be, a party to antisocial exchange under the terms of the (anti)social contract.'[1] 'Antisocial' not only insinuates 'anti-Black' but explicitly states it. It is not so much the act of blind, lawless violence as the social contract itself which installs the racist order and inscribes it on the body of those who refuse to collaborate with the given conditions. The social contract of European modernity is always directed against those whose exploitation and subjugation it legitimises.[2] Its antisocial character consists, however, not only in the fact that it undermines its own premise, but in the fact that it constantly seeks to destroy the very site of the social.

The social, according to Moten, can be found in the community of the expropriated. Those who are expropriated in body and life are slaves whose social life differs from any other form of the social. Which practices and orientations shape the lives of the enslaved, and what philosophical consequences arise from them, can only be examined at the margins of the archive. The historians Emily Owens and Marisa J. Fuentes base their study of enslaved women, and the paradoxes they lived with, on legal history.[3] This does not allow us to narrate the experience of enslavement, but it does allow us to reconstruct courses of life and struggle that are incompatible with the Lockean concepts of freedom, autonomy and agency. Historical work throws these categories of the European bourgeoisie into crisis, along with their moral category of empathy. We can learn that, as Owens says, there are 'other orientations' than freedom with which to structure a life – without the concept losing any of its meaning or relevance.[4] In this respect it is valid to help find a philosophical expression for the dispossessed and to find appropriate terms that act as a negation of Enlightenment philosophy, but not only that. What if the vocabulary of the Enlightenment falls short in describing the personhood of the enslaved, the figure of a 'slave agency'?[5]

Carmélite

The slave Carmélite found herself in a difficult legal situation in Louisiana in 1844. Carmélite was sold by her slave owner Françoise Doubrère to Jean Lacaze, whose brothel she worked in from then on, as a so-called *statu liber*: a form of temporary enslavement that offered enslaved people the prospect of freedom after a determined number of years of work.[6] In Carmélite's case, the rule stipulated that she would have to perform sex work in Lacaze's brothel for seven years and could then live in freedom. In 1851, however, the year that Emily Owens begins her examination of the case, Carmélite finds herself in court. She argues that Lacaze – contrary to the promise of *statu liber* – has not released her after her seven years in the brothel, and that she has also been subjected to abuse. Fearing further abuse and that Lacaze will possibly sell her in this unclear legal position and make her release impossible, she asks to be placed in prison until she can prove her right to freedom in another court case, via the contract between Doubrère and Lacaze. Lacaze's refusal to release Carmélite violated Spanish slavery laws in force at the time and the *statu liber* enshrined in them, but his behaviour, as Owen outlines, was also entirely consistent with other valid legal provisions in Louisiana. 'Misconduct', which included working in a brothel for example, was stated as reason to disqualify enslaved people from the possibility of liberation.[7] Owens considers the possibility that Lacaze was already aware of this when he signed the contract. He would have deliberately involved Carmélite in a legal drama through cunning – the Odyssean 'loophole in the agreement'[8] – from which she could hardly free herself: 'He had put her in an impossible situation, having promised to free her because she worked in a brothel, but subsequently refusing to free her because of her uncouth conduct in that brothel.'[9]

Even beyond the legal archaeology which Owens conducts in her article, this is a vivid illustration of the paradox of liberation from enslavement. The conditions for captivity and freedom were legally determined by the colonial powers – even if they no longer explicitly acted as such, but understood themselves as agents of a just order. The legal granting of freedom was subject to conditions in the case of *statu liber* laws, which emphasised the objectified nature of the bodies of the enslaved. Sexual labour in the brothel corresponds to a kind of equivalent value – freedom was only available on the condition that Lacaze's investment in the purchase of Carmélite's body would first yield a profit through the brothel's income.

Freedom thus means that ownership of Carmélite passes from the slave owner Lacaze to Carmélite, the slave. The legal category of property holds open the possibility for Lacaze to postpone Carmélite's claim to freedom. 'Misconduct' is grounds for a lawsuit because Carmélite's misconduct is considered damage to 'Carmélite's property'. Property, even in the form of people, was protected in such a way in Louisiana in the 1840s that it was usually easy for slave holders, on account of 'misconduct', to legally object to the claims of enslaved people for their freedom. And since Carmélite does not belong to herself and has no legal personal status that would allow her to articulate such claims, she appears before the law as an object. Lacaze's complaint of 'misconduct' commits a category error, but one which carries no weight in a white-dominated world: Carmélite corresponds to her legal object status through the sexual labour she is forced to perform. When Lacaze invokes 'misconduct' against her liberation, he refers to misconduct as a subject, which Carmélite can only become through complying with coercion in the first place. What is duplicitous about Lacaze's complaint, and the legal situation that makes it possible, is that Carmélite's correspondence with object status, as a body forced into sexual labour, legally deprives her of the possibility of ever leaving her position. The rest of her history is undisclosed.

Subjects of Enslavement

> *This self which is unobservable is a mystery. It is imprisoned in the observed. It is constantly struggling to wrest itself from the warp of its public ownerships. Its own language is plain yet secret. Rather, obscured.* —Dionne Brand[10]

Carmélite's case demonstrates how the place of the court and the domain of the law, which hold enormous importance for the manifestation of personhood, become instruments of a particular negation with respect to the person of Carmélite.[11] Given their presence in law as objects, the enslaved are denied their personhood. This fundamental establishment has consequences that go beyond this law's jurisdiction, because as long as former slaves are not ultimately freed from their owners, the latter can repeatedly assert claims of ownership. This means that, by realising property claims, it is precisely the law that dehumanises people by treating them as objects. Closely connected is the fact that enslaved people, in their object status, have no possibility of making legal claims themselves. The only case in which they are granted legally relevant agency is when they are held accountable for criminal acts.[12] This gives rise to a paradox in the body of the enslaved: the demand to follow the law persists, even though they have no right to be treated under the law as such.

As a slave, Carmélite is judged and condemned for her double existence as subject and object: on the one hand, she is claimed as property, while on the other, there is a kind of concession to her agency in her punishment for moral misconduct. Enslavement is to become an object as the property of another person. The enslaved have no rights – and yet they are liable for certain actions and subject to punishment. This relationship forces them into a structure in which they can hardly be imagined as the authors of actions and desires. Everything that happens to them is determined by those in power. All the same, imagining and seeking out the subjectivity of the enslaved is a way to defy this order without overriding it. It means disturbing its unbroken validity through the archives and in the writing of history.

How can we refer to this form of human existence, veiled by absolute power? How can it be described in such a way that it does not only represent an abstract negation in contradiction to the liberal legal subject, but it can be theoretically imagined as a specific relation to the world?

On the one hand, Saidiya Hartman examines life permeated with the violence that enslavement produced, even beyond its formal abolition. On the other hand, she pursues the moments in which the enslaved do not come undone in the objectification of their bodies, their labour power, their kinship, their very existence. Hartman speaks of a slave agency, which at first seems like an oxymoron in the face of all-encompassing violence, but on closer inspection also actualises a mode of existence beyond autonomy and free will.[13] The vocabulary of self-possessing subjectivity cannot explain the resistance and praxis of the enslaved under conditions of absolute domination.

Slaves are commodities who speak[14] – their ability to speak does not mean that they are exempt from circulating as commodities. Their existence is shaped by the potential violence implicit to exchange relationships. The way in which the enslaved have been robbed of themselves disqualifies them from legally representing themselves – they do not belong to themselves. Rather, the 'natal alienation'[15] which constitutes enslavement is a lived objection to the very idea of autonomy. Enslavement is more than exploitation. It is marked by forcing people into a state of 'social death' from which they cannot free themselves. In his comparative study, Orlando Patterson describes the moment of enslavement in these drastic terms: in the instance of victory in war, the capture of the enemy replaces their killing. The defeated become human material at the victor's disposal. Those forced into slavery in this way now live in a state of socially enacted death, postponed only in physical terms.[16]

Carmélite shows what such a social localisation means in concrete terms: an absolute power over the enslaved person, which can be renewed and extended at will. Carmélite's position of social subjugation is constitutive, as is evident in her court case and treatment throughout. The social rules of possessive individuality and racist enslavement, resulting in an 'antisocial contract',[17] are constructed in such a way that self-determination and freedom remain unattainable for her, even when contractually guaranteed – the contract concerning Carmélite is not one that she herself signs. The life of the enslaved is infinitely malleable for those in power.[18]

Absolute Domination

Following Michel Foucault, because the power relations characterising slavery are so absolute, it is difficult to recognise a subject in their midst who is ultimately constituted by a 'clash with power', and visible resistance to it.[19] A subject with clear contours is hard to find here, on account of the all-pervasive character of this absolute power. The philosophical task of grappling with slave subjectivity can therefore only consist of abandoning the desperate search for a 'subject capable of world-historical action'.[20] Instead of such a figuration, traces of other, less monolithic subjectivities come to the fore in the work of Saidiya Hartman and her successors. Doing conceptual justice to this fragile knowledge is a challenge to achieve. On the one hand, working on the history of the enslaved entails a critique of a concept of the subject that is reduced to action, free will and autonomy.[21] On the other hand, such work requires closely observing what traces remain legible – as well as a circumspect, new vocabulary.

Looking at Carmélite's story, Emily Owens questions the meaning of the idea of individual agency for women who found themselves in similar circumstances. Carmélite's behaviour shows signs of determination and an ability to put up a fight. Nevertheless, it seems misguided to understand it in terms of 'action' under the given circumstances. She chooses neither the place from which to navigate nor the instruments of her attempt to escape Jean Lacaze's control. In this context, the self-evident use of the vocabulary of 'action' is also brought into question, with the aim of contradicting a narrative that claims 'that women of color willingly trapped themselves in a prison of their own making'.[22] Such a narrative has often been used in the context of enslavement and the sexual relations that characterised it. Instead, the strategies which find expression in Carmélite's paradoxical call for her own imprisonment, for example, should be understood with reference to the subjects who employ them. This requires a theoretical shift in perspective. From the self-possessing individual's point of view, Carmélite's position seems hopeless. Her plan to improve her situation through imprisonment seems grotesque, because it is likely to fail. And since the archives are silent on the matter, Carmélite's perspective is inaccessible. From the known circumstances, one can at most deduce that, during the legal proceedings, escape from Lacaze's immediate control seems more urgent to her than all else. How, then, can Carmélite's behaviour be conceptually reappraised and re-evaluated if the history of her oppression is taken into account, as well as the fact that neither she, nor what she does, belongs to herself? If one recognises that she has no way on her own of changing or even overcoming the circumstances of her subjection?

That it was made impossible for the enslaved to act independently, in all areas of life – not least in that of sexuality – says something about the slave-holder's relationship to himself as well. If ownership of the self is understood as the basis of self-determination, the possibility of self-determination is destroyed for slave subjectivity. The existence of a bourgeois, self-possessing individual is only possible in the first place because it finds its stable negative in the enslaved. Both modes of existence are mutually dependent, and they shape the Western value system in a dialectical interplay. As Hartman writes: 'The slave is the object on the ground that makes possible the existence of the bourgeois subject and, by negation or contradistinction, defines liberty, citizenship, and the enclosure of the social body.'[23]

The abduction of African people and their complete uprooting during the passage across the Atlantic makes them into objects that, as 'empty shells',[24] lend themselves to any form of inscription. In this case, the lives of the enslaved have exactly the meaning that those in power ascribe to them. This difference between self-possession and self-expropriation, fixed in racial difference, has survived the transatlantic slave trade in the guise of race and gender.

The formations of enslavement are an irreducible part of Western civilisation to this day. As Hortense Spillers puts it in her examination of gender's constitution in the context of slavery: 'My country needs me, and if I were not here, I would have to be invented.'[25] Her Black identity is indispensable to the narrative of the United States. Spillers is concerned with the 'layers of attenuated meaning'[26] that she must penetrate to achieve something truer than the racist images which circulate of Black femininity. Through their historical entanglement in an ontological order, they are more than clichés – they are identities that establish and restrict modes of existence. Spillers writes about herself as one who bears all of this: 'I describe a locus of confounded identities, a meeting ground of investments and privations in the national treasury of rhetorical wealth.'[27] Spillers analyses the bourgeois subject's dependence on the oppression of others as a process of meaning-making. The mythical casting of Black femininity as promiscuous, resilient, maternal, etc., fixes the human commodity in a specific position and adds a layer of significance to its material restriction. Thus the labour and the bodies of the enslaved are no longer merely objects of absolute malleability, but are at the same time forced into specific affective formations on the basis of which their rulers interact with them – supposedly on equal footing. And whatever these images consist of, they affect legal proceedings and further restrict the ability of the enslaved to express themselves.

Bourgeois subjectivity's dependence on enslavement manifests itself in a racial difference that persists beyond the historical epoch of slavery. Even after the abolition of slavery in the US in 1865, bourgeois subjectivity remains dependent on a counterpart that it can subjugate in order to define itself. From then on, this counterpoint is characterised only by its Blackness and is no longer identified by formal enslavement.[28] Hartman therefore speaks of a 'nonevent of emancipation'[29] and shows how, in the racist society that formed after 1865, liberation is postponed to an unforeseeable future.

In order to approach the subjectivity of the enslaved, it is important to dwell on this deferral of liberation, its negativity, to prevent historical distortions. In racial slavery, an interest arises in generating profit from people and their personal histories, robbing them of any meaning and erasing their future. Negated kinship relations and silenced biographies are means of turning people into commodities. These techniques of destruction cannot be counteracted simply by projections from the present which intend to fill in the blanks by seeing people instead of mere victims. We can neither permit capitulation to the history of the victors, who deprived the enslaved of their names and their origins, nor is it adequate to romanticise resistance narratives and the subjects which belong to them.

Between these false alternatives, one must find a practical answer to a philosophical question: how can the dead be narrated as subjects? How can one critique the 'language of political philosophy', a 'language of deeds and actions', without at the same time giving in to the fatalism of powerlessness and speechless violence that validates the project of the colonial victors?[30] What does it mean to defend the dead?[31]

Desperately searching for the will and agency of enslaved women ultimately risks misrecognising the comprehensive forms of subjugation that constitute both enslavement and the non-event of emancipation. Hartman's aforementioned concept of slave agency expresses an open engagement with the traces and remnants of enslaved subjectivity: 'How is it possible to think "agency" when the slave's very condition of being or social existence is defined as a state of determinate negation? In other words, what are the constituents of agency when one's social condition is defined by negation and personhood refigured in the fetishised and fungible terms of object of property?'[32]

Marisa J. Fuentes also considers it necessary from her perspective as a historian to find a new language for the historical examination of slavery and subjugation that does not compulsively assign enslaved subjects' experiences to the categories of agency, decision and willpower.[33] Hartman's assessment that the idea of 'the autonomous self endowed with free will is inadequate'[34] to understand the modes of activity and the variants of selfhood, thus not only has philosophical and conceptual consequences, but also resonates in empirically informed fields of research. The restriction of self-determination to a bourgeois vision – that is, with material, bodily and legal preconditions withheld from the enslaved – presents a fundamental problem. How can subjectivity be examined if it cannot be clearly positioned on a scale between heteronomous oppression and self-achieved freedom? How can this examination succeed without only letting the violence itself speak, having dominated the sources? And finally, how can we avoid reducing the lives of slaves to a 'particular negation' of bourgeois ideas? Perhaps searching for a subject may mean trying to fulfil these multiple demands simultaneously – including those the dead pose for our present, knowing that these demands can hardly be met.[35]

The critique of bourgeois concepts is an important step on the path to a new description of enslaved subjects.[36] If agency is not only an extremely presuppositional realisation of personhood, but only becomes a meaningful concept through its counterpart, the slave, then the claim that it is a universal human characteristic seems mistaken.

Rather, it must be recognised that the assertion of universal validity itself serves to maintain power – and thus is not altruistic. The fact that people are subjected to a way of life to which they do not belong requires us to examine critically both the political system that legitimises this fact, as well as the philosophical idea of self-possession.

This requires a methodological openness which avoids predetermined results. It is neither a matter of saving bourgeois ideals, nor abandoning them in an illusory and helpless theoretical gesture; it is not a matter of these ideals at all, but of describing enslavement as a constellation to which these ideals explicitly do not refer, or refer to only negatively. And just as bourgeois society needed slaves to understand itself, its ideals can serve as a negative foil in approaching enslaved life. Much remains buried due to the precarious source material. But Hartman also warns against finding excuses to leave it at that. Description of violence was often refused for exactly the reasons that made it possible in the first place. Obfuscating the pain of the enslaved and thus denying it was an integral part of the system of slavery. Hartman writes of the fundamental willingness to ignore the pain of Black people, which is still at work today.[37] 'If this pain has been largely unspoken and unrecognised, it is due to the sheer denial of black sentience rather than the inexpressibility of pain.'[38] How the lives of enslaved people can be narrated in their 'irrepressible humanity',[39] instead of only finding linguistic expression through 'routinized violence',[40] is the unavoidable question which accompanies any attempt in this direction.

The term 'slave agency' defies a merely negative determination. Instead of wanting to make goals and motives manifest, Owens, Hartman and Fuentes pursue their historical subjects of interest by looking at how they cope with everyday life and the tactics they use to do so. In an interview, Owens talks about her research and the glimpse of enslaved women that she can catch through precarious archives. In this subjectivity, constrained on all sides, she sees a self-understanding at work for which the categories of bourgeois freedom simply do not offer a promising horizon:

> I follow Walter Johnson's articulation of 'agency' as a project of liberal humanism and try to think about what it might have meant to be someone who would not only be legally and politically and socially inscribed as a non-subject . . . But also to presume that these women understood that, that they weren't walking around thinking that they were little Thomas Jeffersons, they knew exactly what their social location was, and that they were working within that . . . When I look at my archive, I don't see women who ask themselves, 'How do I make an agential choice right now?' . . . I see them looking at a very complicated situation in which they have very little power but they have some . . . and in which lots of material conditions matter, regardless of or in addition to their legal status.[41]

For Owens, finding a language for seemingly fragmented lives is a task of reconstruction. Analogously, slave agency can never define the lives of the enslaved as a concept of irrefutable historical evidence. Slave agency denotes the elusive relationship between the oppressed and the conditions under which they live – and seeks to describe it through collection of material and use of imagination. Owens is not interested in making the principle of autonomous agency more fruitful, or in proving that it carries weight in spite of everything. Instead, she questions its relationship to the subjects whose lives she researches, without describing it as a failure. She does not undertake any moral or political evaluation of agency, but simply states that it is not helpful for enslaved women to orient themselves towards it given the infinitesimal forms of power they possess. Instead of a normatively positive agency, Owens's analysis aims directly at the relational aspects of the lives she investigates. In this way, Hartman's diagnosis, that slave agency is an oxymoron, is expanded in favour of a perspective that deals with this contradiction and not so much with its conceptual persistence.[42] To use the term slave agency in the knowledge of its paradoxical meaning is to embark on a historical perspective in search of what enslaved people *do* without insisting that they *act*. The subjects of Owens's work are not oriented towards genuinely planned actions. Owens emphasises that material needs and their organisation form the horizon of daily activity. Carmélite's case makes it especially clear that the concrete relations in which people find themselves are initially more important than orientation towards an ideal. Despite all the difficulties, therein lies an opportunity to insist on a counter-narrative of modernity: 'The time has come for the primal history of modernity to be reconstructed from the slaves' points of view.'[43]

In this context, another political category comes into view: resistance. This concept clarifies the balancing act necessary for a historical and theoretical reference to slavery. While resistance narratives can surely provide a counter-narrative to the victor's history, they can just as quickly tip over into heroisation. Hartman and Owens aim not only to circumvent the categories of bourgeois autonomy in order to describe slavery with precision, but also to turn away from mirroring bourgeois ideals. What constitutes the enslaved as subjects is not better understood by celebrating all of their conduct as 'resistance'. Such a framing would fail to recognise the concretion of their lives. To counter bourgeois subject narratives means to break with romanticising the subject: 'denaturalisation of this history of the subject as romance, even if a romance of resistance.'[44] Incorporating the concept of resistance, potentially just as romanticised, into a theory of enslavement further escalates this theory's complexity. Slave agency must be distinguished from the extension of domination *and* from the romantic lure of resistance rhetoric.[45]

To speak of resistance opens up the important dimension of relationality. To survive, the enslaved relate to the circumstances imposed on them and in many places vehemently reject them – even if this occurs outside of historical visibility. For Hartman, the medium of narrative is a way to trace these relations and give them a temporal dimension.[46] The search for traces fundamentally shifts engagement with violence and resistance. Instead of pursuing the formation of heroic narratives and measuring resistance by its material success, Iris Därmann suggests the following: 'Resistance can only be measured by the fact that it happened at all and left a trace, which must belatedly be brought to light in history. Otherwise, it is rendered inaudible yet again.'[47] In this respect, it is not only historiographical complications which bear the possibility of saying anything at all about enslaved subjectivity. It requires an affective archaeology to deliberately avoid certain narratives of struggle and resistance, while at the same time insisting that enslaved people, despite their extensive invisibility in the archives, were complex subjects who had various reactions to their circumstances. The intention is to save the dead from the enemy, at the very least[48] – if that does not succeed, at least not to surrender the dead to the enemy in the comfortable silence which archives of violence suggest.

Conceptual attempts to consider the meaning of resistance, in a way that stands up to an ethics of history, are attended by numerous problems in the material itself. No woman who survived the Middle Passage managed to provide a surviving autobiographical account.[49] There are hardly any testimonies that can be assigned to a first-person perspective at all – and amongst them, hardly any have not always been assigned to very specific contexts and functions, such as newspaper reports, travelogues or government documents.[50] Even the autobiographical slave narratives are, as a genre, closely interwoven with the project of white abolitionists and their specific interests. These narratives served, among other things, to convince a white majority society that slaves could be educated. The voice of their authors is not always self-evident, and demands careful attention.[51]

Due to the precarious source material, it can be helpful to examine the relations that characterise slavery as objects of investigation. The legally codified, absolute power relation of human ownership and the concrete practices and techniques that the enslaved use to cope with their everyday lives are equally important. Hartman's method is to read all extant documents against the grain, and to use their secondary mentions to survey the web of meaning in which they are woven. The philosophical relationship one takes up with reference to historical violence is in this sense always a question of representation. How can the irreducible contradictions of enslaved life, which must at the very least have influenced how it was experienced by those who lived it, be narrated retrospectively?

Hartman speaks of 'praxis'[52] to offer a multifaceted, fragmentary conceptual framework for the activities of the enslaved, to which I will return. Därmann, drawing on Hartman among others, explains the concept of 'unserviceability' (*Undienlichkeit*)[53] to refer to the resistances she encounters in the source material. This expression of passivity does more justice to the subjectivity of the enslaved than terms such as 'action', 'self-determination' or 'resistance'. Unserviceability describes concrete practices of evasion, flight and sabotage, and thus aims at a description of actions existing within the minimal leeway which remained for the enslaved to briefly escape the regularity of violence. For Därmann, the term also historically corrects talk of 'passive resistance' to the effect that passivity is not synonymous with non-violence.[54] Evasion can mean cunningly dodging the scene of violence or, in extreme cases, using violence against oneself before someone else does. To live as a commodity is the condition that provides the enslaved with the organisational principle of resistance. There is no escaping the status of commodity, and no commodity can own itself. But the commodity can withdraw from use, becoming unserviceable. According to this principle, Carmélite also attempts to escape the control of her current owner through the lawsuit regarding her prison custody, in order to remove herself from the space of violence that Lacaze created for her.

In her study of the practices of 'unserviceability', Därmann confirms Hartman's conviction that there are other ways to discuss the impossibility of agency than through perplexed silence, in the form of pornographies of violence, or as a euphemistic glorification of the remnants of activity, laboriously assembled into independent actions. On the one hand, Därmann further investigates the moments of social life among the enslaved that Hartman describes as 'praxis', and, on the other, she attends to those acts it would seem brutal to term resistance: self-harm, infanticide and suicide.[55] In these and all other formations of resistance under conditions of 'absolute subjugation',[56] Därmann finds *'the most inexplicable thing* – that, and how, the power of refusal and evasion can arise from the unbearable suffering connected to sheer powerlessness, to violent exploitation, enslavement, mistreatment, humiliation and submission'.[57] When the question of resistance's meaning and motivation is directed at small, concrete acts, and when their ineffectiveness in changing the whole is relentlessly presented, then it suddenly seems even more drastic. At the same time, however, these close-ups open our eyes to how the enslaved 'defied and redefined the terms of absolute subjugation'[58] – that is, how the inventive negation of surrounding circumstances temporarily defangs their concrete negativity. The destruction of tools and other tangible property by the enslaved is just one example of practices that established a relationship of sabotage to a world constantly threatening their own lives.[59]

Negative Subjectification

Racial slavery is the relationship between white, self-possessing colonialists and Black and Indigenous colonised people who do not own themselves. The subjectivity that develops on both sides can only be understood in relation to the other. The master defines who the slave is and, conversely, remains negatively dependent on his existence. While Hartman can claim that her historical work concretely designates the resistant tactics and practices of the enslaved, my philosophical perspective concerns the conceptual manifestations which stabilise racial subjugation to this day, even in unsuspected places. In this history of philosophy, the 'subjects of enslavement' are those fixed in racialised categories and dispossessed of themselves by John Locke, G.W.F. Hegel, and others. Regimes of coldness keep these structures affectively alive.

It is a methodological challenge to establish intellectual proximity to the enslaved without maintaining them forever as pure negative determinations, where Western philosophy and the history of violence have positioned them. The determination of slave subjectivity confronts fugitivity. What can be imagined of it must ultimately remain a projection – historically informed but unable to be foreclosed conceptually. Slaves organise their lives from a logic of survival. In this liminal position, idealistic determinations are superfluous. 'Agency' does not take on a concrete form when a person is under the absolute power of another. In this context, Emily Owens speaks pragmatically of 'organisational principles of life', which can take very different forms, but are primarily committed to survival and never to an ideal of the subject.[60]

In light of all this, one could perhaps speak of a negative subjectification. This expression does not mean that *no* subjectification takes place, rather that it primarily involves factors of impossibility and struggle in adverse circumstances, and counteracts the elevated status of the subject in the Western history of philosophy. Initially, the enslaved subject-object is legally, politically and socially positioned as a 'non-subject'.[61] The paradox of this negative subjectification is to find a subject constantly engaged in struggle against its own effacement.

To assume subjectivity despite its successful annihilation is to attempt theoretically to secure traces of human selves and to make them legible under new auspices. Saidiya Hartman speaks of the 'determinate negation'[62] that the enslaved subject opposes to the bourgeois subject. This determination is filled by the millions of uprooted people on the Middle Passage, which represents an initial moment of enslaved subjectivity. Hortense Spillers speaks of an 'undifferentiated identity', 'culturally unmade' on the passage across the Atlantic, which is simultaneously 'nowhere at all'.[63] The professor of Black studies Omise'eke Tinsley sees those affected by violence as 'fluid bodies under the force of brutality'.[64] Each of these formulations targets slightly different aspects of the subject-theoretical consequences of the transatlantic slave trade, but all are united by their adherence to a self that has been uprooted, although it cannot be grasped as an intact one. In her travelogue from Ghana, Hartman mentions the 'identity produced by negation'[65] – a formation of the self shaped by the 'inheritance passed from one generation to the next' that goes beyond enslavement and finds identity in this experience.[66] Hartman describes herself as a part of 'the afterlife of slavery'. Negative subjectification lives on here in embodied 'history that hurts'[67] and manifests itself as a material lack in the lives of Black people.[68] The question of the memory of the slave trade, which appears to be merely historical, shifts to the open question of what to do when the event of the catastrophe has not come to an end.[69]

It is much more difficult to describe in a philosophically complex way the accumulated practices, circumstances and acts of resistance (as well as their structures of negativity) than it is to conceptually homogenise them prematurely. Multifaceted manifestations of resistance would simply be distorted, even inflated, by conceptualising them. In this respect, the most valuable philosophical contribution may be to survey the limits of the powerful and cherished vocabulary of autonomous subjectivity and to correct certain transgressions. This means to rein in politically the concepts of agency, freedom and autonomy by considering the moments of their erosion. Furthermore, philosophy can critically recalibrate the relationship between colonists, the colonised and abducted people with a view to the 'afterlife of slavery'.[70] This work is not limited to a renewed, careful study of the sources, because the violence of discourse is not only in effect situated there. Concepts also carry violence. Their deconstruction is part of the process by which a future beyond the past and present of slavery becomes for the first time obtainable and conceivable.[71]

Dehumanisation

Self-possessing bourgeois subjects and self-dispossessed enslaved subjects form the dialectic of modern subjectivity. Saidiya Hartman demonstrates how 'scenes of subjection' constitute the dividing line between the two, as well as the interdependency of these subject positions. The white, bourgeois self is dependent on its enslaved counterpart in a number of ways. The concept of freedom is a central category of meaning for bourgeois existence and only takes shape through its negation in a life in which freedom cannot be realised. It is hard to theoretically conceive of the survival of this subjugated, embodied negative of the Western subject. What characterises Blackness above all is that it can be shaped by the ruling powers in any way they choose. Hartman argues that the way in which the enslaved are treated with violence expands the possibility of what it means to be human.[72] The project of slavery is an ongoing inquiry into human resilience and physical persistence. At the same time, the 'ethnoclass (i.e. Western bourgeois)' defines the conceptual boundaries of the human within this project.[73]

Extreme situations of subjugation testify to the difficulty, as well as the necessity, of presuming a subject who suffers through these experiences of violence. In the midst of accounts of colonial appropriation and forced labour, plantation slavery and formal emancipation, this subject is certainly no self-evident phenomenon. It emerges and decays through the effects of colonial violence and rarely finds expression that cannot be interpreted as a direct reaction to that violence.

However, there are subjects whose lives are not touched by enslavement in terms of chronology, but whose lives are still shaped and formed by the 'afterlife of slavery'. The continuity of the 'nonevent of emancipation'[74] and the perspective of an unfinished 'long emancipation'[75] necessitate an engagement with colonial, negative subjectification that goes beyond historical chronology.

If anti-Blackness proves to be a constitutive element of modernity, and thus also the present, then the self-evidence of institutional politics as a site of liberation comes under pressure. How and whether political subjectivity can be discussed, or whether this concept must be left to dissolve in view of the problematic normative factors that determine it, requires further elaboration. Fred Moten and Stefano Harney propose a politics without subjects in order to counter incomplete emancipation through an incomplete politics and a damaged subject.

8 The Self in Disintegration

MANTHIA DIAWARA: *What does departure mean to you?*
ÉDOUARD GLISSANT: *It's the moment when one consents not to be a single being and attempts to be many beings at the same time.*[1]

Hannah Arendt's essay 'Reflections on Little Rock', in which she assesses the efforts in the Southern states of the USA to end segregation in schools, caused a great deal of controversy when it was first published;[2] the text's publication had already been delayed a year because the editors anticipated its explosive potential. In her preliminary remarks, Arendt explains that she considers the delay useful despite the loss of contemporary relevance. She publishes her commentary on the desegregation of Little Rock Central High School 'in the hope that even an inadequate attempt might help to break the dangerous routine in which the discussion of these issues is being held from both sides'.[3]

What are these 'routines' of thought that Arendt considers problematic? Sixty-five years after its publication, Arendt's perspective has been brought into focus again, by Fred Moten and Kathryn Gines among others,[4] because it demonstrates aporias of liberal thought with regard to Black liberation struggles, aporias which remain virulent in the present. The 'routines' identified by Arendt point to the irreconcilable nature of the conflict. The situation giving rise to Little Rock occurred in 1957. Arendt is by no means the only commentator on the case, now described as a milestone of African-American resistance to segregation in public space – 'a civil rights firestorm'.[5] Little

Rock is of interest concerning bourgeois coldness, because coldness reveals itself here as part of a special form of intelligence for which Arendt is exemplary, according to Moten.

Contemporary criticism notes that Arendt greatly overlooks the conditions and historical continuities that structure Little Rock.[6] By insisting on clear categories of political analysis, she misses, first, the surrounding conditions – the racist circumstances that make school integration an event in the first place – and, second, the stubborn element – the decisive behaviour of the students, who cannot be reduced to merely acting as representatives of their parents. Moten understands this as a problem of perceptions – Arendt's view is too clear to indulge in the details of the scene. Ultimately, this view refuses insight into the complexity of the social, and Black sociality in particular, reproducing what Saidiya Hartman calls a 'burdened individuality of freedom.'[7]

Little Rock

> *You said 'groundless thinking.' I have a metaphor which is not quite as cruel, which I have never published for myself. I call it thinking without banister, that is in German, 'Denken ohne Geländer'. That is, as you go up and down the stairs, you can always hold on to the banister, so that you don't fall down. What we have lost is a banister. That is the way I tell it to myself. That is indeed what I try to do.* —Hannah Arendt[8]

On 4 September 1957, nine teenagers approach the Little Rock Central High School building in Arkansas, previously all-white. Elizabeth Eckford, Ernest Green, Gloria Ray Karlmark, Carlotta Walls LaNier, Minnijean Brown-Trickey, Terrence Roberts, Jefferson Thomas, Thelma Mothershed-Wair and Melba Pattillo Beals are the Black teenagers who will implement the 1954 US Supreme Court ruling *Brown vs Board of Education*, stipulating the end of racial segregation in schools. The building is surrounded by countless onlookers, curious, aggressive, shouting.

Surrounded too by soldiers: Orval Faubus, the Governor of Arkansas, has had the national guard positioned in front of the school to prevent the Black students from entering the building and to express his own opposition to the ruling. In her 1995 autobiography, Melba Pattillo Beals recounts the Black teenagers' first attempt to enter Central High and the physical and verbal abuse she and her fellow students were subjected to on 4 September: 'I stood motionless, stunned by the hurtful words. I searched for something to hang on to, something familiar that would comfort me or make sense, but there was nothing.'[9] The most visible culmination of the violence in the media is the military securing of the high school and the unrestrained aggression of the white demonstrators, as documented in many news photographs. The days after this first confrontation are marked by no less turmoil for the Black teens and their families. Attacks on their homes, armed gangs hunting down those willing to integrate, and the participation of security forces in racist violence: it all resembles a permanent death threat.[10] In spite of all this, Beals emphasises that she and her fellow students would choose integration again and again, even under these circumstances, demonstrating the fifteen-year-old's clear political consciousness.[11] In her diary from the time, which forms the basis of her autobiography, Beals repeatedly affirms her belief in the justness of the struggle, reflecting on her role in it. She writes before a court hearing: 'This is the day I hope to meet Governor Faubus face-to-face. I can't decide what to say to him. If only he will listen to me one minute, I know I can make him understand there is nothing so bad about me that he shouldn't allow white children to go to school with me.'[12] The governor, however, does not attend. To enforce the law, President Dwight D. Eisenhower sends troops to Arkansas to protect the students and to escort them into the building on 25 September 1957.[13]

Hannah Arendt's perspective on the events that Melba Beals and the eight other teenagers endured comes, as she herself admits, from a distance. Arendt has never been in the Southern states, nor, she emphasises, does anything draw her there.[14] In this sense, there is little familiarity with the social factors of the integration issue. Despite this, or precisely because Arendt does not limit her capacity to make judgements as she forms her opinion, the web of claims and perspectives regarding Little Rock make Arendt's comments appear to Fred Moten as a 'deeply disagreeable but theoretically productive misunderstanding'.[15] The more obvious aspects of this 'misunderstanding' lie in the general condescension and arrogance with which Arendt pronounces judgement on the behaviour of those involved. The more subtle and interesting 'productive' points concern the question of political subjectivity.

Arendt's hubris stands out as sign of an attitude deeply rooted in white supremacy. Despite admitting unfamiliarity with the immediate aspects of the situation, Arendt considers herself as capable of and legitimate in proclaiming her opinions on Little Rock.[16] Her text is animated and moved by crude gestures of anti-Blackness:[17] she devalues the political judgement of the Black population in question,[18] places her trust in the state to solve the complex situation, and condemns any form of Black vigilante justice while uncritically granting authority to the demonstrably racist police apparatus.[19] She is unaware of any fault of her own in reproducing racist prejudices, considering herself immune to them.[20] In her 'Reply to Critics', formulated after the controversy surrounding her article, Arendt adopts the fictitious position of a 'Negro mother'[21] who sends her child to a school newly freed from segregation. She does this in order to make a serious accusation of all parents involved in Little Rock: that they are instrumentalising their children for political gain.[22] Beal's autobiography shows how false this assumption is, which then reads as absolute arrogance: the teens themselves explicitly requested to participate in the integration programme. Beals only tells her mother and grandmother that she has registered to participate – for fear that her concerned family would forbid it – after she has been selected for Central High.[23] Arendt dramatically under-estimates the political capacity and consciousness of young people.[24] Instead, her statement pulls out all the stops of racist victim blaming. In her view, the violence of white segregationists and white nationalists can be seen as a reaction to 'forced' integration.[25] If it had not been called for, there would be no problem.[26]

Taking a closer look at the characterisation of the problem as a political or social one, as a 'Black problem' or a 'white problem',[27] can open a more systematic discussion of Arendt's anti-Blackness. In Arendt's essay on Little Rock, the distinction between the political and the social, central to her political theory, crystallises around the concept of discrimination. According to Arendt, there is a legitimate, social form of discrimination, concerning the banal fact that people seek their own kind when they come together in a social space.[28] Independent of whether this assessment stands up to closer scrutiny, already it articulates Arendt's conviction that not every space in which people convene has to be structured around criteria of equality, as long as all those involved can agree on it. A political form of discrimination differs from this one, and for Arendt the former is illegitimate because it excludes people from political participation. Arendt extends this problematic to areas of 'public services' like bus and train systems and other business-related things.[29] In short, discrimination in the social is unproblematic for Arendt, but is illegitimate and dangerous in the political.

The two forms of discrimination in turn point to the separation of the political and the private which Arendt develops in *The Human Condition*, published as the same time as her Little Rock essay.[30] The relative seclusion of the two spheres of human existence serves to enable a common space of political decision-making, in which people can emerge as political actors and act 'in the light of publicity'.[31] In the private sphere, on the other hand, they are 'protected from their vulnerability'.[32] The social occupies an intermediate position between these two realms: while the private in Arendt's political model is clearly the domestic sphere, the *oikos*, and the public sphere concerns the area of activities 'in the spotlight', the *polis*, it is the social, society, which somehow permeates both, and which has a subordinate political significance for Arendt. And yet, she sees how this realm, unclear in its designation, is the most natural place for people to be: 'that curiously hybrid realm where private interests assume public significance that we call "society."'[33] The situation in Little Rock is no different. In her essay, however, Arendt is concerned with understanding the situation from the perspective of the political.

Her critique is of the failure of the political insofar as the teens remained in the social realm. She sees her contribution as helping to assess, in light of her conception of the rules of the political in the United States, the political and parental responsibilities of those who have come out publicly for desegregation. So Arendt concludes that white and Black parents are passing on responsibility to formulate solutions to their children, while the equality they must fight for does not occur in schools, but in the law.[34] Rather, Arendt considers the 'forced' overcoming of discrimination, in the social sphere of school, to be wrong and counterproductive. The racial segregation enforced by the Southern states cannot, in Arendt's view, be undone by another form of force.[35] In her view – based on a survey conducted in the state of Virginia – desegregation is not a measure supported by the population, and therefore should be avoided.

In the broader context of Arendt's political philosophy, the social character of the efforts towards desegregation make this a secondary concern. Because school does not belong to the political sphere according to this model, the fight for integration is neither promising nor does it serve progress towards a solution to the 'Negro problem' – it is mere window dressing. For Arendt, school is the equivalent of the world of work for adults,[36] and thus not yet political: 'For each time we leave the protective four walls of our private homes and cross over the threshold into the public world, we enter first, not the political realm of equality, but the social sphere.'[37] Arendt thus denies the topic any political character. As a result, the parents and the NAACP activists involved in the desegregation efforts appear as 'failures of citizenship', because, in Arendt's eyes, they have a false understanding of the state.[38] They are therefore considered unsuitable for Arendt's ideal of citizenship.

This also expresses a curious view of young people; Arendt sees every child as a conformist who 'instinctively seeks authorities'.[39] Arendt would therefore like to see them protected from any contact with the political world of adults. In doing so, she overlooks that these children – teenagers – show themselves to be headstrong in society, which for Arendt is structured much more unclearly than the political and the private. Elizabeth Eckford is the unwitting representation of this headstrongness.

Beals describes her first encounter with Eckford and her reserved presence: 'Elizabeth Eckford was petite, a very quiet, private person who had smiled and waved at me across the hallway at our old school. She was regal in her bearing and, like all of us, very serious about her studies.'[40] Photographs in which Elizabeth openly confronts armed forces in front of the school, while being followed by the 'mothers' league' of Central High, became famous.

In her text, Arendt speaks of a girl whose facial expression she describes as 'not precisely happy'.[41] Judging by her description, she is probably referring to a photograph that does not feature Eckford at all, but which could be seen next to her picture on the front page of *The New York Times* of 5 September 1957.[42] In any case, the images led her to state: 'The girl, obviously, was asked to be a hero.'[43] Arendt is seemingly focused on the aggression that the teens in Little Rock were exposed to, without protection.

> The anger of that huge crowd was directed toward Elizabeth Eckford as she stood alone, in front of Central High, facing the long line of soldiers, with a huge crowd of white people screeching at her back. Barely five feet tall, Elizabeth cradled her books in her arms as she desperately searched for the right place to enter . . . As she turned toward us, her eyes hidden by dark glasses, we could see how erect and proud she stood despite the fear she must have been feeling.[44]

In Beals's account, this moment of confrontation is followed by an outburst of violence. The increasingly aggressive crowd confronts Elizabeth directly.[45] Melba and her mother are also chased by a group of white men hurling death threats and insults until they reach their car. No soldier or police officer intervenes – some even take part in the hunt.[46]

Arendt may have imagined all of this in the moment of her empathetic appeal: 'If I were a Negro mother in the South . . .' Arendt sees the helplessness of children in the face of the white mob, forced into this situation by state measures. Her reaction unfolds from this image: 'If I were a Negro mother in the South I would feel that the Supreme Court ruling, unwillingly but unavoidably, has put my child into a more humiliating position than it had been in before.'[47] In this unprotected confrontation with the chaos of white rage, Arendt sees a degradation which in her eyes signals the loss of political agency. In her view, Eckford is at the mercy of the violence surrounding her without being able to classify it politically. What she doesn't see is how Eckford stands at odds with this classification of roles: Eckford enters the scene with her own imagination and her own story.

In his text 'Refuge, Refuse, Refrain', Moten places Elizabeth Eckford at the centre of Arendt's misunderstanding without seeking to decipher Eckford's behaviour. Moten sees Eckford as the 'visage of another imagining', the presence of an imagination which Arendt sees but does not see.[48] Moten occupies himself with Little Rock in order to better understand Arendt's unbroken authority 'on the scene that is supposed to be the American political and intellectual field'.[49] He evokes a new encounter between Eckford and this American political and intellectual field shaped by Arendt, one which also concerns Arendt's omission. In her gesture of intrusive empathy – 'If I were a Negro mother' – she refuses to analyse the hate-filled desire that threatens Eckford.[50] She articulates her purported solidarity with the civil rights movements as political counsel that in no way responds to the racial tension that structures Little Rock. And – what is systematically most significant – Arendt misjudges the social as a space of hindered agency and devalues it. Although, according to Moten, it is precisely there and only there that Black creative force is to be found. The misunderstanding lies in the transition between the social in which Elizabeth Eckford operates, and the political which Hannah Arendt seeks.

Moten suspects that Arendt is already deceived by the dark glasses that hide Eckford's eyes.[51] Eckford eludes the gaze of enemies and onlookers and thus already frustrates one of Arendt's notions of political agency.[52] While Arendt understands that those who are not 'seen and heard'[53] cannot be read politically either, she relegates Eckford to the role of child in need of rescue. But she has no idea who Eckford is, nor what the thoughts and feelings of a 'Negro mother', into whose shoes she has paternalistically inserted herself, might be.[54] In doing so, she misses a more complex analysis. Moten sees the student as caught in the spell of Arendt's 'reparative fantasy'.[55] When Arendt begins to consider the situation from the mother of Eckford's perspective, she demands that this fictional mother forget her social interests and make a political decision. For Arendt, this can only mean to protect children from politics and to end the social unrest caused by integration efforts. This means coming to terms with the fact that there are no political instruments available to fight this fight.[56]

Arendt's argumentative determination, often emphasised positively as a philosophical quality, carries a heavy burden of racist coldness. Arendt is in the right, but from the wrong position. She clearly but coldly sees difficult circumstances which run counter to the systematics of her philosophy. In the imagined role of the 'Negro mother', she exercises cold empathy, remaining blind to what this mother embodies outside of her political theory. She discards the social as the space of a hidden, insurgent activity in which there is more to find than merely an entryway to the political. Instead, a sociality could be discovered here that consciously withholds itself from the political.[57] The civil rights fought for at Little Rock and elsewhere, as well as those that were denied, are mostly constituted in a 'hermaphroditic realm' that is neither political nor private, and which Arendt would rather theoretically neglect on account of its complexity.[58]

What philosophical view could credit Elizabeth Eckford with more than Hannah Arendt does, freeing her from Arendt's organising fantasy? How can we – as distant, clueless sympathisers – look at Eckford without wanting to understand her exhaustively, without participating in the violence of those who would like to rip the sunglasses off her face?

Cold Political Reason

Can Hannah Arendt's negation of Elizabeth Eckford's autonomy through her appraisal of the situation itself be read as a part of Eckford's performance? Fred Moten is particularly interested in such a recalibration of Eckford's position, refusing to lionise her in a limited reading or to subjugate her as a victim. He formulates a new question: 'It's not whether anyone could ever stand in for the many that are gone, and that still come, to send Elizabeth Eckford. At stake, in the fact and question of her neglect and regard, is whether we can feel (with) her in having seen (through) her.'[59] Moten proposes something seemingly simple here: to *see* and to *feel* Eckford. Given the fact that Eckford cannot be deciphered as a political subject who becomes transparent through her intentions and self-disclosure, the question of whom to see, and whom to feel with, is a problematic one. The prepositions of this feeling and seeing are in parentheses. The possible dimensions of meaning in these parentheses are rich and intelligible as a reaction to the illegibility of Eckford's subjectivity. Moten suggests that we should understand Eckford's uncertain presence as an appeal, and to take a new look at the permeability and the impossibility of fixing Eckford's position in events. The 'seen (through)' suggests how Arendt passes over Eckford in her consideration, but also means that sight can change when it brushes against something and renounces its fixity.

Because Eckford does not 'appear' to her, Arendt undermines the possibility of this change. Eckford exists as a negation of Arendt's political theory – as a negative subject that has been pushed into a position by the supposed agency of others: her parents. Moten writes: 'Neither the "Negro Girl" nor her actions appear to Arendt.'[60] What does it mean to see and feel with Eckford in the face of Arendt's formed gaze and the unformed performance that refuses to provide self-disclosure? It would be wrong to fixate on Eckford as a representative 'for the many that are gone' – as one who carries Black suffering. Where is Eckford positioned in the political space when there she is simply a kid for Arendt? Or in what other space could she be found? Eckford does not stand before the National Guard as the unequivocal representation of a Black liberation struggle, as we can reassuringly see her in retrospect. Rather, her performance manifests an open-ended challenge to political categories.

Moten's intellectual leitmotif, the project of understanding the monstrosity of white civilisation, is directed here at the political theory of Arendt, who reveals her shadows in confrontation with Eckford. For Moten, it is unimportant whether Eckford shows herself, acts, rebels or protests. Because none of these categories is accurate, he describes her presence as 'nonperformance'.[61] Eckford is part of the scene. All attention is directed at her, but she is neither as helpless as Arendt suspects, nor does she pursue a goal that can be adequately described as political struggle. In the midst of the seemingly clear conflict over 'segregation', Eckford remains unreadable. Nonperformance realises itself through the acceptance of the actor: on the one hand, the acceptance of being an object, and on the other, of emerging as a resistant object. Nonperformance is the suspension of participation in the dominant social rules and the renunciation of individual self-assertion. The artist and philosopher Adrian Piper, whose reflections on performance Moten discusses,[62] uses self-objectification as a strategy for entering a hostile place without being permeated by it. Nonperformance functions as resistance to deformation by others ('deformation, to being messed up or messed with by others'[63]):

> My solution was to privatise my own consciousness as much as possible, by depriving it of sensory input from that environment; to isolate it from all tactile, aural and visual feedback. In doing so, I presented myself as a silent, secret, passive object, seemingly ready to be absorbed into their consciousness as an object. But I learned that

> complete absorption was impossible, because my voluntary objectlike passivity implied aggressive activity and choice, an independent presence confronting the Art-Conscious environment with its autonomy. My objecthood became my subjecthood.[64]

Piper develops a theory of performativity that explains what Eckford can be, apart from being inscribed in narratives of resistance and victimhood: an object that becomes a subject by refusing its own disclosure. Moten sees in this gesture the aporia of Black life in an anti-Black world. Piper articulates the felt antagonism[65] that induces her – much like Eckford – to accept her objectification as a Black woman, while simultaneously rejecting the schemata of appearance thus imposed on her. Such an immunisation against the encroachment of hostile spaces into one's thinking and being mirrors the strategic coldness towards institutions discussed above. Piper does not protect herself as a subject of integrity. She merely tries to limit the scope of the environment in which she finds herself by remaining cold to that environment.[66] A strategic sensory restriction allows her to evade the danger of being absorbed as an object by such a space. Moten writes of the sensory self-curtailment that enables this, which makes the 'refusal of collaboration' possible: 'ears shut, eyes pinched, a refusal of collaboration, as positive resistance to the "self-consciousness of art-consciousness".'[67]

The comparison between Piper and Eckford reveals the logic of what is only recognisable from the outside as a threat. Eckford and Piper's decisions – to be where they are – follow from a knowledge of omnipresent violence, which concretely surrounds them. The threat is no exception, which is why possibilities for containing it belong to everyday life. Piper and Eckford are practiced in nonperformances, using gestures as a form to situate themselves as 'objects in the world alongside others'.[68] They reject the 'political assimilation' that would make them addressable as subjects concerned with integrity and disrupt the desire for a political struggle legible to white people.[69] By no means does this make the situation any safer in a hostile space – quite the opposite. Thus to renounce self-protection only avoids self-extinction because it is proceeded by a self-abandonment.[70] And in the form of a 'consent not to be a single being' at that.[71]

Nonperformance formulates an objection to Arendt's political philosophy. When entry into the sphere of the political, so important for Arendt, is obscured or even denied, when those entering shed their subjectivity before they do so or come empty-handed,[72] Arendt's attempt to read the actor with a clear view inevitably comes to nothing. Eckford's behaviour is directed against the anti-Blackness that surrounds her, because her presence dares the 'violence of silent consensus' to be heard.[73] This is no game. It is the most passive provocation of white supremacy and entices Arendt to domesticate the nonperformance as well. For the reason Eckford renounces self-protection without being forced to do so is the aspect of Little Rock that 'political theory's cool reason' *cannot* understand.[74]

In Arendt's view of Eckford, Moten senses this 'coldness', which is not unlike the coldness of the social space Eckford enters in Little Rock.[75] And Arendt is an incarnation of bourgeois coldness, which appears here as the political reason of the clear-eyed. It is Arendt's pressing need to relegate the actors in Little Rock to reason. She justifies her assessments with the diagnosis that 'oppressed minorities were never the best judges on the order of priorities in such matters', and therefore 'even an inadequate attempt might help to break the dangerous routine in which the discussion of these issues is being held from both sides'.[76] Arendt hopes to provide clarity by providing the – in her eyes – helpless actors of Little Rock with a political strategy, one with correct, viable priorities. At the same time, this form of clarity counteracts the dangers which, according to Arendt, emanate from Black academic self-empowerment[77] and the political participation of those 'who have not the slightest notion of what the *res publica*, the public thing, is'.[78]

Driven by fear for the political community, Arendt tries to correct the imagination of those she fears till it finally corresponds to her own again as a 'regulated political *Einbildungskraft* [faculty of imagination]'.[79] Moten sees being 'clear-eyed' as an intellectual weapon to enforce this correction. In the Black mother she imagines, Arendt would instil a 'regulated imagination, the purified worldview, of the clear-eyed'.[80]

The clear view is the visual articulation of intelligence – firmly grounded in the arsenal of white rationality. Its coldness lies in the ability to present the political world as an objectifiable field, and thereby erroneously to integrate those who do not reveal their concerns fast enough. The clear view is the intellectual property of those who belong to themselves. It is the institutionalised fear of the chaos that threatens to ensue when the white world ends. Its everyday manifestation is 'common sense', which, according to Arendt, gives members of a society the certainty that they live in a shared reality.[81] Arendt's corrective gesture towards Little Rock is thus an invitation to orient oneself patiently towards this shared reality – even if it includes segregation and racism. This also means that it is always political clarity which decides when and how to wage struggles.

The deferral of emancipation is grounded and justified by reason. This is where the monstrous quality of Arendt's thinking reveals itself: it is always directed towards a theory of politics and seldom towards the ambivalence of the situation. Arendt relies on her own intelligence at every moment. Thus she occupies a position of authority in which she is always right, but sometimes only in one aspect of reality.[82] To this intelligence, it is incomprehensible how Eckford can reject the self-protection that this same intelligence would enable her to have. How can one dwell where one isn't wanted? In addition to a paternalistic form of empathy, Arendt's coldness is also a sign of her greatest competence, namely her sharp intelligence.

In the appendix to *On Violence*, Arendt's political attitude, fixated on intelligence, is expressed in an involuntary remark. She talks about the problematic tendency to equate all formerly colonised countries, thereby creating an undifferentiated political platitude. She justifies her concerns by saying that the equally general Marxist slogan 'Workers of the world, unite!'

has been refuted.[83] The idea that a call for revolution can be refuted philosophically and rendered useless is a form of reality denial, the kind espoused by intelligence.

Arendt's phrase 'thinking without banister'[84] also expresses how she approaches Little Rock without knowledge of its conditions, relying solely on the sharpness of her mind. Her clear view, which always sees the totality of the political community before it, would forbid sending Eckford to a white school, where she is unwanted and at the mercy of direct violence.[85] But the clear view has a pre-structured horizon. A banister remains and Arendt hardly notices it. Her clear view trusts in the order of the bourgeois state and gives its preservation the highest priority. Moten rightly fears that loyalty to one's own intelligence entails a problematic loyalty to the state alongside it; since the state values and rewards the intelligent, it benevolently passes on its own authority to those who are committed to intelligence.[86] And Moten's view?

A Politics of the Blurred View

The critique of Hannah Arendt's unapologetic political classification raises the question not only of which concepts could replace her position, but also what kind of thinking, consciously departing from rigorous categories, would need to be learned in order to do so. Fred Moten finds this thinking in a 'double vision', the sensory equivalent of W.E.B Du Bois's 'double-consciousness, this sense of always looking at one's self through the eyes of others'.[87] Such a doubled relationship to the world emerges from the social position that Blackness occupies – through dirty glasses:

> I'm sorry if this is all a blur. I'm so used to my own astigmatism that maybe I can't even talk to anybody anymore. To make matters worse, I've never been able to keep my glasses clean. For the last forty-five years it's all been a blur and the dirty lenses Gaines provides in *Librettos* redouble the

> wounded, blessed assurance of my unsure, double vision. I think I'm seeing what I think I'm seeing, which makes me wonder if I'm seeing what I think.[88]

For forty-five years, Moten's dirty glasses have prevented him from taking on Arendt's view. His blurred vision gives rise to a new method of thinking. Instead of a clearly contoured view of the world, Moten's analysis is guided by a 'double-vision'. At the same time, this 'double-vision' prevents fixing Elizabeth Eckford in a clearly contoured manifestation. While Arendt determines the courses of action for individual political actors with her incorruptible clarity, it is thanks to Moten's astigmatism that he does not want to see such an actor in Eckford. Instead, he regards her performance as an act not bound to any sharp delineation of the self: 'Eckford's untitled nonperformance at Little Rock Central is consent not to be a single being.'[89] In Moten's work, the 'consent not to be a single being' is more than just a description of Eckford's appearance at Little Rock. As the title of Moten's theory trilogy, borrowed from Édouard Glissant, it represents a kind of refrain which, analogous to Arendt's 'thinking without banister', recurs over and over as a methodological motif – and perhaps even means much the same. 'Consent not to be a single being' expresses an objection to possessive individuality.[90] Moten completes a turn towards the social when he follows his thought's refrain, while Arendt sees the mind balancing in its solo brilliance.

Eckford dispenses with this balancing act. Seeing Eckford comprehended in constant breakdown allows one to consider her renunciation of self-protection in a new light. Eckford finds herself in an 'vicious dialectic of desire and aversion, protection and endangerment'.[91] Standing in front of the high school, her presence is contested, and it is exactly this contestation that is enjoyed by the white supremacists. By allowing the white mob and the state of Arkansas to visually demonstrate their opposition, Eckford's presence enables the constitution of the white order once again. Eckford is thus an object of relished violence – she remains an object even in the white liberal desire to protect her from this violence.[92] Her object status enables the realisation of a white capacity – whether through violence or rescue. Frank B. Wilderson III describes this relation as 'parasitic' because it draws the white capacity to act from the concrete and painful incapacity of the Black body.[93]

This sympathetic objectification is particularly evident in Arendt's relationship to images from the news. Arendt's indignation at the scene indicates that she would have liked to see Elizabeth Eckford saved through a superior intelligence. Arendt sees her defencelessness as a provocation, for which she blames Eckford's parents. But Eckford is not free to withdraw from the fray. The affective structure which confronts her at the scene of Little Rock always already deploys her as an object in the midst of violence. For Adrian Piper, this seems to be the twist on offer to her: 'My objecthood became my subjecthood.'[94]

With reference to Saidiya Hartman, this position could be understood as the 'burdened individuality of freedom'.[95] Hartman establishes this concept to describe the negative freedom of formerly enslaved people. Despite the legal shift after abolition, such people were still deprived of the essential resources to be able to realise 'their' freedom. Eckford appears as the bearer of a 'burdened individuality' because Arendt's gaze imposes on her the burden of proving she is capable of participation in civil society. Eckford is expected to behave in accordance with the liberal paradigm of freedom. When Arendt judges the ability of the oppressed to self-organise and accuses the nine students' parents of instrumentalising their children, she presents the parents with the task of proving 'their worthiness for freedom'. And this before the 'nation's duty to guarantee, at minimum, the exercise of liberty and equality' is even invoked on their behalf.[96] Arendt sees the Black children and their parents exactly in the position of the slaves who were released to destitute freedom: as supplicants of bourgeois society, who must first learn the appropriate conduct and achieve the correct property relations before their membership of that society can be considered. Arendt demands that the Black population integrate from a place of destitution, thereby overlooking the fundamental difference between a social position of poverty and one of racialised poverty: 'To be a poor man is hard, but to be a poor race in a land of dollars is the very bottom of hardships.'[97]

It is not easy conceptually to dispose of the notion of political subjectivity and its prerequisites as established by Arendt. Moten's aesthetically informed deconstruction of Arendt requires the reader to recognise the coldness of the bourgeois even where it seeks to establish equality and progress. Eckford's nonperformance cannot be apprehended with a democratically trained sensory apparatus. In Arendt's view, Eckford and her parents squander their claim to bourgeois participation through a lack of intelligence or strategy. But instead of replacing this problematic Arendtian logic of political subjectivity with another one, Moten's intention to linger on Eckford perhaps already honours the demand of critique.[98] His refrain against possessive individuality represents an alternative to Arendt's political system. The question of 'whether we can feel (with) her in having seen (through) her' is answered by the blurred view, which does the utmost justice to Eckford's divided existence.[99] We can see and feel Eckford if we do not demand that she show herself to us in a particular way. A politics of the blurred view accommodates Eckford and, in the form of her 'consent not to be a single being', also provides relief for those burdened by the liberal paradigm of freedom.

A blurred view is the epistemological prerequisite for being able to name the 'nonevent of emancipation' as such.[100] The blurred view is a way to avoid becoming blind – through the regulative politics of bourgeois freedom – to another possible form of freedom. Emancipation is not complete. And because, 'The incomplete emancipation fears the more complete one',[101] the liberal concept of freedom constantly threatens to refute doubts about its usefulness by resorting to cold political reason. Because these doubts are also Eckford's, the blurred view can be conceived as a tool to curb Arendt's political epistemology of anti-Blackness. Or, to paraphrase Sylvia Wynter, to take action against an understanding of 'normality' that defines itself by its distance from Blackness.[102] This struggle is also an intellectual one.

The blurred view concerns politics in general, and the question of what limitations this category is subject to. Moten and Stefano Harney write that politics resembles an 'attack on the common' and carries the danger of a 'recourse to self-possession'.[103] The only option is to '[look] for politics in order to avoid it'.[104] *The Undercommons*, their manifesto-like collection of essays, reflects Moten's engagement with Arendt's political model as a silent negation. The 'attack on the common' consists in the universalised assumption of individual agency, which is undermined by Eckford.

Moten and Harney are concerned with the possibility of a different, wilder political navigation that takes its starting point in the situation of the Black object-subject. This must resemble a theory of 'revolution without politics, which is to say revolution with neither a subject nor a principle of decision'.[105] Politics is contrasted, performatively and in terms of content, with the concept of 'the surround' – 'that strange, somehow hermaphroditic realm between the political and the private'[106] – which corresponds to the concept of the social in Arendt's philosophy. Moten and Harney's implicit reference to Arendt reiterates the distinction between the perspective of modern statehood and that of those excluded and objectified by it. Within Arendt's system, Moten and Harney's position can be read as a valorisation of the social in relation to the political. In fundamental agreement with Arendt's basic distinction between these two spheres, they shift attention and situate the hope of liberation in the social – there, where it is formulated in a more interesting fashion. Arendt is able to identify the difference, which has such importance for her. This is what makes her misunderstanding productive – Moten and Harney use the line between political and social life, so precisely calibrated by Arendt, to call for a revolution against the political.

The revolution of the surround without a subject relies on movements of withdrawal, flight and the presence of the new in the old. In doing so, no *concept* of freedom is realised; rather, this revolution operates against the conceptual immobilisation of fugitive movements. No conceptual ideal should curtail the openness of a sociality in motion.[107]

Moten and Harney do not see themselves, or those who feel identified by the 'we' of the 'undercommons', as being responsible for politics.[108] Their social philosophy finds its horizon in trust in 'actually existing social life', which dispenses with the corrective aspect of politics.[109] Existing social life is enough to imagine felicitous social life. This conviction justifies the renunciation of a concept of politics that, according to Moten and Harney, merely seeks to regulate the social from within. Accordingly, the new that helps to overcome the liberal political subject is already in the world – especially in its dysfunctional parts. The new lies 'already . . . around and below the forts, the police stations, the patrolled highways and the prison towers'.[110] And, contrary to the assumption that this new would only prove useful through its appearance on the stage and through its explicit framing as politics, Harney and Moten reject the duty of representation as a misunderstanding. The only measure of change is what is done and how it is done: 'There is no way for us to differentiate ourselves from the enemy except through practice.'[111]

In *The Undercommons*, an avoidance strategy of political subjectivity is formed that aims to shake off the 'burdened individuality of freedom' – which means shaking off individuality above all. The mode of existence that Moten and Harney describe renounces the demands of liberal freedom by permanently evading them – intellectually, physically, legally. They sketch out a struggle that is directed against political institutions as a whole, that is, against the structuring forces of (post-) colonial reason. The 'undercommons' are to be understood as an elaborate negation of political theory and at the same time as the revocation of a colonial ceasefire.

This radical counter-project to liberal politics considers the question of colonial subjectivity, beginning with its primal scene. The text begins with the figure of the settler and his eternal gestures of intervention, organisation and appropriation from the 'surrounded fort'.[112] The fort as power centre in the settler state 'is besieged by what still surrounds it, the common beyond and beneath – before and before – enclosure'.[113] The colonial antagonism is presented here as centre versus periphery. The colonial order spreads out from the centre, which it created itself, and calls itself politics. Outside of it, those living in the surround lack a systematic language with which to escape the dominance of political decisions. Their eyes therefore fall on flight, theft and invisibility – activities that no longer want to be called politics. Through their theoretical work Moten and Harney's intention is to protect the surround, where this all takes place.[114]

Coda: End of a World

The opposition of political reason and social self-defence is neither purely abstract nor a phenomenon of the past. In the moment of protest, the blurred view turns against the reasons for its blurriness: the material devastations of anti-Blackness inhibit life. They are 'the hold',[115] the belly of the slave ships in which the presence of police violence, social precarisation and Black death take place as norm.[116] This constitutes a reality of incessant siege, whose unliveability is voiced in protest against state violence – sometimes in confrontation with the state itself. What Hannah Arendt misunderstands as revenge, but what must be rightly called self-defence, erupts here.[117] In Arendt's eyes, revolutionary violence is not only futile, but it also makes it impossible to act in a way that could actually interrupt the course of things.[118] Arendt is not surprised by 'the violated dream of violence'.[119] As if answering Arendt, the activist Tamika Mallory, speaking during the 2020 George Floyd uprising in Minneapolis, sets it right: 'Violence is what we learned from you.'[120]

Christina Sharpe's careful question about a possibility out of impossibility indicates that there is no escape from the totality of white supremacy, for anyone. 'What happens when we proceed as if we *know* this, antiblackness, to be the ground on which we stand, the ground from which we to attempt to speak, for instance, an "I" or a "we" who know, an "I" or a "we" who care?'[121] Which self or which 'we' can answer the catastrophe? The question of a shared reality is the burden that the 'I's and 'we's now bear. Anti-Blackness is the ground on which everyone stands. But how can we find an appropriate relation to it that does not exhaust itself in the limits of identity?

In the summer of 2020, independent of foundational research on white civilisation, the possibility of such an affective and political readjustment arises: the insurrectionary manifestation of Black objection to the Western sense of justice turns against the regulatory power of cold political reason. The intransigence of the protests in the United States, and the global solidarity with them, ineluctably inscribe this antagonism in the field of global political struggles.

Fred Moten reflects on the rhetoric of 'crisis' in this context. Linguistic markers such as 'riot' and 'crisis' resemble a call for state regulation.[122] Moten writes in 2018 – before that summer of 2020, but already under the first Trump administration – that the stabilisation of the status quo is upheld by the use of the word 'riot'.[123] The language used to label events legitimises state intervention and thus itself has a policing function.[124] But while the vocabulary of 'riot' and 'crisis' brings the legitimation of state violence in its wake, it also makes a promise. The crisis itself becomes recognisable as a generative moment because, by definition, it defies regulation.[125] Against Arendt's critique of violent protest, Moten seeks to understand, in the context of the Black radical tradition, what constitutes the riot as an independent form. An adequate understanding of the role of violence suggests that it is always present on both sides – that of the oppressor and that of the insurgent. Once historical and colonial – as well as everyday structural – violence is understood as part of the energy that initiates protest, to frame the riot as self-defence instantly makes sense. Black Lives Matter is a reaction to anti-Blackness. A 'we' of negative subjectification is constituted by disrupting the machine of white supremacy. According to Moten, this is therefore 'generative violence':

> To rise to the defense of this sacred, ordinary, generative violence – to protect it from the ongoing murder – is often to risk a kind of appropriation of the very propriative force one seeks to combat with an otherwise animating fugitivity. Such uprising can take the form of burnin' and lootin', but, even more easily, such appropriation can take the form of a critical account of the justificatory causes of burnin' and lootin'. Meanwhile, what always remains or, more precisely, what must be understood as the irreducible remainder that animates such physical acts as well as such critical accounts, are everyday and everynight things. It's not about the looting of loot or the assault of persons who take shape as shops and wares, or about the insurgents' loss of or exclusion from citizenship or belonging that supposedly makes the former inevitable; it is, rather, all about insurgence as the performative declaration of what we are and what we have and what we give.[126]

To defend violence as creative is dangerous, because such a linguistic containment contradicts the fleeting dynamics that constitute violent protest. One cannot actually speak of such dynamics with the categories of legitimate and illegitimate action. Violence as 'sacred, ordinary, generative' can take shape as burning and looting without this becoming a formulated practice. Moten is interested in the everyday nature of moments that initiate outbreaks of violence, uprisings, self-defence. They do not concern looting itself, they are not justified through or affected by the gain or loss of civil status, which is only named as the apparent starting point for unrest.[127]

Moten is concerned with understanding violence as part of the structures of civilisation and its specific eruptions as forms of self-assurance: 'what we are and what we have and what we give.' In other words, violence, according to Moten, should not be subjected to a critical evaluation that seeks to locate it morally. Rather, it is best considered performatively. Riot itself is the only statement of those who are not responsible for politics.[128] In a moment filmed by David Jones at the end of May 2020, Kimberly Jones opposes the condemnation of forms of resistance justified by a supposed social contract with the simple observation that this contract has long since been broken under the conditions of white supremacy and continues to be broken: 'You broke the contract when you killed us in the streets and didn't give a fuck. You broke the contract when for four hundred years, we played your game and built your wealth.'[129] Much more could be said about riot, since it constitutes a breaking point of political positioning. Riot, violence, is always the point of departure for distinguishing democracy from anti-democracy – and with that, inside from outside, speech from silence, citizen from barbarian.

It cannot remain that way. Because then it will remain as it is. The roots of anti-Blackness in European political morality are so dogged and old that they cannot be gently dislodged. The 'performative declaration' of the riots refuses to be responsible for a politics of softness. It declares that it is not responsible for a political reconstruction. Violent protest pulls up the roots under which the dead lie in order to defend them.[130]

It is not only bourgeois individuals who keep whiteness alive through social existence. The world itself, as a complex of meaning, as an ultimately coherent system of affects, interests and ideas, metaphysically guarantees the preservation of white bodies and minds.[131] The world 'houses some bodies more than others'.[132] So if the white bodies that inhabit it are unable to break the dynamics of their own constitution, then nothing more than the end of the world can bring about their end: 'The paradox is that human extinction provides the answer and the corrective to the modern project of whiteness.'[133] In the summer of 2020, Saidiya Hartman pursues a social-metaphysical reflection in which freedom from white supremacy is only thinkable in connection with humanity's extinction. She refers to W.E.B. Du Bois's 1920 science-fiction short story

'The Comet', in which he describes the end of the world. After a comet strike, the entire population of New York is wiped out – except for Jim, a young Black messenger, and Julia, a rich young white woman. In the face of catastrophe, in the midst of death, they are able to encounter the other in a way that would never otherwise have been possible.[134] Only the end of the world, Hartman comments on the story, ends the white supremacy that separates the two in the social world: 'The stranglehold of white supremacy appears so unconquerable, so eternal that its only certain defeat is the end of the world, the death of Man.'[135] Hartman pauses in the resonance chamber of this possibility. 'I know this is all very heavy,' Hartman writes. 'But it is timely.'[136]

Theodor W. Adorno, too, reflects on what ends when freedom begins. The lip service paid to revolution from within the midst of bourgeois society ensues all too often out of fear – the fear of bringing liberation to completion – and not out of a genuine desire for revolution. Bourgeois consciousness 'has always been wavering and ambivalent'[137] when the 'radicalisation of the concept of freedom . . . cut[s] the ground from underneath the bourgeois categories of exchange, free competition and whatever else formed the part of bourgeois ideology'.[138] It wants to leave everything behind that inhibits freedom, but finds itself in a situation where it 'takes fright at its own courage and fears that a freedom made real might lead to chaos'.[139] Fear is precisely named here; perhaps Adorno knows it himself.

With Moten and Fumi Okiji we could diagnose that this fear is preserved in Adorno's aesthetic judgement: 'In Adorno's jazz essays the limitations of this narrow conception of subjectivity-as-bourgeois are brought into relief.'[140] As a bourgeois, Adorno pronounces judgement on music that is not only aesthetically alien to him, but which also conveys a knowledge about the world which irksomely haunts him. His racist and distorted reception of jazz[141] appears to trace the 'dissonance of emancipation', the proclamation of which he does not want to hear.[142] There is an 'insight Adorno's deafness carries':[143] what is expressed in the dissonance rejected by Adorno is the fact that jazz as 'black music' cannot help but undertake 'a critical reflection on the integrity of the world', which puts the bourgeois self in question.[144] 'Incomplete emancipation fears the more complete one.'[145]

9 Freedom

The day the slave decides to act out the threat of death that always hangs over her by risking her life is the first day of wisdom. And whether or not one survives it, is perhaps less important than the recognition that unless one is free – unless one is free – love cannot and will not matter. —Hortense Spillers[1]

When freedom is spoken of, its realisation is usually still to come. The formal emancipation of the enslaved, their self-possession acquired through abolition, is merely the bourgeois element of freedom's meaning. Saidiya Hartman traces the concept of freedom in the context of slavery and racist oppression during the period of Reconstruction after the American Civil War. Those who bear the 'burdened individuality of freedom' experience freedom as the mere absence of chains – but not as entry into a carefree life.[2] Hartman pursues the meanings which freedom assumes when the resources necessary for its realisation – rights, property – are withheld from the supposedly liberated. Emancipation, which was formally accomplished with the end of slavery but effectively unrealised, places the recipients of freedom on a social threshold: 'being freed from slavery and free of resources, emancipated and subordinated, self-possessed and indebted, equal and inferior, liberated and encumbered, sovereign and dominated, citizen and subject.'[3] For slaves released into freedom, existence rested on a self-preservation through work which itself resembled bondage.[4]

The formerly enslaved did not only find themselves in a situation of absolute destitution. The end of the nineteenth century saw a high concentration of racist terror, especially in the Southern states. White vigilante racism reached brutal heights when 'justice' was 'restored' by the lynch mob.[5] The forms of violence to which Black people were subjected did not substantially differ from those of slavery – only now they were perpetrated against so-called freedmen.[6] How could the concept of 'freedom', and a meaningful relationship to it, continue to exist at all in the face of material dependence on the slave-owning class and in the midst of rampant racist violence? How could the survivors of slavery still believe in freedom's realisation? 'How does one survive the common atrocities of slavery yet possess a sensibility, a feeling, an impulse, and an inexplicable, yet irrepressible, confidence in the possibilities of freedom?'[7]

Freedom is not a natural category, as an analysis of the subjectivity of the enslaved demonstrates. Not even as a concept can its necessity or its meaning remain undisputed. Emily Owens is therefore inclined to relegate freedom to the background when she approaches the organisation of enslaved women's lives. She notes that 'her subjects' are hardly concerned with freedom directly and that, although this says nothing about the normative status of freedom, freedom was not relevant to them in their daily lives.[8]

According to Theodor W. Adorno, the philosophical concept of freedom may certainly rise above empirical existence,[9] but it must be measured against historical realities, 'that is to say, with everything that Auschwitz represents'.[10] The concept of freedom is fragile. First, because it always oscillates between the reality of actual unfreedom and philosophical reflection, which rises above the given. Second, because, as Owens discerns, it has no practical, life-organising use as long as its bourgeois realisation in the 'right to individuality' is denied, and it reveals itself instead as the 'freedom to starve'.[11] In order to describe the lives of the enslaved, it may therefore be useful to set the concept of freedom aside and instead work with categories directly related to what we can know about enslavement. Freedom however remains a breaking point, or more precisely a mediating moment that connects bourgeois and enslaved subjects. The 'long-standing and intimate affiliation of liberty and bondage', writes Hartman, does not allow for imagining bourgeois freedom as utterly independent of subjugation. Freedom and autonomy always result from a property-based self-understanding that also includes the possession of objectified, unfree selves.[12]

Adorno, who does not want carelessly to assign freedom to a deficient reality, and Hartman, who considers the paradoxical relationship of the formerly enslaved to freedom, reveal delicate aspects of this concept. The role of freedom as a coveted yet deferred promise requires a 'reality check'. Freedom must confront the negativity of survival. What meaning and what effect does freedom have for those who live in its negation? How is the concept of freedom appropriated and transformed into something that makes sense from the perspective of the enslaved and the formally liberated? If, according to bourgeois conceptions, freedom for freedmen merely means being 'free from bondage but not from social, economic and political degradation', then it is worth seeking out manifestations of the concept of freedom that contradict, expand or dispel bourgeois notions.[13] Hartman describes how the desire to be free seeks paths of articulation and in doing so changes what freedom can mean. The liberated seek freedom as if it were a concrete place that could be reached, even if it lies far away.[14] Mobility itself, no matter how miserable it must have appeared, awakened the hope of a 'tangible freedom' waiting at the end of the journey.[15] If freedom continues to exist in the face of suffering in 'extreme situations of the political' (Iris Därmann's focus), then it does so in the form of freedom dreams and longings for freedom which are repeatedly actualised – through fugitive contact with moments of relief.

Perhaps this fugitive form of freedom cannot be adequately described with theoretical tools alone. Philosophy, in its craft, is too fixed on the unlimited validity of its statements, their 'reality', for it to conceptually recognise moments of shorter duration.[16] What freedom could mean in positive terms may only be deduced along the lines of its constant impossibility.

Adorno sees this as the primary philosophical task: 'Freedom is solely to be grasped in determinate negation, in accordance with the concrete form of unfreedom.'[17] The 'determinate negation', on whose basis freedom can perhaps still be glimpsed, could be the history of violence that Hartman and others study. This dimension also appears in Adorno's work. His engagement with the concept of freedom begins, among other places, in his course on G.W.F. Hegel's philosophy of history.[18] Here he works through the question of whether 'a theory of history is possible without latent idealism' – a question that also plays a recurring role in the historiography of the Middle Passage.[19] In this context, the concept of freedom takes on the function of a meaning of history. Adorno fights to preserve the Hegelian system, while at the same time questioning it from the perspective of historical catastrophes and incomplete emancipations. Thus, a 'negative identity of history' crystallises – a counter-image to Hegel's universal-historical world spirit, which embodies historical progress.[20] The negativity of world events also determines the question of freedom. Given the rarity of its realisation, how can anything be said about freedom at all? Where can thinking be freedom? Adorno works through the efforts of the 'bourgeois class to transparently ground' freedom, in order to find 'a common formula for freedom and oppression' instead of a theory of freedom's necessity.[21] This formula is to be understood in such a way that it simultaneously expresses the content of freedom and the existing relations of violence which make it impossible. And this is precisely what produces the opacity of the concept of freedom.

In order to help realise a dialectical freedom that satisfies this formula without too much idealistic excess, the merely bourgeois notion of freedom must be conceptually broken open. On the one hand, it unveils its limits through a historical method which focuses on the moments of its prevention; on the other, it is expanded through micrological studies that seek out freedom in its delicacy. The fugitive forms which Därmann, Hartman and Adorno want to be understood as vanishing realities of freedom pose a challenge to the Western-trained philosophical eye. They are by no means always recognised by the systematically trained gaze; Adorno can be read as a theorist who therefore wants to commit philosophy to the identification of the negative.[22] Only in this way can the desirable be thought successively, dialectically. His formulation of, 'It is to be achieved only negatively' is the result of his extensive engagement with what philosophy stands to contribute to freedom.[23] Philosophy can study the obstruction of freedom,[24] insist that it cannot be gained through self-consciousness alone,[25] and repeatedly defer it to a utopian future. All of this serves to not diagnose the condition of freedom a moment too soon. Freedom is only real when all suffering has been reconciled and all are sated: 'There is tenderness only in the coarsest demand: that no one shall go hungry anymore.'[26]

The negative invocation of freedom continues in Afro-pessimist thought. Calvin L. Warren, Jared Sexton, Tyrone S. Palmer and others transform the historical premise that Blackness represents the negation of bourgeois freedom into an ontology which not only temporally defers freedom into the unknown, but also comprehends its violent obstruction in the present as a condition of Western civilisation.[27] In this perspective, freedom and Black life form an ontological contradiction. At the same time, this contradiction forms the starting point for the struggle for freedom, one which has no alternative, despite everything. Sexton expounds on what it means to be situated in this aporia. It's not a matter of *if* one could be free, but of fighting a battle that can't be won. '*If* you can't be free is a monumentally misleading conditional. You cannot be free, no one can, you can only fight for freedom, pursue the struggle. You cannot be free, so you pursue it. You cannot be free, so you *must* pursue it, but how?'[28] The Afro-pessimist position radicalises Adorno's warning against a premature, merely apparent redemption. Afro-pessimist thought charges his sentence about the 'incomplete emancipation' which 'fears its completion' with concrete meaning: the contention that the white, bourgeois world and all of its concepts stand in the way of actual freedom can only entail the demand to destroy this world.

In an interview following the murder of Michael Brown at the hands of police in Ferguson, Missouri in 2014, Frank B. Wilderson III speaks about the political rift between the white left and the Afro-pessimist position. He makes it clear how the white left's orientation towards freedom is a question of improving material circumstances, while for Black people it can only result in a different world. Saving the world then stands opposed to the radical call to abandon it to destruction: 'Because what are they trying to do? They're trying to build a better world. What are we trying to do? We're trying to destroy the world. Two irreconcilable projects.'[29]

The Middle Passage forms a historical negativity, to which any attempt to understand the colonial afterlife of the present must inevitably refer. There is no present other than the one constituted by the transatlantic slave trade, hence destruction and liberation are here closely linked. Without drawing a substantive comparison between the suffering of the transatlantic slave trade and that of the Shoah, it can be said, in structural terms, that the Middle Passage occupies a similar position for Afro-pessimism as the mass extermination of Jews in the twentieth century did for Adorno.[30] The human world can only be meaningfully understood from the perspective of the catastrophes it has inflicted on itself, for these are the clearest expressions of the violence that its orders produce. Palmer reads Dionne Brand's image of a 'Door of no Return'[31] as the articulation of a negative historical origin. The door through which Africans stepped, brought out of the slave dungeons onto ships, marks the 'threshold to the world' as we know it. Palmer insists that the door exists – 'despite all efforts to change it by its carpenters or passengers' – and that it relentlessly actualises the ontological-affective colonial reality that founded it.[32] To disavow this reality obscures the violence it stems from and reproduces the 'cognitive schema of captivity'[33] that degrades Black people to the 'antithesis of the human'.[34] Afro-pessimism takes into account this logic, established in the Middle Passage, in order to understand the ontological quality of racism. For the concept of freedom, that means eking out an existence outside of political possibilities and beyond the realm of the imaginable. Even more vehemently than Adorno, Palmer warns against confusing the traces of alleviation – particularly explored in discourses around care, affect and 'other worlds'[35] – with freedom's realisation. Concrete conditions – including, among others, the prison–industrial complex and the European border regime – must always be taken as the basis for thinking freedom.

I think that Hartman also answers the question of freedom, and the philosophical possibilities of addressing it, in the spirit of the negative. For her, however, the ethics of utopian displacement is less important for the task of philosophy than observing how freedom functions for the unfree as an image, dream or horizon. The enslaved and oppressed situate freedom itself outside the here and now, or in transit, but never completely out of reach. Standing on the other side of this philosophical negation, however, is the affective material of hope, desire and wishes, which fill freedom with meaning, regardless of its conceptual history. It is this immediate orienting function of freedom that Hartman attempts to express in her book *Wayward Lives, Beautiful Experiments*. In the form of a speculative historiography, she deals with the lives of young Black women in the ghettos of New York at the beginning of the twentieth century. Freedom promises these women 'the good life' from afar, contrary to all impossibility. In the divided present, the promise of freedom unfolds as a collective attempt promptly to realise something of this good life within everyday precarity. In so doing, they are driven by the desire to be ready for freedom. 'This collective endeavor to *live free* unfolds in the confines of the carceral landscape. They can see the wall being erected around the dark ghetto, but they still want to be ready for the good life, still want to get ready for freedom.'[36] If freedom has weight, it is because those who need it have an idea of what it consists in. This is evident when Melba Pattillo Beals writes in her diary in the midst of the chaos of the Little Rock Central High integration that, 'Freedom is not integration. Freedom is being able to go with Grandma to the wrestling matches.'[37]

The 'wayward lives' which Hartman portrays in her book know freedom as a space between danger and exultation: as anarchic intention and as lack of institutional possibilities; as desire and bountiful intimacy; as the dream of glory and as decisive self-aggrandising. Freedom is – in fantasy – the permanence of this feeling – and in reality the chase after its fleeting realisation. Freedom cannot be brought under a concept when racist violence incessantly mocks its realisation. At the same time, violence and the everyday dealings of racialised subjects carry new meanings into the concept of freedom.

While bourgeois society conceived of the actualisation of individual autonomy in the bourgeois state as freedom, it persists negatively, even as longing, for people regulated by this state. From then on, the autonomous self must be regarded as a constellation of economic conditions, racial and gender identifications, and a striving for mastery over nature as well as universal cognitive capacity. The successful realisation of this self is measured up against subjugated others who do not belong to themselves and, as a foil to bourgeois society, assure the latter of its existence. A self burdened with this negative subjectification organises its relation to the world through practice in a field that 'cannot count on a "proper" (a spatial or institutional localisation)'.[38]

The (non)performance is faced with the appearance of a self as transparent subjectivity. 'Thinking without banister' meets 'consent not to be a single being' – in an encounter that, with Moten, might be read as a 'mutual, negative positioning of master and slave'.[39] A subject theory that seeks a 'common formula for freedom and oppression'[40] does not want an essentialist separation of two versions of the subject – one dominating and one oppressed. It seems rather to denaturalise bourgeois conceptions of selfhood. Adorno and Max Horkheimer initiated this project of denaturalisation in *Dialectic of Enlightenment*, but failed to recognise its depth in light of the close connection between the European bourgeoisie, colonialism and a history of violence. In this context, subjectivity is a category that insists on making survival conceivable. To describe enslaved women, about whom we know almost nothing, as subjects is to insist that they lived and had some kind of understanding of their circumstances – although their suffering is indescribable and irreconcilable. Freedom, then, would be the possibility of escaping violence without thereby exercising new violence. 'How is love possible for those dispossessed of the future and living under the threat of death? Is love a synonym for abolition?'[41]

IV

Oceanic Philosophy

Damaged personas labour in a broken world.
—Hubert Fichte[1]

A conclusion, which will not smooth over the contradictions running through this book, can only consist of considerations as to how this discipline can move forward despite Western philosophy being interwoven with the colonial legacy of the European continent. The question of philosophy in the face of catastrophe is also a starting point for *Negative Dialectics*. Theodor W. Adorno presents negative dialectics as an 'anti-system'.[2] This is to be understood as a fundamental critique of idealist philosophy. I read Adorno with the intention of lending new volume to this anti-systematic attitude in his thinking and thereby demonstrating its compatibility with Black studies and its undermining critique of Western modernity. The limits of commonality between these two traditions of thought have become clear in Adorno and Max Horkheimer's attachment to the bourgeois subject. The limitations of critical theory can be traced where 'Moten's thinking always starts from jazz while Adorno's is always against it'.[3]

The resistance to systematic philosophy, which among other things finds expression in the disintegration of coherent subjectivity, translates into three impulses. 'Destruction', 'care' and 'illegibility' are motifs that drive philosophy – and the self that it endeavours – beyond itself. They are proposals for radicalisation and, at the same time, offerings for where philosophy might be situated in a society based on the division of labour.[4]

10 Blackness and Negative Dialectics

Both Fred Moten and Theodor W. Adorno are interested in thinking as form[1] – in the condensations, boundaries, variations and tones of philosophical thought. For both, it is precisely not about systems but about multiform efforts to approach reality mimetically and musically. For Adorno, these different lines of thought usually find their way back to a common score; for Moten, coherence is not central to their validity. In his work, thinking is well acquainted with long solos and dissonances. There are a few moments in the work of both that particularly emphasise that it was 'by no means a missed encounter'[2] between critical theory and Black studies. In what follows, first, Adorno's work on contradiction and the 'primacy of the object'[3] encounter Moten's reflections on the 'resistance of the object'[4] as a similarly unyielding engagement with subject and object. Second, the constant border crossing of (philosophical) thought in the direction of other forms of expression generates a shared horizon that sometimes calls philosophy's very right to exist into doubt. They come to different conclusions in terms of the scope of philosophy's tasks and available tactics. I briefly highlight these moments of encounter to conclude my examination of Blackness and negative dialectics with a final chord that does not resolve them, but that does, to some extent, harmonise them.

Resistance and Contradiction

The centrifugal forces of the history of violence affect the possibilities and impossibilities of philosophical conceptualisation. The concept of freedom has proven to be a place where the ideal of freedom's individual realisation encounters its material impossibility and a less systematic reconfiguration of the word. The meaning of freedom from the perspective of absolute unfreedom is different from its meaning seen from the perspective of civil society's democratic institutions.

Nevertheless, Adorno's negative dialectics and Moten's para-conceptual practice[5] are capable of responding to these contradictions and understanding their inescapable existence as the very points of departure for thinking. Resistance and contradiction are the moments of greatest condensation for a thinking committed to the materiality of suffering.

Adorno's central question in *Negative Dialectics* is: how can concepts, despite their distance from objects, be applied to them as non-violently as possible? How can philosophy take into account the excess that experience always contains, in relation to concepts, in its form, method and practice? For this to succeed, post-idealist philosophy must recognise identity-based thinking as one of its contributions to the horrific conditions of the twentieth century. On the other hand, negative dialectics is supposed to maintain the dynamics of dialectical thinking and lead to the greatest possible agility and open vision, while also preventing it from carelessly transcending its own limits through the awareness of what it cannot grasp – the non-identical. All this is achieved in the form of philosophical concept formation. Concepts are structural elements of thought, which Adorno describes as inherently dialectical. Concepts are both the tool and the result of philosophy – for successful concept formation, knowledge of the concept's history is just as necessary as its quality of pointing beyond the given. In reality, philosophy constantly strives for what is without concept.[6] It aims for what it cannot reach, and this contradiction represents its most important methodological challenge. Concepts are units that, because they claim to be substantial, must always fail to recognise the non-identical, but on the other hand can assume forms which implicitly refer to the nonconceptual. To 'open up the nonconceptual with concepts, without making them alike' is therefore, according to Adorno, the 'Utopia of knowledge'.[7]

This is where the 'primacy of the object'[8] is articulated, which Adorno makes his guiding principle: although their failure is predetermined, concepts are constantly working on the objective and unformed world, constitutively withdrawn from language. 'Auschwitz' remains a cipher for the unimaginable, and to renounce it in language does not represent an alternative. The concept creates order, although what it orders is in constant motion.[9] Concepts inevitably skate on thin ice, and the philosophising subjects who work with them take ever more risk in their relentless pursuit of the non-identical. The non-identical calls the integrity of subjects into question.[10] According to Adorno, knowledge cannot be attained without danger.[11] Concept formation thus represents an endless aspiration to which philosophy can do justice only when it abandons the safe terrain of its 'school concept' and ventures towards a 'world concept',[12] where different skills are required than those needed to develop a conceptual order.[13] What Adorno genuinely calls 'thinking' is characterised by an at times desperate clinging to the unattainable negative, the non-identical; it mobilises affective and speculative forces, going 'beyond the concept, by means of the concept'[14] to brave oceanic infinity.[15]

If successful, philosophical concepts partake of a yearning that, according to Adorno, is inherent in works of art: 'What the philosophical concept will not abandon is the yearning that animates the nonconceptual side of art, and whose fulfilment shuns the immediate side of art as mere appearance.'[16] The nonconceptual is, qua yearning but also through play and speculation, a dynamic part of philosophical practice that helps bring thoughts to life.[17] These elements are mimetic. Yearning and play refer to something real, which language assimilates in order to achieve it. The enslaved's adherence to freedom could be understood *as a concept*. As a mimetic insistence.

In view of this tension between free play and the rigour of a history of concepts, Adorno speaks of squaring the circle, which the concept demands of philosophers.[18] Thus the yearningly speculative aspect of philosophy reaches its limits: it must not be confused with poetry, because 'poetry in philosophy means everything that is not strictly relevant'.[19] Already in his habilitation dissertation in 1931, Adorno warns: 'Philosophical form requires the interpretation of the real as a binding nexus of concepts.'[20] And concepts are 'walls between philosophy and that yearning [*Sehnsucht*]'.[21] Adorno is disturbed by the equation of philosophy and poetry or art because this endangers philosophy's commitment to the reality of material conditions, and thus also its socio-critical power.[22] Adorno insists on being fixed within the factual, and this, in his view, is what a philosophical concept should muster, despite its dialectical permeability towards traces of the non-identical, full of yearning. In this context, the factual denotes the number of philosophical truths pertaining to the respective concept. Only after contemplating and taking into account this material from the history of philosophy is it legitimate to leap into speculation. Conceptual work thus requires a philosophical education which enables philosophers to survey and work through the field of pertinent reference systems before becoming creative themselves.[23] Speculation can then be introduced as an expansive tool to 'keep on thinking . . . in a motivated, consistent way, going beyond the point where one's thinking is backed up by facts'.[24] Adorno imagines a philosophy that makes appropriate use of lines of flight from yearning and speculation.[25] Once added to the history of concepts, these resources allow for the development of theories that 'go all out'[26] and allow for 'complete intellectual union with the object'.[27] For Adorno, tying these free-floating aspects to constant self-reflection is the prerequisite for a philosophy that does not fail instantly on account of its fallibility.

Moten's para-conceptual practice stands in contrast. Adorno goes diving for the sediment, while for Moten, the bottom of the ocean is clearly unreachable – it is not the goal of thinking either. Turning away from Adorno's insistence on philosophical qualification, Moten devotes himself to things through an 'antiprofession and professoriate of deviance'.[28] Deviance as a counterpoint to the professionalisation of philosophy means, after the anti-idealist critique of form, allowing more for thought than its dialectical optimisation. Moten's lines of flight move arbitrarily and tend to shatter concepts, rather than to solidify them. Concepts serve a higher purpose. They help to ascertain the possibility of communal life: 'the concepts are ways to develop a mode of living together, a mode of being together that cannot be shared as a model but as an instance.'[29] For Moten, the problem of identity thinking is different than it is for Adorno. Instead, 'rituals of renomination',[30] constitutive fugitivity and the negation of the name represent elements of enslavement that determine Moten's ontological point of departure. Blackness means that nominal, familial belonging is made impossible, and that the movement of flight is necessary for survival. Moten's philosophical practice proceeds accordingly, first by accumulating concepts and then by continuously replacing one concept with the next, grasping the fugitivity of the object as a sign of its complexity. The goal of his thinking is not to reduce the object to something controllable, but to express movement. It is about the failure of the concept, about the attempt to not become a successful participant in the order of the world: 'trying hard not to succeed in some final and complete determination either of themselves or of their aim, blackness, which is, but so serially and variously, that it is given nowhere as emphatically as in rituals of renomination, when the given is all but immediately taken away.'[31]

Blackness is the highest condensation of Moten's theoretical interest, nowhere better expressed than in those rituals where everything given is just as soon withdrawn again. Instead of a dialectical balance, which always moves towards openness and facticity, Blackness is the method and object of an unfixed and unfixable performance. But the primacy of the object prevails even here, namely as resistance ('resistance of the object'). In Moten's usage, the resistance of the object represents a concretisation of what remains vague in Adorno. Contrary to what the mere priority of the object and its dialectical function within the formation of the concept may suggest, the resistance of the object – and its very priority – can be observed historically. It is the resistance of the enslaved.

This absolute specification, in addition to the claim to anchor thinking in singularity, has to do with Moten's literal reading of Marx. The turn of the resistant object goes back to a passage in *Das Kapital* where Marx seeks to clarify the difference between use value and exchange value by positing such a possibility: 'If commodities could speak . . .'[32] Unlike Marx, Moten sees this possibility not as a mere thought experiment, but as realised in enslaved bodies. The philosopher Ruth Sonderegger makes clear that Moten's 'subjunctive questioning' has fundamental implications.[33] On closer inspection, Marx's assumption that commodities 'lack the power to resist man' applies neither to slaves nor to the 'wanton women' that he mentions as examples of 'tender things' on the market.[34] Even if the circulation of commodities suggests otherwise, slaves, women, are capable of resistance, and they do resist. Again, this concept of resistance is not intended to ascribe an agency which slaves did not have – at least not in this context. But Moten insists that objects 'can and do resist'[35] in order to remove what Adorno calls the 'non-identical', the mystical veil. The anti-systemic concretion can be understood as an objection to an all too distant, generalising engagement with suffering, its expression and its peculiarity. Moten says more about abstract and concrete aspects of thought: 'The tragic in any tradition, especially the black radical tradition, is never wholly abstract. It is always in relation to quite particular and material loss.'[36] When Adorno states that, 'Suffering is objectivity that weighs upon the subject',[37] he replaces what *weighs* with a concept – that of suffering. In Moten's work, in contrast, the 'quite particular and material loss' always refers to a concrete object with irreducible characteristics.[38] In the case of the Black radical tradition, the expropriation of the enslaved is the prerequisite for being able to think the resistance of the object: 'The history of blackness is testament to the fact that objects can and do resist.'[39]

Objects resist not only when those objects are people wanting to escape the violence done to them, but also in that objects do not allow themselves to be subsumed under or contained by concepts. Adorno understands the non-identical as something like resistance against linguistic containment. In his philosophy, he hopes to do justice to the non-identical through unyielding work on concepts that are aware of their limitations. While 'Great philosophy was accompanied by a paranoid zeal to tolerate nothing else and to pursue everything else with all the cunning of reason', philosophy according to Adorno should not give up its pursuit, but always be aware: 'The slightest remnant of nonidentity sufficed to deny an identity conceived as total.'[40] Moten reminds us that the disruption of the non-identical which thinking waits for, according to Adorno, only initially exists as a painful facticity. Nothing that is thought is merely abstract. Everything that enters thinking as a singularity, that is, everything that thinking wants to process, also exists beyond concepts. Moten portrays philosophy's dialectical treatment of singularity as movement that, hoping for a way out, runs along the paths of despair until it encounters its own inevitability.[41] Some would see it as accurate to describe Adorno's work[42] as 'an endless dialectical struggle with despair as inevitability'.[43] Painful singularity insists on facticity by forming a presence in thinking that never lets the thinker forget that the pain she works on is not curable in its medium. And perhaps it is true that negative dialectics surrenders to this despair, understanding it as the primary impetus for conceptual work.

Moten wonders, among other things, how this is to be endured. To be able to remain 'in the grip' of despair requires a 'faith in resurrection, ghosts, spirits, spectres, a powerful faith in . . . some mystical . . . force rising from the abyss that blocks any notion . . . of progress or perfectability'.[44] This form of forceful negativity can only, according to Moten, be avoided with a spiritual attitude. (Here he refers to the poet Amiri Baraka, and not to Adorno.) To endure the tragic, one needs a faith that rejects linearity, for example in the form of progress, and replaces it with interruptions. Some of these would be miracles. In any case, the point is to hold open the possibility of deviating from the expectable. There are tactics and practices for this: Moten contemplates an 'anarchisation' that would enable an 'improvisation of Enlightenment'.[45] Instead of adhering to 'self-reflection on enlightenment, not its revocation',[46] as Adorno does, Moten sees improvisation as a way to avoid the blockade produced by the alternative between despair and progress. For the fearless, the question is: 'what if we let the music . . . take us'?[47]

Adorno and Moten part ways when it comes to strategies for thinking this diagnosed despair. Adorno does not see this task as a dialectical cul-de-sac, but rather as the philosophical miracle of the self-indictment of contradiction, 'index of the untruth of identity',[48] which it is a philosophical duty to persist with.[49] Moten's thinking begins with the observation that objects resist, and in doing so reveal themselves as music (jazz), performance, which, when observed, are always more than mere monuments to despair.

In the end, philosophy is just one activity in a society based on the division of labour.[50] Like any other work, it maintains a relationship to survival. Its reproductive task might be determined precisely by the fact that it 'disturbs the immediacy of life in a sensitive way, in a way that may even have consequences'.[51] It not only disturbs the immediacy of that which remains external to it, it has also dedicated itself, at least in Adorno's conception, to the task of repeatedly and willingly disrupting its own tendency to harden in certain formulas of truth. Truth only endures if it can circulate. Whether it does so is decided in the relationship between philosophy and practice. Despite all his reservations about blind, action-oriented practice,[52] Adorno is also aware of this: 'Paradoxically, the desperate fact that the practice that would matter is barred which grants to thought a breathing spell it would be practically criminal not to utilise. Today, ironically, it profits thought that its concept must not be absolutised: as conduct, it remains a bit of practice, however hidden this practice may be from itself.'[53] Here is a humble reference to thought as something that bridges the blockade of practice and thereby itself becomes a practice, one capable of restoring access to action. To find ways out and to uncover intellectual possibilities for escape then become the tasks of thinking. Oriented towards mobility in this way, thinking itself becomes practice: 'Thinking is a doing, theory a form of practice; already the ideology of the purity of thinking deceives about this.'[54] Philosophy can best realise its embeddedness in practical processes, and its possibilities for contributing to them, when it confronts institutional, conceptual and ethical limits and goes beyond itself. When it deals with suffering that it cannot itself alleviate, or applies unified concepts to things that are constitutively disjointed, philosophy is forced to ask itself about the means of thinking, and perhaps even to change. In the moment of radical self-questioning, it anchors itself in practice to protect itself from false appropriations. For there is no other way to differentiate oneself from the enemy than through practice.[55] What does that mean for philosophy, whose only practice consists in dealing with concepts, and perhaps the way in which these concepts touch down in the world? Adorno expresses the hope that concepts will ultimately fight for the good: 'The concept ought really to be the good aspect of the thing.'[56]

Something must fall apart, '*not into nothing*, but rather into the informal, deformed, enforming somethings that they were and never were.'[57] Disintegration and deformation are steps on the path to overcoming monolithic orders of meaning – in simultaneously terrifying and gentle 'rituals of renomination, when the given is all but immediately taken away'.[58] Where the conceptually given is everything, and where it just as soon withdraws, here, the self disintegrates. But this is philosophy.

Notes

Introduction: The Self at Sea

1 Adorno 2006a, pp. 192–93.
2 Brand 2011, p. 9.
3 Adorno 2005c, p. 45.
4 Robinson 2000, p. 14.
5 Sloterdijk 2018, p. 40.
6 Reckwitz 2008, p. 176; cf. Sloterdijk 1987, p. 136.
7 Fanon 1963, p. 162.
8 Ibid., pp. 139–40.
9 Adorno, Adorno and Horkheimer 2010, p. 110.
10 Adorno and Horkheimer 2002, p. 36.
11 Harris 2018, p. 2.
12 See ibid.; Moten 2003; Hartman 1997; Harney and Moten 2013.
13 Moten 2003, p. 8.
14 Hartman 2020.
15 Moten 2003; 2017; Sellami 2020; Hartman 1997, p. 14; Sonderegger 2020, p. 81.
16 Okiji 2018.
17 James 2021.
18 Traverso 2016, p. 173.
19 Ibid.
20 Ibid., p. 166; Sonderegger 2020, p. 80.
21 Adorno 1966.
22 Claussen 1972.
23 Marcuse 2004, p. 49.
24 Traverso 2016, p. 174.
25 Bartonek 2011; 2021; Kramer 2017; Oberle 2018.
26 Danowski and Viveiros de Castro 2017.
27 Piesche 2017; Eigen and Larrimore 2006; Sandford 2018; Sonderegger 2018; 2019; Hostettler 2020; Bernasconi 2000; Buck-Morss 2011; Tibebu 2011; Kirkland 2018; Lettow 2021.
28 Harney and Moten 2020; 2021.
29 Adorno 1973a, p. 25.
30 Hartman 1997.
31 Wynter 2003; Ferreira da Silva 2007.

Part I: The Aegean

1 Horkheimer 1992, p. 214.
2 Federici 2004; 2012; Lorey 2015.
3 Spivak 1988; Dhawan 2014; Cooper, Dhawan and Newman 2019; Khader 2019.

4 The authors of *Dialectic of Enlightenment* include Margerete 'Gretel' Adorno, née Karplus. Gretel Adorno's contribution to the transcription of *Dialectic of Enlightenment*, and to Adorno's work in general, has gone underappreciated – also due to the scant research to date on the women of the Frankfurt School – but seems large enough, at least in the case of *Dialectic of Enlightenment*, to consider her a co-author and to name her here, contrary to official practice (cf. von Boeckmann 2004).

1. The Self

1 Adorno and Horkheimer 2002, p. 46.
2 Homer 2018, p. 302.
3 Ibid., p. 303.
4 Ibid., p. 305.
5 Ibid.
6 Ibid., p. 302.
7 Ibid., p. 306.
8 Ibid., p. 307.
9 Ibid.
10 Ibid.
11 Adorno and Horkheimer 2002, p. 43.
12 Ibid., p. 38.
13 Homer 2018, p. 306.
14 Ibid.
15 Adorno and Horkheimer 2002, p. 46.
16 Ibid.
17 Ibid.
18 Ibid., p. 38.
19 Ibid., p. 46.
20 Ibid., pp. 46–47.
21 Ibid., p. 48.
22 Ibid., p. 38.
23 Homer 2018, p. 256.
24 Adorno and Horkheimer 2002, p. 38.
25 Ibid., p. 39.
26 Mettin 2021, p. 93.
27 Adorno, Adorno and Horkheimer 2010, p. 51.
28 Adorno and Horkheimer 2002, p. 46.
29 Ibid., p. 69.
30 Mettin 2021, p. 94.
31 Adorno 1970; Bertram 2014; Menke 2013; Rebentisch 2003; Witzgall and Stakemeier 2015; Stakemeier 2017.
32 Rancière 2013, pp. 25–26.
33 Shock, and the mobilisation of a protective shield against it, are the departure points for Freud in developing his theory of trauma, which Benjamin expands on in his writing to a form of social pathology: 'We describe as

"traumatic" any excitations from outside which are powerful enough to break through the protective shield. It seems to me that the concept of trauma necessarily implies a connection of this kind with a breach in an otherwise efficacious barrier against stimuli. Such an event as an external trauma is bound to provoke a disturbance on a large scale in the functioning of the organism's energy and to set in motion every possible defensive measure. At the same time, the pleasure principle is for the moment put out of action. There is no longer any possibility of preventing the mental apparatus from being flooded with large amounts of stimulus, and another problem arises instead – the problem of mastering the amounts of stimulus which have broken in and of binding them, in the psychical sense, so that they can then be disposed of.' Freud 1920, pp. 29–30.

34 Benjamin 2006, p. 317; Benjamin 1974, p. 613.
35 Benjamin 2006, p. 318.
36 Ibid.
37 Ibid.
38 Ibid.
39 Ibid.
40 Ibid., p. 319.
41 Ibid.
42 Benjamin 2008.
43 Benjamin 2006, p. 316.
44 Benjamin 2005, pp. 731–32.
45 Ibid., p. 732.
46 Benjamin 2006, p. 331.

2. Homecoming

1 Homer 2018, p. 5.
2 Frame 2005, p. 105.
3 Adorno and Horkheimer 2002, p. 61.
4 Horkheimer 1991, p. 405; trans. in Van Gelder 1998.
5 Adorno 2021, p. 357.
6 Ibid.
7 Ibid.
8 Adorno 1991, p. 429.
9 Ibid., p. 498.
10 Adorno 1977, p. 380.
11 Adorno 1973a, pp. 360–61
12 Cf. Adorno 2003.
13 Frame 2005, p. ix.

Part II. The Mediterranean

1 Süder Happelmann 2019, p. 190.
2 Kailouli and Schreijäg 2020.

3 Cf. Danewid 2017; Di Maio 2012; Grimaldi 2019; Khalil Saucier and Woods 2014; Proglio et al. 2021. The term is based on Paul Gilroy's book *The Black Atlantic* (Gilroy 1995).

4 Danewid 2017; cf. also Wekker 2016.

3. Europe

1 Rotkopf 2020.

2 Danewid 2017, p. 3.

3 Sea-Watch e.V. 2019a; 2019b.

4 NDR 2019; Kailouli and Schreijäg 2020.

5 Kailouli and Schreijäg 2020, 28′ 40″.

6 Deutsche Welle 2020.

7 CNN 2017.

8 Kailouli and Schreijäg 2020, 31′ 11″ and 58′ 50″.

9 See https://www.tagesspiegel.de/politik/anlegeverbot-in-italien-soll-auch-fur-sea-watch-3-gelten-5332357.html (last accessed 15 July 2025).

10 Kailouli and Schreijäg 2020, 1h 9′.

11 Ibid., 1h 14′ 50″.

12 Materla and Steffen 2019; Deutsche Welle 2019; and see https://www.bild.de/politik/inland/politik-ausland/rackete-im-bild-interview-wir-muessen-klima-fluechtlinge-aufnehmen-63280720.bild.html (last accessed 15 July 2025).

13 Di Cesare 2019.

14 Ehrmann 2021, p. 425.

15 Danewid 2017, p. 8.

16 Dadusc and Mudu 2020, p. 6.

17 Ibid.

18 Ibid., p. 7.

19 See https://www.spiegel.de/politik/ausland/carola-rackete-und-matteo-salvini-sea-watch-kapitaenin-hat-italien-verlassen-a-1278080.html (last accessed 15 July 2025); Materla and Steffen 2019; Di Cesare 2019; Zeit Online 2019; WDR 2020.

20 Khalil Saucier cited in Danewid 2017, p. 11.

21 Dadusc and Mudu 2020, p. 8.

22 Compare 'Violence, Mourning, Politics' in Butler 2004 and Butler 2010.

23 Butler 2005.

24 Danewid 2017, p. 4.

25 Ibid., p. 5.

26 Ibid.

27 Fassin 2012, p. 4.

28 The critique of empathy will be taken up again in Chapter 10.

29 Danewid 2017, p. 13.

30 This also includes the EU emphasising its 'humanist heritage' (Von der Leyen 2021) and holding out the prospect of a permanent solution

for suspended sea rescue. The exact relationship between rescue and 'strong external borders' remains unclear however (ibid., p. 18). From the EU's perspective, responsibility for the thousands of Mediterranean deaths lies with the 'brutal business model of people smugglers' (European Union 2020). The EU president describes her own role counterfactually as follows: 'Europe will always remain true to its values and reach out to people fleeing persecution or war – this is our moral duty. The same applies to saving lives at sea.' (Von der Leyen 2019, p. 19).

31 Fassin 2012.

32 Mezzadra 2020, p. 430.

33 Dadusc and Mudu 2020, pp. 18–19.

34 Ibid., pp. 19–20.

35 Ibid., p. 20.

4. Critique

1 Horkheimer 1991.

2 'Kulturindustrie, Aufklärung als Massenbetrug' in Adorno, Adorno and Horkheimer 2010, p. 128.

3 Cf. Jeffries 2016, p. 33 ff. and Claussen 2003, p. 27 ff.

4 Adorno and Horkheimer's work contains passages that reproduce or even actively systematise racism, starting with a few sentences on cannibalism in *Dialectic of Enlightenment*, which explicate it on the basis of Edvard Westermarck's theory of the stages of civilisation in the non-European world (Adorno, Adorno and Horkheimer 2010, pp. 58–59). In addition, Adorno's essays 'Perennial Fashion – Jazz' (Adorno 1977) and 'On Jazz' (Adorno 2003b) are now much-discussed subjects, and evidence of elitist bourgeois, and above all anti-Black, tendencies in Adorno's sense of taste and his aesthetic. Okiji and Moten take Adorno's observations of a resistant force in jazz as the starting point to further explore this critical capacity (Okiji 2018; Sellami 2020). In his essay 'The American Way of Life' (1964), Horkheimer presents a perspective on racial discrimination in the USA that testifies to fully naturalised racism. In his opinion, 'civilisational differences' and the Black population's unwillingness to assimilate are responsible for ongoing discrimination (Horkheimer 1985, p. 242 ff.). In general, the statements of the two reflect the established bourgeois position which legitimises racism through 'stages of civilisational development'. Such a view does not deny that Black people can assimilate to a white bourgeois way of life under appropriate conditions. However, this assimilation is the only conception of legitimate political and social participation and, second, bourgeois society's production and reproduction of poor living conditions for racialised and migrant others is almost never considered.

5 Fanon 2013, p. 26.

6 Robinson 2000.

7 Jenkins and Leroy 2021.
8 Mbembe 2017, p. 62.
9 Ferreira da Silva 2007.
10 Wynter 2003.
11 Arendt 2018, p. 51.
12 Ibid., p. 40.
13 Arendt 2011, p. 405 ff.
14 Andreetta, Vetters and Yanaşmayan 2022; Vetters 2007, 2019; Vetters, Eggers and Hahn 2017.
15 Weber 2009, p. 125 ff.
16 Habermas 2019.
17 Adorno 2003c, p. 128.
18 Adorno 2005b, p. 110.
19 Adorno 2003c, p. 127.
20 Adorno 2005b, p. 112.
21 Ibid., p. 126.
22 Ibid., p. 113.
23 Weber 2009, p. 125.
24 Adorno 2005b, p. 122.
25 Arendt 2011, p. 518.
26 Arendt 1973, p. 244.
27 Graeber 2017, p. 21.
28 Ibid., p. 72.
29 Ibid., p. 90.
30 Ibid.
31 Arendt 2009, p. 231. Eichmann is known to have claimed, in connection with his law-abiding behaviour, that 'he had followed Kant's moral precepts his whole life'. Arendt contextualises this statement with Hans Frank's reformulation 'of the categorical imperative in the Third Reich . . . "Act in such a way that the Führer, if he knew your action, would approve it"' (ibid., p. 232). Arendt's analysis of Eichmann was revised by later research and the thesis that Eichmann knowingly played the role of the obedient official in order to be absolved of the burden of responsibility (Stangneth 2011). So from this perspective also, bureaucracy proves to be an effective means of obscuring individual agency. Eichmann embraced this. Here it is clear that the coldness of bureaucracy is not itself produced by anti-Semitic motivation, rather it functions as the medium of its reproduction and implementation.
32 Schmid 1997, p. 41.
33 Graeber 2017, p. 14 ff.
34 Ibid., p. 11.
35 Ibid., p. 19, Weber 2009, p. 126.
36 Graeber 2017, p. 12.
37 Weber 2009, pp. 126, 128.
38 Ibid., p. 351.
39 Weber 2019, p. 347.
40 NSU Watch 2020, p. 35.

41 Ibid., p. 36.
42 Billstein 2020.
43 Since 2020, the German Federal Ministry of the Interior has been dealing with the suspected cases, but again under the problematic assumption that there are 319 individual cases without connection or network structure; see https://www.bmi.bund.de/SharedDocs/pressemitteilungen/DE/2020/10/lagebild-rechtsextremismus.html (accessed 15 July 2025).
44 NSU Watch 2020, p. 29.
45 Ayata 2016, p. 217.
46 NSU Watch 2020, p. 81.
47 Fraser 1990.
48 Ayata 2016, p. 215.
49 NSU Watch 2020, p. 81.
50 Ibid., p. 82 ff.
51 Ibid., p. 83.
52 Ibid., p. 82.
53 Ayata 2019.
54 Nandy 2003.
55 Ibid., p. 8.
56 Agamben 2011, p. 120.
57 Agamben 2007, p. 46.
58 Ibid., p. 37.
59 Nandy 2003, p. 9.
60 Agamben 2011, p. 117.
61 Benjamin 1965.
62 Benjamin 1996, p. 237.
63 Ibid.
64 Ibid., p. 348.
65 Loick 2012, p. 190.
66 Benjamin is more likely to treat the critique of violence as a means – represented by pacifism – as 'childish anarchism' (Benjamin 1965, p. 41). Loick elucidates: 'A justification of non-violence, if one considers it absolutely necessary, is out of the question for Benjamin for epistemological reasons, as becomes clear at the end of his text' (Loick 2012, p. 190); and Derrida explains: 'A purely moral critique of violence thus proves to be as unjustified as it is powerless' (Derrida 1991, p. 88).
67 Benjamin 1965, p. 45.
68 Adorno, Adorno and Horkheimer 2010, p. 62.
69 Benjamin 1965, p. 55.
70 Tuck and Yang 2012.
71 Benjamin 1996, p. 249.
72 Benjamin 1965, p. 64.
73 Derrida works on Benjamin's 'signature' in the final passage and understands it as a driving force in which Benjamin finally replaces his own with that of a god (Derrida 1991, p. 114). Loick interprets this passage as an epistemological problem that reveals the

impossibility, which Adorno diagnosed, of making statements on the condition of actual liberation [*vollzogener Befreiung*] from a non-liberated perspective: 'Only the standpoint of justice itself, which as universal redemption could end history as it has existed up till now, whether it be coded as the arrival of the Messiah or as communism, could unlock the world history of knowledge so far' (Loick 2012, p. 190).

74 Derrida 1991, p. 76.
75 Benjamin 1996, pp. 242–43.
76 Ibid., p. 243.
77 Weber 2019, p. 344.
78 Loick 2017, p. 12.
79 Loick speaks of a 'radical transformation of law' (ibid., p. 18), which also entails a renewal of what counts as political action, informed by feminism and decoloniality: 'Political action can no longer be reduced to action that can converted into a legal currency and addresses itself to the state, but it also encompasses all those forms that directly address the level of civil society, the economy or intimate relationships' (ibid., p. 21).
80 Ibid., p. 13.
81 Martinot and Sexton 2003.
82 Ibid., p. 177.
83 Ibid., p. 179.
84 Ibid.
85 Maurel 2025, p. 103.
86 Habermas 2019, p. 56.
87 Ibid., p. 55.
88 Ibid., pp. 69–70.
89 Ibid., p. 84.
90 Ibid., p. 97.
91 Ibid., pp. 94–95.
92 Ibid., p. 96.
93 Koselleck 1973, p. 68; trans. Grace Nissan.
94 Habermas 2019, p. 96.
95 Koselleck 1973, p. 90; trans. Grace Nissan.
96 Habermas 2019, p. 105.
97 Koselleck 1973, p. 8; trans. Grace Nissan.
98 Adamczak 2019, pp. 218–19.
99 Boltanski and Chiapello 2003, p. 236 ff.; Negri et al. 1998.
100 Reckwitz 2008, p. 176.
101 Fest 2007, p. 22; Reckwitz 2008, p. 174.
102 Marasco 2015, pp. 84–85.
103 Gilmore 2018; cf. also Gilmore 2022.
104 Adorno 1977, p. 694.
105 Dorlin 2020, p. 225.
106 See https://dictionary.cambridge.org/de/worterbuch/englisch/virtue-signalling (accessed 15 July 2025); Westra 2021, p. 156.

107 Ahmed 2006; 2012.
108 Barthes 1981, p. 112.
109 Ibid., p. 102.
110 Steyerl 2007, p. 72.
111 Deleuze and Guattari 1992; 2000.
112 Barthes 1972, p. 124.
113 Adorno and Horkheimer 2002, p. 70.
114 Reitz 2003.
115 Dorlin 2020, p. 225.
116 Steyerl 2007, p. 72.
117 Sloterdijk 2018, p. 157; trans. Grace Nissan.
118 Nietzsche 1997, p. 4.
119 Ibid., p. 2.
120 Adorno 1973a, p. 115.
121 Georg 2019, p. 174.
122 Nietzsche 2013d, p. 172.
123 Horkheimer 1968 and Habermas 1968, cited in Georg 2019, pp. 169, 178.
124 Sedgwick 2003, p. 123 ff.
125 Nietzsche 1974, p. 169.
126 Georg 2019, p. 181.
127 Ibid.
128 Nietzsche 1995, p. 36.
129 Ibid., p. 57.
130 Ibid., p. 56.
131 Ibid., p. 56.
132 Ibid., p. 58.
133 Deleuze 1983, p. 5.
134 Ibid., p. 6.
135 Deleuze and Guattari 1974; 1992; Foucault 2002.
136 Horkheimer 1978, p. 142.
137 Dorlin 2020, p. 185.
138 Ibid., p. 142.
139 Ibid., p. 188.
140 Steyerl 2007, p. 72.
141 Adorno 1951, p. 28.
142 Ibid.
143 Kant 1999; Foucault 1992, pp. 11–12.
144 Anderson 1993; Steyerl 2007.
145 Alexander et al. 2018; Brüggmann 2020.
146 Fraser 2005, p. 100.
147 Maurel 2025, p. 55.
148 Maurel and Rehberg 2019, p. 30.
149 Ibid., p. 79.
150 Ibid., p. 86.
151 Wüschner 2016.
152 Slaby and von Scheve 2020.

5. Coldness

1 Bernhardt 2021.
2 Knoch 2021.
3 Harney and Moten 2020.
4 Adorno 1977.
5 Lethen 2018.
6 Lorde 2007.
7 Adorno 2005a, p. 201.
8 Adorno 1977, p. 685.
9 Ibid., p. 682.
10 Ibid., p. 681.
11 Ibid., p. 686.
12 Adorno 2005a, p. 191.
13 Ibid., p. 196.
14 Knoch 2021, p. 153.
15 Adorno 2005a, p. 193.
16 Ibid., p. 195.
17 Mussell 2013, p. 62.
18 Adorno and Horkheimer 2002, p. 67.
19 Ibid.
20 Foucault 2009.
21 Adorno 2002, pp. 80–81. The sentence could be reformulated as follows: *Those representatives of bourgeois coldness*, who unmasked compassion, ultimately negatively espoused the Revolution *in an analogous way* to the Stoic apathy in which bourgeois coldness, the counterpart of compassion, has modelled itself, likewise more loyal, however wretchedly, to the universal it had rejected than the commonality all participate in, which adapted itself to the world. (Thanks to Philipp Wüschner for his grammatical skill.)
22 Hogh 2017, p. 28.
23 Adorno and Horkheimer 2002, p. 65.
24 Adorno 1977, p. 778.
25 Adorno 2005a, p. 202.
26 Ibid.
27 Ibid.
28 Slaby and von Scheve 2020.
29 Lethen 2018, p. 7.
30 Hogh 2017, p. 33.
31 Lethen 2002, p. xi.
32 Slaby, Mühlhoff and Wüschner 2019.
33 Plessner 2002, pp. 14, 28, 45.
34 Lethen 2018, pp. 69, 101–2.
35 Ibid., p. 94.
36 Ibid., p. 69.
37 Ibid., p. 64.
38 Gruschka 1994.
39 Knoch 2021, p. 155.

40 Lorde 2007, p. 73.
41 Federici 2012, p. 18.
42 Federici 2015.
43 Lorde 2007, pp. 26, 103.
44 Ibid., p. 27.
45 Ibid., p. 71.
46 Dorlin 2020, p. 168.
47 Ibid.
48 Ibid., p. 172.
49 Ibid., p. 170.
50 Ibid., p. 182.
51 Lorde 2007, p. 26.
52 Palmer 2017.
53 Mühlhoff 2019, p. 119.
54 Adorno 1990, p. 226.
55 Harney and Moten 2020.
56 Ibid., 1h 32′ ff.
57 Ibid.
58 Adorno 2005c, p. 39.
59 Harney and Moten 2020, 1h 38′.
60 Moten 2017, pp. 152, 158, 168.
61 Ibid., p. 169.
62 Adorno 2021, p. 356.
63 Ibid.
64 Mussell 2013, p. 60.

Part III: The Atlantic

1 Hartman 2007, p. 32.
2 Walcott 1990.
3 Okpewho 2002, p. 35.
4 Wynter 1995, p. 5.
5 Walcott 1990, p. 325.
6 Ibid.
7 Hartman 2008, p. 2.
8 Ibid., p. 11.
9 Ibid.
10 Ibid., p. 9.
11 Olney 1984; Gates Jr and Andrews 2000.
12 Hartman 2007, p. 103.
13 Hartman 1997, p. 62.
14 Hartman 2007, p. 6.
15 Broeck 2018.
16 Hartman and Wilderson III 2003; Wilderson III 2010; Warren 2018.
17 On the concept of Blackness, see: Moten 2017, p. 202; Moten 2018b, pp. 241, 243; Harris 2018, p. 2; Gray 2022.
18 Jackson 2018; cf. also Jung and Vargas 2021.

19 Jackson 2020, p. 3.
20 Adorno 2021, p. 18.
21 Därmann 2020, p. 36.
22 Dorlin 2020; Därmann 2021.
23 Hartman 2007, p. 103.
24 Hartman 1997, p. 52 ff.
25 Three categories come into play here: what is sought is an 'understanding of self', which in turn makes possible a 'subjectivity', which is ultimately capable of outlining a 'black political subject' (Gilroy 1995, p. 53).

6. Property of Self

1 Locke 1977, p. 30.
2 Därmann 2020, p. 101.
3 Locke 1977, p. 28; cf. Därmann 2020, chapter 4.
4 Macpherson 1975; Diefenbach 2018; Bhandar 2018, p. 164.
5 Bhandar 2018, p. 159.
6 Ibid., p. 153.
7 Harris 1993, p. 1,726; Loick 2018a.
8 Bhandar 2018, pp. 2, 3.
9 Bhandar 2020, p. 55.
10 Bhandar 2018, chapter 1.
11 Ibid., p. 85.
12 Weber 2009.
13 Bhandar 2018, pp. 77, 101.
14 Ibid., p. 99.
15 Harney and Moten 2021, p. 29.
16 Ibid.
17 Bhandar 2018, p. 101.
18 Ibid., pp. 81, 103.
19 Bhandar 2020, p. 57.
20 Bens 2021.
21 Von Redecker 2020b, p. 35; Von Redecker 2020a.
22 Harney and Moten 2021, p. 16.
23 Därmann 2020, pp. 81, 95.
24 Bhandar 2018, p. 168.
25 Cf. Arneil 1996; Diefenbach 2018.
26 Därmann 2020, p. 89.
27 Locke 1689, p. 32.
28 Ibid., p. 33.
29 Bhandar 2018, pp. 47, 82.
30 Ibid., chapter 3; Harney and Moten 2021.
31 Därmann 2020, p. 92.
32 Locke 1689, p. 33.
33 Ibid.
34 Bhandar 2018, p. 48 ff.

35 Därmann 2020, p. 92.
36 Bhandar 2018, p. 167.
37 Ibid., p. 166.
38 Harney and Moten 2021, p. 14.
39 Bhandar 2018, p. 167.
40 Harney and Moten 2021, p. 29.
41 Ibid., p. 28.
42 Därmann 2020, p. 99.
43 Ibid., p. 98.
44 Ibid., pp. 100–101.
45 Harris 1993, p. 1,714.
46 Ibid.
47 Ibid., p. 1,724.
48 Bhandar 2018, p. 177.
49 Harris 1993, p. 1,716.
50 Hartman 1997, p. 62.
51 Harris 1993, p. 1,721.
52 Ibid., p. 1,734.
53 Ibid., p. 1,739.
54 Bhandar 2018, p. 161.
55 Harney and Moten 2021, p. 17; cf. Walcott 2021.
56 Harris 1993, p. 1,767.
57 Ibid., p. 1,770.
58 Ibid., p. 1,777.
59 Ibid., p. 1,758.

7. Expropriation of the Self

1 Harney and Moten 2021, p. 34.
2 Rousseau 2011; Federici 2015; Lorey 2015.
3 Fuentes 2016.
4 Owens 2019b.
5 Hartman 1997, p. 52 ff.
6 Cf. Owens 2017, pp. 180–81.
7 Ibid., p. 181.
8 Adorno and Horkheimer 2002, p. 46.
9 Owens 2017, p. 181.
10 Brand 2011, p. 51.
11 Hartman 1997, p. 52.
12 Ibid., p. 126.
13 Ibid., p. 53.
14 Moten 2003, p. 5; Sonderegger 2020.
15 Patterson 1982; Därmann 2020.
16 Patterson 1982, p. 44.
17 Harney and Moten 2021, p. 34.
18 Jackson 2020, p. 3.
19 Foucault 2001, p. 22.

20 Hartman 1997, p. 14.
21 Ibid., p. 53.
22 Diana Williams cited in Owens 2017, p. 182.
23 Hartman 1997, p. 62.
24 Ibid., p. 21.
25 Spillers 1987, p. 65.
26 Ibid.
27 Ibid.
28 Hartman 1997, p. 187.
29 Ibid., p. 116.
30 Därmann 2021, p. 55.
31 Sharpe 2016, p. 10.
32 Hartman 1997, p. 52.
33 Owens 2017, p. 182.
34 Hartman 1997, p. 53.
35 Hartman 2008, p. 2.
36 Hartman 1997, p. 6.
37 Sharpe 2016, p. 10; Palmer 2017.
38 Hartman 1997, p. 51.
39 Smallwood 2008, p. 34.
40 Hartman 1997, p. 4.
41 Owens 2019b; cf. Johnson 2003.
42 Hartman 1997, p. 52.
43 Gilroy 1995, p. 55.
44 Hartman 1997, p. 54.
45 Ibid., p. 55.
46 Hartman 2008, p. 13.
47 Därmann 2021, p. 113
48 Benjamin 1965, p. 82; Hartman 1997, p. 14.
49 Hartman 2008, p. 3.
50 Hartman 1997, p. 55.
51 Cf. Olney 1984, p. 156; Gilroy 1995, p. 70; Moten 2003, introduction; Douglass 2011.
52 Hartman 1997, chapter 2.
53 Därmann 2020.
54 Ibid., p. 23.
55 Ibid., chapters 1, 4, 6; Därmann 2021, chapters 2, 5.
56 Hartman 1997, p. 63.
57 Därmann 2020, p. 133.
58 Hartman 1997, p. 63.
59 Ibid., p. 51.
60 Owens 2019b.
61 Ibid.
62 Hartman 1997, p. 52.
63 Spillers 1987, p. 72.
64 Tinsley 2008, p. 197.
65 Hartman 2007, p. 103.
66 Ibid., p. 103; Hartman 2002, p. 758.

67 Hartman 1997, p. 77.
68 Hartman 2007, p. 6.
69 Hartman 2002, p. 758.
70 Därmann 2020, pp. 23–24.
71 Hartman 2002, p. 760.
72 Hartman 1997, p. 34.
73 Wynter 2003, p. 260.
74 Hartman 1997, p. 116.
75 Walcott 2021, pp. 1, 37.

8. The Self in Disintegration

1 Diawara and Glissant 2011, p. 5.
2 Arendt 1959b.
3 Ibid., p. 45.
4 Kathryn T. Gines changed her name to Kathryn Sophia Belle in 2017 and now publishes under this name.
5 Beals 1995, p. xviii. Melba Pattillo Beals was, like Elizabeth Eckford, part of the group of Black students who were integrated in Little Rock Central High School; she uses this expression in her autobiography in discussion of the integration of Little Rock.
6 Allen 2004; Gines 2014; Moten 2018b.
7 Hartman 1997, chapter 4.
8 Nagel 2020.
9 Beals 1995, p. 48.
10 Ibid., chapter 6.
11 Ibid., p. 3.
12 Ibid., pp. 92–93.
13 For a detailed description of the events, see ibid.
14 Arendt 1959b, p. 46.
15 Moten 2018b, p. 68.
16 Gines 2014, p. 4.
17 Moten 2018b, p. 66.
18 Arendt 1959b, p. 46.
19 Ibid., p. 272.
20 Ibid., p. 259.
21 Arendt 1959a.
22 Arendt 2000, p. 276.
23 Beals 1995, p. 32; Anderson 2010, p. 8.
24 Arendt 2000, p. 274.
25 Ibid., p. 264.
26 Gines 2014, p. 14.
27 Ibid., pp. 2–3.
28 Arendt 2000, p. 267.
29 Ibid., p. 269.
30 Arendt 2002.
31 Arendt 2018, p. 71.

32 I adopted this formulation after conversations with Marie With, who deserves thanks.
33 Arendt 1959b, p. 51.
34 Arendt 2000, p. 265.
35 Ibid., p. 270.
36 Ibid., p. 273.
37 Arendt 1959b, p. 51.
38 Allen 2004, p. 26.
39 Arendt 1959b, p. 56.
40 Beals 1995, p. 34.
41 Arendt 2000, p. 275.
42 Gines shows, with reference to Danielle Allen's research, that Arendt is mistaken in her interpretation of the image. According to Allen, her description refers to the 9 May 1959 edition of *The New York Times*, with two photographs on the front page: one of Elizabeth Eckford confronting the National Guard and one of Dorothy Counts, the only Black child to attend Harding High School in Charlotte from then on – not Little Rock. Arendt wrongly attributes both images to Little Rock Central High School (Allen 2004, p. 197). Furthermore, the 'white friend of her [Dorothy's] father' is not absent in the way Arendt suggests – he was parking his car at the time (Gines 2014, p. 17). Gines sees a certain projection at work here about Black families and parenting: 'It seems that the facts about the Counts family and their friends do not line up with Black families as they apparently existed in Arendt's imagination. It did not occur to Arendt that Dr. Counts was valedictorian of his high school class before earning several degrees with honors' (ibid., p. 18). Other interpreters of Arendt's essay do not notice the error (Lebeau 2004), which Allen attributes to Arendt's authority.
43 Arendt 1959b, p. 50.
44 Beals 1995, p. 49.
45 Anderson 2010, p. 2.
46 Beals 1995, p. 50.
47 Arendt 2000, p. 276.
48 Moten 2018b, p. 74.
49 Ibid.
50 Ibid., p. 77.
51 Ibid., p. 76.
52 Arendt 2002, p. 217.
53 Arendt 1959b, p. 47.
54 Ralph Ellison cited in Allen 2004, p. 27.
55 Moten 2018b, p. 78.
56 Ibid., p. 111.
57 Ibid., p. 185.
58 Arendt 2000, p. 266.
59 Moten 2018b, p. 95.
60 Ibid., p. 75.
61 Ibid., p. 80.

62 Piper 1996.
63 Moten 2003, p. 240.
64 Piper 1996, p. 27, cited in Moten 2018b, pp. 80–81.
65 Palmer 2020, p. 272.
66 Moten 2003, p. 233.
67 Ibid., p. 240.
68 Moten 2018b, p. 81.
69 Ibid.
70 Ibid., p. 118.
71 Ibid., p. 81.
72 Ibid., p. 82.
73 Ibid., p. 92.
74 Ibid., p. 88.
75 Ibid., p. 77.
76 Arendt 1959b, p. 45.
77 Arendt 2008, p. 22; Gines 2014, chapter 7.
78 Arendt 1970, p. 78.
79 Moten 2018b, p. 80.
80 Ibid., p. 77.
81 Arendt 2008, p. 12.
82 Moten contextualises this tendency in a problematic discourse where intelligence is seen as a moral duty (Moten 2018b, p. 254; Erskine 1969; Trilling 2008). What would happen to the non-intelligent in light of this orientation? They lack the ability to authorise themselves and thus also to engage in moral discourse: 'The unintelligent do not stand out from the multitude. They have not authorised themselves. They do not have a story. They are not moral beings. They have failed their moral obligation insofar as they are unable to recognise that they (might) have one' (Moten 2018b, p. 255).The non-intelligent do not receive attention because they do not stand out through their agency. They remain trapped in an undetected form of nonperformance. And this is precisely where Moten seeks them out.
83 Arendt 2008, p. 117.
84 Arendt first used this slogan, closely associated with her work, at a conference in Toronto in 1972, the transcripts of which have not yet been published: 'You said groundless thinking. I have a metaphor, which is not quite that cruel, and which I never published but kept for myself, I call it "thinking without banister", that is in German *Denken ohne Geländer*. That is: as you go up and down the stairs, you can always hold on to the banister, so that you don't fall down. What we have lost is a banister. That is a way I tell it to myself. That is indeed what I try to do' (Nagel 2020).
85 Gines 2014, p. 21.
86 Moten 2018b, p. 255.
87 Du Bois 1986, p. 8.
88 Moten 2017, p. 261.
89 Moten 2018b, p. 81.
90 Moten 2017; 2018b; 2018a; cf. Diawara and Glissant 2011.

91 Moten 2018b, p. 80.
92 Ibid.; Harney and Moten 2021, p. 64.
93 Wilderson III 2010, p. 45.
94 Piper 1996, p. 27, cited in Moten 2018b, pp. 80–81.
95 Hartman 1997, p. 117.
96 Ibid., p. 118.
97 Du Bois 1986, p. 12.
98 Harney and Moten 2013, p. 19.
99 Moten 2018b, p. 95.
100 Hartman 1997, p. 116.
101 Adorno 2007, p. 125.
102 Wynter 2003, pp. 261–62.
103 Harney and Moten 2013, p. 17.
104 Ibid., p. 19.
105 Ibid., p. 18.
106 Arendt 2000, p. 266.
107 Harney and Moten 2013, p. 19.
108 Ibid., p. 20.
109 Ibid.
110 Ibid., p. 18.
111 Harney and Moten 2020.
112 Harney and Moten 2013, p. 17.
113 Ibid.
114 Ibid.
115 Sharpe 2016, p. 90.
116 Ibid., p. 7.
117 Arendt 2008, p. 23.
118 Ibid., p. 34.
119 Arendt 1970, p. 21.
120 See https://x.com/bengarvin/status/1266448204176003072 (last accessed 15 July 2025).
121 Sharpe 2016, p. 7.
122 Hall et al. 1978.
123 Moten 2018a, p. 185.
124 Ibid., p. 184.
125 Ibid.
126 Ibid., p. 185.
127 Osterweil 2020, p. 3.
128 Harney and Moten 2013, p. 19.
129 Jones 2022, p. 15; Jones 2020.
130 Sharpe 2016, p. 10.
131 Palmer 2020, pp. 252–53.
132 Ahmed 2010, p. 12.
133 Hartman 2020.
134 Du Bois 1920, p. 270.
135 Hartman 2020.
136 Ibid.
137 Adorno 2006a, p. 196.

138 Ibid., p. 195.

139 Ibid., p. 196.

140 Okiji 2018, p. 22.

141 'Zeitlose Mode. Zum Jazz' in Adorno 1977 and 'Über Jazz' in Adorno 2003b.

142 Moten 2018b, p. 79.

143 Moten 2003, p. 179.

144 Okiji 2018, p. 13.

145 Adorno 2007, p. 124.

9. Freedom

1 Spillers 2017.

2 'In short, the advent of freedom marks the transition from the pained and minimally sensate existence of the slave to the burdened individuality of the responsible and encumbered freedperson' (Hartman 1997, p. 117).

3 Ibid.

4 Ibid., p. 126.

5 Violence against Black people in the Southern states did not in any way cease after the abolition of slavery. During the Reconstruction era, white paramilitary organisations made constant attempts to restore antebellum power relations – as shown, for example in W.E.B. Du Bois's *Black Reconstruction in America*, as a conflict of interests between abolition and industry: 'Abolition-democracy demands for Negroes physical freedom, civil rights, economic opportunity and education and the right to vote, as a matter of sheer human justice and right. Industry demands profits and is willing to use for this end Negro freedom or Negro slavery, votes for Negroes or Black Codes' (Du Bois 1969, p. 325). This era saw at least 2,000 lynchings, the most brutal expression of racial terror against men, women, and children (Equal Justice Initiative 2020).

6 Hartman 1997, p. 121.

7 Ibid., p. 64.

8 'I don't hear my subjects a lot talking about freedom . . . And I have started to presume that they don't think freedom is relevant to them. Not that it's good or bad or that they can't have it, but that it's just not the organising principle of their lives' (Owens 2019b).

9 Adorno 1973a, p. 221.

10 Adorno 2006a, p. 203.

11 Ibid., pp. 85, 201.

12 Hartman 1997, p. 115.

13 'If "freedom" meant free from bondage but not from social, economic and political degradation, what does it mean to survive under such conditions?' (Fuentes 2010, pp. 565–66.)

14 '. . . like it was a place or a city' (Hartman 1997, p. 151).

15 'This desire set thousands on the road in search of a distinct and tangible freedom. The ambulant expressions of freedom are consistently detailed in slave testimony. The search for a parent, child, or lover and the longing to return to the place of one's birth or simply instantiate being free through the exercise of this nascent mobility' (ibid.).

16 Adorno therefore warns against a notion of philosophy as poetry. Philosophy is then beholden to concepts and their truth content, whereas artworks 'do not obey the power of the universality of ideas' (Adorno 1989, p. 21).

17 Adorno 2021, p. 230.

18 Adorno 2006b.

19 Ibid., p. 16.

20 Ibid., p. 136. The 'negative identity' arises essentially from Adorno's engagement with Benjamin's theses on the philosophy of history.

21 Adorno 2021, p. 213.

22 A formulation which Adorno finds for this with reference to moral philosophy is, 'since in philosophy there is no sense in discussing what does not cause difficulties' (Adorno 2015, p. 29).

23 Adorno 2021, p. 18.

24 'Yet the *principium individuationis* is by no means the metaphysically ultimate and unalterable, and thus it is not freedom either. Freedom is a moment, rather, in a twofold sense: it is entwined, not to be isolated; and for the time being it is never more than an instant of spontaneity, a historical node, the road to which is blocked under present conditions' (ibid., p. 219).

25 Adorno 1973a, p. 222.

26 Adorno 2005c, p. 156.

27 Sexton 2017; 2019; Warren 2018; Palmer 2020.

28 Sexton 2017.

29 Wilderson III 2014, p. 20.

30 On their distinction, see Weheliye 2014, p. 37.

31 Brand 2011.

32 The quotations come from a lecture by Tyrone S. Palmer in the workshop 'Affect and Blackness' at SFB Affective Societies, Freie Universität Berlin in June 2021.

33 Ibid.

34 Wilderson III 2010, p. 9.

35 Cf. King, Navarro and Smith 2020; Quashie 2021.

36 Hartman 2019, p. 24.

37 Beals 1995, p. 83.

38 De Certeau 1988, p. xix.

39 Moten 2003, p. 21.

40 Adorno 1990, p. 214.

41 Hartman 2020.

Part IV: Oceanic Philosophy

1 Fichte 2001, p. 19.
2 Adorno 1973a, p. 10.
3 Sonderegger 2020, p. 81; trans. Nicholas Grindell.
4 Adorno 2007, p. 134.

10. Blackness and Negative Dialectics

1 Sonderegger 2020; Sellami 2020.
2 Sonderegger 2020.
3 Adorno 1990, p. 188.
4 Moten 2003.
5 The prefix *para* means 'besides'. Moten operates alongside concepts and resists their urge to fix meanings. *Para* has an important meaning in Black studies, for example as 'paraontology' (Chandler 2018) and 'para-semiosis' (Judy 2020).
6 Adorno 1973a, p. 20.
7 Adorno 1990, p. 21.
8 Adorno 1973a, p. 184 ff.
9 Ibid., p. 156.
10 Ibid., p. 184.
11 Adorno 2007, pp. 127–28.
12 Adorno 1990, p. 4.
13 Adorno 1973a, p. 17.
14 Adorno 2021, p. 27.
15 Adorno 2007, pp. 118–19.
16 Adorno 1990, p. 15.
17 Adorno 2007, p. 134.
18 Ibid., p. 140.
19 Adorno 1989, p. 4.
20 Ibid., p. 3.
21 Adorno 2007, p. 140.
22 Adorno 1962, p. 11.
23 Demirović 1999.
24 Adorno 2007, p. 95.
25 Cf. Deleuze and Guattari 1974, p. 440; Deleuze and Guattari 2000, p. 50.
26 Adorno 2007, p. 143.
27 Dankemeyer 2020, p. 323.
28 Moten 2017, p. 184.
29 Harney and Moten 2013, p. 105.
30 Moten 2017, p. vii.
31 Ibid.
32 Marx 1982, p. 176.
33 Sonderegger 2020, p. 85.
34 Marx 1982, p. 178.
35 Moten 2003, p. 1.

36 Ibid., pp. 89, 94.
37 Adorno 1990, pp. 17–18.
38 Moten 2003, p. 94.
39 Ibid., p. 1.
40 Adorno 2008, p. 126; Adorno 2003, p. 170; Adorno 1990, p. 22.
41 Moten 2003, p. 99.
42 Ibid.; Marasco 2015.
43 Moten 2003, p. 99.
44 Ibid.
45 Ibid., p. 93.
46 Adorno 2007, p. 201. What is interesting here is the difference between Adorno's lecture, in which the sentence sounds like a demand, and the formulation in *Negative Dialectics*, where it simply says, 'The self-reflection of enlightenment is not its revocation'. (Adorno 1990, p. 158).
47 Moten 2003, p. 96.
48 Adorno 1990, p. 17.
49 Adorno 1973a, p. 17.
50 Adorno 2007, p. 134; Dankemeyer 2020, p. 333.
51 Adorno 1973, p. 33.
52 Adorno 1977, pp. 759, 764.
53 Adorno 1990, p. 245.
54 Adorno 2005a, p. 261.
55 Harney and Moten 2020.
56 Adorno and Horkheimer 2011, p. 30.
57 Moten 2017, p. 156.
58 Ibid., p. vii.

Bibliography

Adamczak, Bini. 2019. *Beziehungsweise Revolution. 1917, 1968 und kommende*. 4th edn. Berlin: Suhrkamp.

Adorno, Gretel, Theodor W. Adorno and Max Horkheimer. 2010. *Dialektik der Aufklärung. Philosophische Fragmente*. Frankfurt am Main: S. Fischer.

Adorno, Theodor W. and Max Horkheimer. 2011. *Towards a New Manifesto*. Translated by Rodney Livingstone. London: Verso Books.

Adorno, Theodor W. 1951. *Minima Moralia. Reflexionen aus dem beschädigten Leben*. Vol. 4 of *Gesammelte Schriften*. Frankfurt am Main: Suhrkamp.

— 1962. *Kierkegaard. Konstruktion des Ästhetischen*. Vol. 2 of *Gesammelte Schriften*. Frankfurt am Main: Suhrkamp.

— 1966. 'Theodor W. Adornos Gutachten für Angela Davis'.

— 1970. Ästhetische Theorie. Vol. 7 of *Gesammelte Schriften*. Frankfurt am Main: Suhrkamp.

— 1973a. *Negative Dialektik. Jargon der Eigentlichkeit*. Vol. 6. of *Gesammelte Schriften*. Frankfurt am Main: Suhrkamp.

— 1973b. *Philosophische Terminologie*. Vol. 1. Frankfurt am Main: Suhrkamp.

— 1977. *Kulturkritik und Gesellschaft*. Vol. 10 of *Gesammelte Schriften*. Frankfurt am Main: Suhrkamp.

— 1981. *Negative Dialectics*. London: Continuum.

— 1989. *Kierkegaard: Construction of the Aesthetic*. Edited and translated by Robert Hullot-Kentor. Minneapolis: University of Minnesota Press.

— 1990. *Negative Dialectics*. Oxfordshire: Routledge.

— 1991. *Notes to Literature*. Edited by Rolf Tiedemann and translated by Shierry Weber Nicholsen. New York: Columbia University Press.

— 1997. *Noten zur Literatur*. Vol. 11 of *Gesammelte Schriften*. Frankfurt am Main: Suhrkamp.

— 2002. *Dialectic of Enlightenment: Philosophical Fragments*. Redwood City: Stanford University Press.

— 2003a. *Kindheit in Amorbach. Bilder und Erinnerungen*. Edited by Reinhard Pabst. Frankfurt am Main and Leipzig: Insel.

— 2003b. *Musikalische Schriften IV*. Vol. 17 of *Gesammelte Schriften*. Frankfurt am Main: Suhrkamp.

— 2003c. *Soziologische Schriften I*. Vol. 8 of *Gesammelte Schriften*. Frankfurt am Main: Suhrkamp.

— 2005a. *Critical Models: Interventions and Catchwords*. Translated by Henry W. Pickford. New York: Columbia University Press.

— 2005b. *The Culture Industry: Selected Essays on Mass Culture*. Oxfordshire: Routledge.

— 2005c. *Minima Moralia: Reflections from Damaged Life*. New York: Verso.

— 2006a. *History and Freedom: Lectures 1964–1965*. Cambridge: Polity.

— 2006b. *Zur Lehre von der Geschichte und von der Freiheit*. Edited by Rolf Tiedemann. 5th edn. Frankfurt am Main: Suhrkamp.

— 2007. *Vorlesung über Negative Dialektik. Fragmente zur Vorlesung 1965/66*. Edited by Rolf Tiedemann. Frankfurt am Main: Suhrkamp.

— 2008. *Lectures on Negative Dialectics: Fragments of a Lecture Course 1965/1966*. Translated by Rolf Tiedemann and Rodney Livingstone. Cambridge: Polity.

— 2015. *Probleme der Moralphilosophie*. 2nd edn. Frankfurt am Main: Suhrkamp.

— 2020. 'Education after Auschwitz'. *Filosofiya Osvity / Philosophy of Education* 25(2): 82–99.

— 2021. *Negative Dialectics*. Translated by Dennis Redmond. Self-published.

Agamben, Giorgio. 2007. *Die Beamten des Himmels. Über Engel*. Translated by Andreas Hiepko. Frankfurt am Main: Verlag der Weltreligionen and Insel.

— 2011. 'ANGELS'. *Angelaki* 16(3): 117–23.

Ahmed, Sara. 2006. 'The Non-Performativity of Anti-Racism (Institutional Speech Acts)'. *Borderlands e-Journal* 5(3).

— 2010. *The Promise of Happiness*. Durham and London: Duke University Press.

— 2012. *On Being Included: Racism and Diversity in Institutional Life*. Durham, NC: Duke University Press.

Aitken, Robbie and Eve Rosenhaft. 2013. *Black Germany: The Making and Unmaking of a Diaspora Community, 1884–1960*. Cambridge University Press.

Alexander, Victoria D., Samuli Hägg, Simo Häyrynen and Erkki Sevänen, eds. 2018. *Art and the Challenge of Markets. Volume 2: From Commodification of Art to Artistic Critiques of Capitalism*. Sociology of the Arts. Cham: Palgrave Macmillan.

Allen, Amy. 2019. *Das Ende des Fortschritts*. Translated by Frank Lachmann. Frankfurt am Main and New York: Campus.

Allen, Danielle S. 2004. *Talking to Strangers Anxieties of Citizenship since Brown v. Board of Education*. Chicago: University of Chicago Press.

American Academy in Berlin. 2019. 'Artist Talk with Arthur Jafa: A Series of Utterly Improbable, Yet Extraordinary Renditions'. https://www.youtube.com/watch?v=xh_j1ahLzwl.

Anderson, Benedict R. O'G. 1993. *Imagined Communities: Reflections on the Origin and Spread of Nationalism*. 2nd expanded edn. London: Verso.

Anderson, Karen. 2010. *Little Rock: Race and Resistance at Central High School*. Princeton University Press.

Andreetta, Sophie, Larissa Vetters and Zeynep Yanaşmayan. 2022. 'The Making of Procedural Justice: Enacting the State and (Non) Citizenship'. *Citizenship Studies*, November: 1–17.

Arendt, Hannah. 1959a. 'A Reply to Critics'. *Dissent* (Spring 1959): 179–81.

— 1959b. 'Reflections on Little Rock'. *Dissent* (Winter 1959): 45–56.

— 1970. *On Violence*. Boston, MA: Mariner Books.

— 1973. *The Origins of Totalitarianism*. Boston, MA: Houghton Mifflin Harcourt.

— 2000. *In der Gegenwart. Übungen zum politischen Denken II*. Munich: Piper.

— 2002. *Vita activa oder Vom tätigen Leben*. Munich: Piper.

— 2008. *Macht und Gewalt.* 18th edn. Munich: Piper.

— 2009. *Eichmann in Jerusalem. Ein Bericht von der Banalität des Bösen.* 4th expanded edn. Munich: Piper.

— 2011. *Elemente und Ursprünge totaler Herrschaft. Antisemitismus, Imperialismus, totale Herrschaft. Ungekürzte Taschenbuchausgabe.* 14th edn. Munich: Piper.

— 2018. *The Human Condition: Second Edition.* Ilinois: University of Chicago Press.

Arens, William. 1980. *The Man-Eating Myth: Anthropology and Anthropophagy.* Oxford University Press.

Arndt, Susan. 2017. '"Rassen" gibt es nicht, wohl aber die symbolische Ordnung von Rasse. Der "Racial Turn" als Gegennarrativ zur Verleugnung und Hierarchisierung von Rassismus'. In *Mythen, Masken und Subjekte. kritische Weißseinsforschung in Deutschland*, edited by Maureen Maisha Eggers, Grada Kilomba, Peggy Piesche and Arndt, 3rd edn, 340–76. Münster: Unrast.

Arneil, Barbara. 1996. *John Locke and America: The Defence of English Colonialism.* Oxford: Clarendon Press.

Arps, Jan Ole. 2020. 'Identitätspolitik. Moria ist das Ende der europäischen Idee? Moria ist die Idee'. *analyse&kritik* 663, 15 September 2020. https://www.akweb.de/politik/moria-ist-europaische-identitaetspolitik.

Ayata, Bilgin. 2016. 'Silencing the Present'. In *Postkoloniale Politikwissenschaft. Theoretische und empirische Zugänge*, edited by Aram Ziai, 211–35. Bielefeld: transcript.

— 2019. 'Affective Citizenship'. In *Affective Societies: Key Concepts*, edited by Jan Slaby and Christian von Scheve, 330–39. London and New York: Routledge.

Ayim, May, Katharina Oguntoye and Dagmar Schultz, eds. 1986. *Farbe bekennen. Afro-deutsche Frauen auf den Spuren ihrer Geschichte.* Berlin: Orlanda.

Baraka, Amiri [LeRoi Jones]. 1963. *Blues People: Negro Music in White America.* New York: William Morrow and Company.

— 1967. *Black Music.* New York: William Morrow and Company.

Barskanmaz, Cengiz. 2015. 'Das Kopftuch als das Andere. Eine notwendige postkoloniale Kritik des deutschen Rechtsdiskurses'. In *Der Stoff, aus dem Konflikte sind*, edited by Petra Rostock and Sabine Berghahn, 361–92. Bielefeld: transcript.

Barthes, Roland. 1972. *Mythologies: The Complete Edition, in a New Translation.* Translated by Richard Howard. New York: Macmillan.

— 1981. *Mythen des Alltags.* Translated by Helmut Scheffel. 6th edn. Frankfurt am Main: Suhrkamp.

Bartonek, Anders. 2011. *Philosophie im Konjunktiv. Nichtidentität als Ort der Möglichkeit des Utopischen in der negativen Dialektik Theodor W. Adornos.* Würzburg: Königshausen & Neumann.

— 2021. 'Marronage and Non-identity'. Part of 'Rethinking Adorno and Race, Part 2: Freedom through Fugitivity and Negation', *The Adorno and Identity Seminars*, 26 February. https://adorno-identity.net/documents.

Baumann, Mechthild. 2016. 'Frontex. Fragen und Antworten'. *bpb.de*. https://www.bpb.de/gesellschaft/migration/kurzdossiers/179679/frontex-fragen-und-antworten.

BDG Network, ed. 2018. *The Black Diaspora and Germany / Deutschland und die Schwarze Diaspora*. Münster: edition assemblage.

Beals, Melba Pattillo. 1995. *Warriors Don't Cry: A Searing Memoir of the Battle to Integrate Little Rock's Central High*. New York: Washington Square Press.

Bempeza, Sofia, Christoph Brunner, Katharina Hausladen, Ines Kleesattel and Ruth Sonderegger. 2019. *Polyphone Ästhetik*. Vienna: transversal.

Benjamin, Walter. 1965. *Zur Kritik der Gewalt und andere Aufsätze*. Frankfurt am Main: Suhrkamp.

— 1974. *Abhandlungen*. Edited by Rolf Tiedemann and Hermann Schweppenhäuser. Vol. 1. of *Gesammelte Schriften*. Frankfurt am Main: Suhrkamp.

— 1977. *Aufsätze, Essays, Vorträge*. Edited by Rolf Tiedemann and Hermann Schweppenhäuser. Vol. 2 of *Gesammelte Schriften*. Frankfurt am Main: Suhrkamp.

— 1986a. *Illuminations*. Random House Digital, Inc.

— 1986b. *Reflections: Essays, Aphorisms, Autobiographical Writings*. New York and London: Harvest/Harcourt Brace Jovanovich.

— 1991. *Berliner Kindheit um neunzehnhundert. Fassung letzter Hand und Fragmente aus früheren Fassungen*. 4th edn. Frankfurt am Main: Suhrkamp.

— 1996. *Selected Writings, 1: 1913–1926*. Edited by Marcus Bullock and Michael W. Jennings. Cambridge, MA: Harvard University Press.

— 2005. *Selected Writings, 2: 1931–1934*. Edited by Michael W. Jennings Howard Eiland, and Gary Smith. Cambridge, MA: Harvard University Press.

— 2006. *Selected Writings, 4: 1938–1940*. Edited by Howard Eiland and Michael W. Jennings. Cambridge, MA: Harvard University Press.

— 2008. *The Work of Art in the Age of Its Technological Reproducibility, and Other Writings on Media*. Edited by Michael W. Jennings, Brigid Doherty, and Thomas Y. Levin. Cambridge, MA: Harvard University Press.

Bens, Jonas, Aletta Diefenbach, Thomas John, Antje Kahl, Hauke Lehmann, Matthias Lüthjohann, Friederike Oberkrome et al. 2019. *The Politics of Affective Societies*. Bielefeld: transcript.

Bens, Jonas. 2021. 'Was ist kapitalistisches Eigentum. Ein sozial- und kulturanthropologischer Ansatz?'. Habilitation lecture, Freie Universität Berlin, 20 October.

Bernasconi, Robert. 2000. 'With What Must the Philosophy of World History Begin? On the Racial Basis of Hegel's Eurocentrism'. *Nineteenth-Century Contexts* 22(2): 171–201.

Bernhardt, Fabian. 2021. 'Affektive Stasis'. Working Papers des SFB 1171 'Affective Societies. Dynamiken des Zusammenlebens in bewegten Welten'. https://doi.org/10.17169/refubium-29346.

Bertram, Georg W. 2014. *Kunst als menschliche Praxis. Eine Ästhetik*. Berlin: Suhrkamp.

Bhandar, Brenna. 2018. *Colonial Lives of Property: Law, Land, and Racial Regimes of Ownership*. Durham, NC: Duke University Press.

— 2020. 'Die kolonialen Leben des Eigentums, abolitionistische Kämpfe und alternative Imaginationen'. *Texte zur Kunst* 117, 52–70.

Billstein, Thomas. 2020. *Kein Vergessen. Todesopfer rechter Gewalt in Deutschland nach 1945*. Münster: Unrast.

Blanchot, Maurice. 2005. *Die Schrift des Desasters*. Translated by Gerhard Poppenberg and Hinrich Weidemann. Munich: Fink.

Blumenberg, Hans. 1997. *Schiffbruch mit Zuschauer*. Frankfurt am Main: Suhrkamp.

Boeckmann, Staci Lynn von. 2004. 'The Life and Work of Gretel Karplus/ Adorno: Her Contributions to Frankfurt School Theory'. Doctoral dissertation: University of Oklahoma.

Boltanski, Luc and Ève Chiapello. 2003. *Der neue Geist des Kapitalismus*. Translated by Michael Tillmann. Konstanz: UVK.

Brand, Dionne. 2011. *A Map to the Door of No Return: Notes on Belonging*. Toronto: Vintage Canada.

Broeck, Sabine and Carsten Junker, eds. 2014. *Postcoloniality – Decoloniality – Black Critique: Joints and Fissures*. Frankfurt am Main and New York: Campus.

Broeck, Sabine. 2003. 'Traveling Memory: The Middle Passage in German Representation'. *The Massachusetts Review* 44(1/2): 157–66.

— 2018. *Gender and the Abjection of Blackness*. Albany: SUNY Press.

Brüggmann, Franziska. 2020. *Institutionskritik im Feld der Kunst. Entwicklung – Wirkung – Veränderungen*. Bielefeld: transcript.

Buck-Morss, Susan. 2011. *Hegel und Haiti. Für eine neue Universalgeschichte*. Translated by Laurent Faasch-Ibrahim. Berlin: Suhrkamp.

Buckel, Sonja, Laura Graf, Judith Kopp, Neva Löw and Maximilian Pichl, eds. 2021. *Kämpfe um Migrationspolitik seit 2015. Zur Transformation des europäischen Migrationsregimes*. Bielefeld: transcript.

Bundesministerium des Innern, für Bau und Heimat. 2018. 'Masterplan Migration. Maßnahmen zur Ordnung, Steuerung und Begrenzung der Zuwanderung'. https://www.bmi.bund.de/SharedDocs/topthemen/DE/topthema-masterplan-migration/topthema-masterplan-migration.html.

Bundesministerium für Wirtschaft und Energie. 2020. 'Klima schützen & Wirtschaft stärken. Vorschlag für eine Allianz von Gesellschaft, Wirtschaft und Staat für Klimaneutralität und Wohlstand'. https://www.bmwi.de/Redaktion/DE/Publikationen/Wirtschaft/klima-schuetzen-wirtschaft-staerken.html.

Burton, Orisanmi. 2005. *Gefährdetes Leben. Politische Essays*. Translated by Karin Wördemann. Frankfurt am Main: Suhrkamp.

— 2007. *Kritik der ethischen Gewalt*. Translated by Reiner Ansén and Michael Adrian. Frankfurt am Main: Suhrkamp.

— 2009. *Raster des Krieges. Warum wir nicht jedes Leid beklagen*. Translated by Reiner Ansén. Frankfurt am Main and New York: Campus.

— 2015. 'To Protect and Serve Whiteness'. *North American Dialogue* 18(2): 38–50.

Butler, Judith. 2004. *Precarious Life: The Powers of Mourning and Violence*. London: Verso.

— 2005. *Giving an Account of Oneself*. New York: Fordham University Press.

— 2010. *Frames of War: When Is Life Grievable?* London: Verso.

Carter, J. Kameron. 2008. *Race: A Theological Account*. New York: Oxford University Press.

Castro Varela, María do Mar and Nikita Dhawan. 2015. *Postkoloniale Theorie. Eine kritische Einführung*. 2nd expanded and revised edn. Bielefeld: transcript.

Cattaneo, Cristina. 2020. *Namen statt Nummern. Auf der Suche nach den Opfern des Mittelmeers*. Zurich: Rotpunktverlag.

Celikates, Robin. 2004. 'Politik und Polizei Jacques Rancière, Zur Logik von Entpolitisierungsprozessen'. *Texte zur Kunst* 55. https://www.textezurkunst.de/55/politik-und-polizei.

Certeau, Michel de. 1988. *Die Kunst des Handelns*. Translated by Ronald Voullié. Berlin: Merve.

— 1988. *The Practice of Everyday Life*. Translated by Steven Rendall. Berkeley: University of California Press.

Chandler, Nahum Dimitri. 2018. 'Paraontology: Or, Notes on the Practical Theoretical Politics of Thought'. Society for the Humanities Annual Culler Lecture in Critical Theory, Ithaca, New York, 29 October. https://vimeo.com/297769615.

Christides, Giorgos, Emmanuel Freudenthal, Steffen Lüdke and Maximilian Popp. 2020. 'Frontex in illegale Pushbacks von Flüchtlingen verwickelt'. *Der Spiegel*, 23 October. https://www.spiegel.de/ausland/fluechtlinge-frontex-in-griechenland-in-illegale-pushbacks-verwickelt-a-00000000-0002-0001-0000-000173654787.

Christides, Giorgos, Steffen Lüdke and Maximilian Popp. 2021. 'Pushbacks in Griechenland. Frontex wusste von Menschenrechtsverletzungen – und tat nichts'. *Der Spiegel*, 15 July. https://www.spiegel.de/ausland/gefluechtete-in-griechenland-frontex-wusste-von-menschenrechtsverletzungen-und-tat-nichts-a-6efe96dc-b4f6-47e9-b4a9-f9b789d2da17.

Ciccariello-Maher, George. 2017. *Decolonizing Dialectics: Radical Américas*. Durham, NC: Duke University Press.

Claussen, Detlev, ed. 1972. *Am Beispiel Angela Davis. Der Kongress in Frankfurt*. Frankfurt am Main: Fischer Taschenbuch.

— 2003. *Theodor W. Adorno. Ein letztes Genie*. Frankfurt am Main: S. Fischer.

CNN, Nima Elbagir, Raja Razek, Alex Platt and Bryony Jones. 2017. 'People for Sale: Where Lives Are Auctioned for $400'. *CNN*, 15 November. https://www.cnn.com/2017/11/14/africa/libya-migrant-auctions/index.html.

Cochrane, Glynn. 2018. *Max Weber's Vision for Bureaucracy: A Casualty of World War I*. Cham: Springer International Publishing.

Community Statement. 2015. 'Community Statement "Black" Studies an der Universität Bremen'. http://www.fb10.uni-bremen.de/inputs/pdf/Communitystatement_BlackStudiesBremen_dt_Unterz815.pdf.

Cooper, Davina, Nikita Dhawan and Janet Newman. 2019. *Reimagining the State: Theoretical Challenges and Transformative Possibilities*. London and New York: Routledge.

Dadusc, Deanna and Pierpaolo Mudu. 2020. 'Care without Control: The Humanitarian Industrial Complex and the Criminalisation of Solidarity'. *Geopolitics* 27(4): 1,205–30.

Danewid, Ida. 2017. 'White Innocence in the Black Mediterranean: Hospitality and the Erasure of History'. *Third World Quarterly* 38(7): 1,674–89.

Dankemeyer, Iris. 2020. *Die Erotik des Ohrs. Musikalische Erfahrung und Emanzipation nach Adorno*. Berlin: Edition Tiamat.

Danowski, Déborah and Eduardo Viveiros de Castro. 2017. *The Ends of the World*. Hoboken, NJ: John Wiley & Sons.

Därmann, Iris. 2020. *Undiendlichkeit. Gewaltgeschichte und politische Philosophie*. Berlin: Matthes & Seitz.

— 2021. *Widerstände. Gewaltenteilung in statu nascendi*. Berlin: Matthes & Seitz.

Davies, Merryl Wyn, Ashis Nandy and Ziauddin Sardar. 1993. *Barbaric Others: A Manifesto on Western Racism*. London: Pluto Press.

Davis, Angela Yvonne. 1971. *Lectures on Liberation*. New York Committee to Free Angela Davis.

Deleuze, Gilles and Félix Guattari. 1974. *Anti-Ödipus*. Translated by Bernd Schwibs. Frankfurt am Main: Suhrkamp.

— 1992. *Tausend Plateaus. Kapitalismus und Schizophrenie*. Edited by Günther Rösch. Berlin: Merve.

— 2000. *Was ist Philosophie*? Translated by Bernd Schwibs and Joseph Vogl. Frankfurt am Main: Suhrkamp.

Deleuze, Gilles. 1983. *Nietzsche and Philosophy*. Translated by Hugh Tomlinson. New York: Columbia University Press.

— 1991. *Nietzsche und die Philosophie*. Translated by Bernd Schwibs. Hamburg: Europäische Verlagsanstalt.

Demirović, Alex. 1999. *Der nonkonformistische Intellektuelle. Die Entwicklung der Kritischen Theorie zur Frankfurter Schule*. Frankfurt am Main: Suhrkamp.

Derrida, Jacques. 1991. *Gesetzeskraft. Der 'mystische Grund der Autorität'*. Translated by Alexander García Düttmann. Frankfurt am Main: Suhrkamp.

Deutsche Welle. 2019. 'Wer ist die Frau, die Salvini herausfordert?' *DW.COM*, 28 June. https://www.dw.com/de/wer-ist-die-frau-die-salvini-herausfordert/a-49380009.

— 2020. '"Raus aus der Hölle!" Flüchtlinge berichten aus Libyen'. *DW.COM*, 24 April. https://www.dw.com/de/raus-aus-der-h%C3%B6lle-fl%C3%BCchtlinge-berichten-aus-libyen/av-50621385.

Deutschlandfunk. 2021. 'Nach Tod von George Floyd. Erster Tag im Prozess gegen Derek Chauvin'. https://www.deutschlandfunk.de/informationen-am-morgen.1764.de.html.

Dhawan, Nikita, ed. 2014. *Decolonizing Enlightenment: Transnational Justice, Human Rights and Democracy in a Postcolonial World.* Berlin: Verlag Barbara Budrich.

— 2019. 'Die affirmative Sabotage der Aufklärung. Die postkoloniale Zwickmühle'. *Zeitschrift für Politik* 66(2): 183–98.

Di Cesare, Donatella. 2019. 'Carola Rackete. Im Namen eines höheren Gesetzes'. *Die Zeit*, 5 July. https://www.zeit.de/2019/28/carola-rackete-sea-watch-kapitaenin-menschenrechte-heldin.

Di Maio, Alessandra. 2012. 'Mediterraneo nero. Le rotte dei migranti nel millennio globale'. In *La città cosmoplita. Altre narrazioni*, edited by Giulia de Spuches and Vincenzo Guarrasi. Palermo: G.B. Palumbo.

Diawara, Manthia and Édouard Glissant. 2011. 'Édouard Glissant in Conversation with Manthia Diawara'. Translated by Christopher Winks. *NKA: Journal of Contemporary African Art* 28(1): 4–19.

Diefenbach, Katja. 2018. 'Possessive Individualism and Trans-Atlantic Slavery as Mirrored in Early Modern Philosophy'. In *The Beast and the Sovereign*, edited by Hans D. Christ, Iris Dressler, Paul B. Preciado and Valentín Roma and translated by Steven Lindberg, 166–76. Leipzig: Spector Books.

Dilger, Hansjörg and Matthias Warstat, eds. 2021. *Umkämpfte Vielfalt.* Frankfurt am Main and New York: Campus.

Doherty, Lillian Eileen. 1995. *Siren Songs: Gender, Audiences, and Narrators in the Odyssey.* Ann Arbor: University of Michigan Press.

Dorlin, Elsa. 2020. *Selbstverteidigung. eine Philosophie der Gewalt.* Translated by Andrea Hemminger. Berlin: Suhrkamp.

Dotson, Kristie. 2012. 'How Is This Paper Philosophy?' *Comparative Philosophy* 3(1): 3–29.

Dougherty, Carol. 2001. *The Raft of Odysseus: The Ethnographic Imagination of Homer's Odyssey.* Oxford University Press.

Douglass, Frederick. 2011. *Narrative of the Life of Frederick Douglass: An American Slave.* Cambridge University Press.

— 2016. *The Portable Frederick Douglass.* Edited by John Stauffer and Henry Louis Gates Jr. New York: Penguin Books.

Du Bois, W.E.B. 1920. *Darkwater: Voices from within the Veil.* New York: Harcourt, Brace and Howe.

— 1969. *Black Reconstruction in America 1860–1880.* New York: Atheneum.

— 1986. *The Souls of Black Folk.* New York: Library of America and Vintage Books.

Dübgen, Franziska. 2019. 'Blinde Flecken der Politischen Philosophie?. Impulse der Critical Philosophy of Race für die Analyse von Normativität, Politik und Recht'. *Deutsche Zeitschrift Für Philosophie* 67(4): 619–33.

Eggers, Maureen Maisha. 2017. 'Rassifizierte Machtdifferenz als Deutungsperspektive in der Kritischen Weißseinsforschung in Deutschland'. In *Masken, Mythen und Subjekte. kritische Weißseinsforschung in Deutschland*, edited by Eggers, Grada Kilomba, Peggy Piesche and Susan Arndt, 3rd edn. Münster: Unrast.

Ehrmann, Jeanette. 2021. 'Schwarzes Mittelmeer, Weißes Europa. Kolonialität, Rassismus und die Grenzen der Demokratie'. *Zeitschrift für praktische Philosophie* 8(1).

— 2023. *Tropen der Freiheit. Die Haitianische Revolution und die Dekolonisierung des Politischen*. Berlin: Suhrkamp.

Eigen, Sara and Mark Larrimore. 2006. *The German Invention of Race*. Albany: SUNY Press.

El-Tayeb, Fatima. 2001. *Schwarze Deutsche. Der Diskurs um 'Rasse' und nationale Identität 1890–1933*. Frankfurt am Main and New York: Campus.

— 2021. 'NaDiRa_lecture series: Things are different here. With Prof. Dr. Fatima El-Tayeb'. DeZIM-Institut, 31 May. https://www.youtube.com/watch?v=YsR2d9rNVV8.

Equal Justice Initiative. 2020. 'Reconstruction in America'. EJI Reports. https://eji.org/report/reconstruction-in-america.

Erskine, John. 1969. *The Moral Obligation to Be Intelligent and Other Essays*. Freeport, NY: Books for Libraries Press.

Essi, Cedric. 2017. '"Mama's Baby, Papa's, Too": Toward Critical Mixed Race Studies'. *Zeitschrift für Anglistik und Amerikanistik* 65(2): 161–72.

Essner, Cornelia. 2002. *Die 'Nürnberger Gesetze' oder die Verwaltung des Rassenwahns 1933–1945*. Paderborn: Schöningh.

European Union. 2020. 'Europa rettet Menschenleben und kämpft gegen Schlepper'. European Commission, Germany, 1 July. https://ec.europa.eu/germany/about-us/reasons/refugees_de.

Fanon, Frantz. 1963. *The Wretched of the Earth*. Translated by Constance Farrington. New York: Grove Press.

— 2013. *Schwarze Haut, weiße Masken*. Translated by Eva Moldenhauer. Berlin and Vienna: Turia + Kant.

— 2017. *Die Verdammten dieser Erde*. Translated by Traugott König. 17th edn. Frankfurt am Main: Suhrkamp.

Fassin, Didier. 2012. *Humanitarian Reason: A Moral History of the Present*. Berkeley: University of California Press.

Federici, Silvia. 2004. *Caliban and the Witch*. New York: Autonomedia.

— 2012. *Revolution at Point Zero: Housework, Reproduction, and Feminist Struggle*. Oakland: Common Notions/PM Press.

— 2015. *Caliban und die Hexe. Frauen, der Körper und die ursprüngliche Akkumulation*. Edited by Martin Birkner and translated by Max Henninger. 3rd expanded edn. Vienna: Mandelbaum.

Ferreira da Silva, Denise. 2007. *Toward a Global Idea of Race*. Minneapolis: University of Minnesota Press.

— 2009. 'No-Bodies: Law, Raciality and Violence'. *Griffith Law Review* 18(2): 212–36.

— 2014. 'Toward a Black Feminist Poethics: The Quest(ion) of Blackness toward the End of the World'. *Black Scholar* 44(2): 81–97.

Fest, Joachim. 2007. *Bürgerlichkeit als Lebensform. Späte Essays*. Leipzig: Rowohlt.

Fichte, Hubert. 2001. *Ketzerische Bemerkungen für eine neue Wissenschaft vom Menschen. Rede in der Frobenius-Gesellschaft, Frankfurt, am 12. Januar 1977*. Hamburg: Europäische Verlagsanstalt.

Florvil, Tiffany Nicole. 2020. *Mobilizing Black Germany: Afro-German Women and the Making of a Transnational Movement*. Champaign: University of Illinois Press.

Forensic Architecture. 2012. 'The Left-to-die Boat' (film), 11 April. https://forensic-architecture.org/investigation/the-left-to-die-boat.

Foucault, Michel. 1977. 'Intellectuals and Power: A Conversation between Michel Foucault and Gilles Deleuze'. In *Language, Counter-Memory, Practice: Selected Essays and Interviews*, 205–17. Ithaca, NY: Cornell University Press.

— 1992. *Was ist Kritik?* Translated by Walter Seitter. Berlin: Merve.

— 2001. *Das Leben der infamen Menschen*. Translated by Walter Seitter. Berlin: Merve.

— 2002. 'Nietzsche, die Genealogie, die Historie'. In *Schriften in vier Bänden. Dits et Écrits: Band 2, 1970–1975*, translated by Michael Bischoff, 166–91. Frankfurt am Main: Suhrkamp.

— 2009. *Hermeneutik des Subjekts*. Translated by Ulrike Bokelmann. Frankfurt am Main: Suhrkamp.

Frame, Douglas. 2005. *The Myth of Return in Early Greek Epic*. Washington, DC: Center for Hellenic Studies.

Fraser, Andrea. 2005. 'From the Critique of Institutions to an Institution of Critique'. *Artforum* 44(1): 100–106.

Fraser, Nancy. 1990. 'Rethinking the Public Sphere'. *Social Text* 25/26: 56–80.

Freud, Sigmund. 1920. 'Beyond the Pleasure Principle'. In *Beyond the Pleasure Principle, Group Psychology and Other Works*, 1–64. *The Standard Edition of the Complete Psychological Works of Sigmund Freud*, XVIII. London: The Hogarth Press.

— 1925. *Gesammelte Schriften*. Vol. 6. Leipzig: Internationaler psychoanalytischer Verlag.

Fuentes, Marisa J. 2010. 'Power and Historical Figuring: Rachael Pringle Polgreen's Troubled Archive'. *Gender & History* 22(3): 564–84.

— 2016. *Dispossessed Lives: Enslaved Women, Violence, and the Archive*. Philadelphia: University of Pennsylvania Press.

Funk, Viktor and Fabian Scheuermann. 2021. 'EU-Grenzschutz mit Frontex: Militarisierung am Mittelmeer'. *FR.de*, 22 May. https://www.fr.de/politik/eu-grenzschutz-militarisierung-am-mittelmeer-90656538.html.

Gates Jr, Henry Louis and William L. Andrews, eds. 2000. *Slave Narratives*. New York: Library of America.

Georg, Jutta. 2019. 'Theodor W. Adorno, Max Horkheimer, Jürgen Habermas und Alfred Schmidt. Kritische Theorie und Nietzsches bürgerliches Denken'. In *'Ein Leser, wie ich ihn verdiene'. Nietzsche-Lektüren in der deutschen Philosophie und Soziologie*, edited by Eike Brock and Georg, 169–97. Stuttgart: J.B. Metzler.

Geulen, Christian. 2020. '"Rasse", Rassismus und Antirassismus'. *Recht und Politik* 56(3): 252–58.

Gilmore, Ruth Wilson. 2006. *Golden Gulag: Prisons, Surplus, Crisis, and Opposition in Globalizing California*. Berkeley: University of California Press.

— 2018. 'Making Abolition Geography in California's Central Valley'. *The Funambulist*, 20 December. https://thefunambulist.net/magazine/21-space-activism/interview-making-abolition-geography-california-central-valley-ruth-wilson-gilmore.

— 2022 'Was tun?' In *Abolitionismus. Ein Reader*, edited by Daniel Loick and Vanessa Thompson. Frankfurt am Main: Suhrkamp.

Gilroy, Paul. 1995. *The Black Atlantic: Modernity and Double Consciousness*. 2nd edn. London: Verso.

Gines, Kathryn T. 2014. *Hannah Arendt and the Negro Question*. Bloomington: Indiana University Press.

Glissant, Édouard. 2010. *Poetics of Relation*. Ann Arbor: University of Michigan Press.

Graeber, David. 2015. *The Utopia of Rules*. New York: Melville House.

— 2017. *Bürokratie: Die Utopie der Regeln*. Translated by Hans Freundl and Henning Dedekind. 2nd edn. Munich: Wilhelm Goldmann.

Gray, Biko Mandela. 2022. 'Blackness'. *Political Theology Network*, 19 April. https://politicaltheology.com/blackness.

Grimaldi, Giuseppe. 2019. 'The Black Mediterranean: Liminality and the Reconfiguration of Afroeuropeanness'. *Open Cultural Studies* 3(1): 414–27.

Grimm, Jacob and Wilhelm Grimm. 1971. 'List'. In *Deutsches Wörterbuch von Jacob und Wilhelm Grimm*. Leipzig.

Gruschka, Andreas. 1994. *Bürgerliche Kälte und Pädagogik. Moral in Gesellschaft und Erziehung*. Wetzlar: Büchse der Pandora.

Guenther, Lisa. 2013. *Solitary Confinement: Social Death and Its Afterlives*. Boston: University of Minnesota Press.

— 2019. 'Seeing like a Cop: A Critical Phenomenology of Whiteness as Property'. In *Race as Phenomena*, edited by Emily S. Lee, 189–206. New York and London: Rowman & Littlefield.

Gumbs, Alexis Pauline. 2020. *Dub: Finding Ceremony*. Durham, NC: Duke University Press.

Gutiérrez Rodríguez, Encarnación. 1999. *Intellektuelle Migrantinnen. Subjektivitäten im Zeitalter von Globalisierung: Eine postkoloniale dekonstruktive Analyse von Biographien im Spannungsverhältnis von Ethnisierung und Vergeschlechtlichung*. Wiesbaden: Verlag für Sozialwissenschaften.

Gutiérrez y Muhs, Gabriella, Yolanda Flores Niemann, Carmen G. Gonzalez and Angela P. Harris. 2012. *Presumed Incompetent: The Intersections of Race and Class for Women in Academia*. Denver: University Press of Colorado.

Ha, Taylor. 2020. 'Black History Month Speaker Reflects on Du Bois' Postapocalyptic *The Comet* 100 Years Later'. Fordham Newsroom (blog), 26 February. https://news.fordham.edu/inside-fordham/lectures-and-events/black-history-month-speaker-reflects-on-du-bois-postapocalyptic-the-comet-100-years-later.

Habermas, Jurgen. 1968. *Friedrich Nietzsche Erkenntnistheoretische Schriften. Mit einem Nachwort von Jürgen Habermas*. Frankfurt am Main: Suhrkamp.

— 1989. *The Structural Transformation of the Public Sphere: An Inquiry into a Category of Bourgeois Society*. Translated by Thomas Burger. Cambridge, MA: MIT Press.

— 1995. *Theorie des kommunikativen Handelns*. Frankfurt am Main: Suhrkamp.

— 2019. *Strukturwandel der Öffentlichkeit. Untersuchungen zu einer Kategorie der bürgerlichen Gesellschaft*. 16th edn. Frankfurt am Main: Suhrkamp.

Hadden, Sally E. 2001. *Slave Patrols: Law and Violence in Virginia and the Carolinas*. Cambridge, MA: Harvard University Press.

Hall, Stuart, Chas Critcher, Tony Jefferson, John Clark and Brian Roberts. 1978. *Policing the Crisis: Mugging, the State, and Law and Order*. London and Basingstoke: Macmillan.

Hall, Stuart. 2020. 'The West and the Rest: Discourse and Power [1992]'. In *Essential Essays Volume 2*, 141–84. Durham, NC: Duke University Press.

Hanewinkel, Vera. 2015. 'Fluchtmigration nach Deutschland und Europa: Einige Hintergründe'. *bpb.de*, 15 December. https://www.bpb.de/gesellschaft/migration/kurzdossiers/217369/fluchtmigration-hintergruende.

Hanke, Christine. 2015. *Zwischen Auflösung und Fixierung. Zur Konstitution von 'Rasse' und 'Geschlecht' in der physischen Anthropologie um 1900*. Bielefeld: transcript.

Hark, Sabine and Paula-Irene Villa. 2017. *Unterscheiden und herrschen. Ein Essay zu den ambivalenten Verflechtungen von Rassismus, Sexismus und Feminismus in der Gegenwart*. Bielefeld: transcript.

Hark, Sabine. 2015. 'Die Vermessung des Schweigens. Oder: Was heißt sprechen? Dimensionen epistemischer Gewalt'. In *Dominanzkultur Reloaded*, edited by Iman Attia, Swantje Köbsell and Nivedita Prasad. Bielefeld: transcript.

Harney, Stefano and Fred Moten. 2013. *The Undercommons: Fugitive Planning and Black Study*. Wivenhoe: Minor Compositions.

— 2016. *Die Undercommons*. Edited by Isabell Lorey and translated by Birgit Mennel and Gerald Raunig. Vienna: transversal.

— 2020. 'FUC 012 Fred Moten & Stefano Harney – the university: last words'. https://www.youtube.com/watch?v=zqWMejD_XU8.

— 2021. *All Incomplete*. Wivenhoe: Minor Compositions.

Harris, Cheryl I. 1993. 'Whiteness as Property'. *Harvard Law Review* 106(8): 1707–91.

Harris, Laura. 2018. *Experiments in Exile: C.L.R. James, Hélio Oiticica, and the Aesthetic Sociality of Blackness*. New York: Fordham University Press.

Hartman, Saidiya and Frank Wilderson III. 2003. 'The Position of the Unthought'. *Qui Parle* 13: 183–201.

Hartman, Saidiya. 1997. *Scenes of Subjection: Terror, Slavery, and Self-Making in Nineteenth Century America*. Oxford University Press.

— 2002. 'The Time of Slavery'. *South Atlantic Quarterly* 101(4): 757–77.

— 2007. *Lose Your Mother: A Journey Along the Atlantic Slave Route*. New York: Farrar, Straus and Giroux.

— 2008. 'Venus in Two Acts'. *Small Axe: A Caribbean Journal of Criticism* 12(2)/26: 1–14.

— 2019. *Wayward Lives Beautiful Experiments: Intimate Histories of Social Upheaval*. New York: W.W. Norton & Company.

— 2020. 'The End of White Supremacy, An American Romance'. *BOMB Magazine*, 8 June. https://bombmagazine.org/articles/the-end-of-white-supremacy-an-american-romance.

— 2022. *Aufsässige Leben, schöne Experimente. Von rebellischen schwarzen Mädchen, schwierigen Frauen und radikalen Queers*. Translated by Anna Jäger. Berlin: Claassen.

Haslanger, Sally. 2008. 'Changing the Ideology and Culture of Philosophy: Not by Reason (Alone)'. *Hypatia* 23(2): 210–23.

Hegel, Georg Wilhelm Friedrich. 1988. *Phänomenologie des Geistes*. Edited by Hans-Friedrich Wessels and Heinrich Clairmont. Hamburg: Felix Meiner.

— 1994. *Vorlesungen über die Philosophie der Weltgeschichte. Band 1. Die Vernunft in der Geschichte*. Edited by Johannes Hoffmeister. Hamburg: Felix Meiner.

Heller, Charles. 2019. 'Wo die Überquerung ins Stocken kommt. Die Bekämpfung der "flüssigen Gewalt" von Grenzen im Mittelmeer. Ein Interview mit Charles Heller'. *Texte zur Kunst* 114: 83–95.

Heng, Geraldine. 2018. *The Invention of Race in the European Middle Ages*. Cambridge University Press.

Hess, Sabine, Bernd Kasparek, Stefanie Kron, Mathias Rodatz, Maria Schwertl and Simon Sontowski, eds. 2017. *Der lange Sommer der Migration*. Berlin and Hamburg: Assoziation A.

Higgins, Charlotte. 2017. 'The *Odyssey* Translated by Emily Wilson Review: A New Cultural Landmark'. *Guardian*, 8 December. https://www.theguardian.com/books/2017/dec/08/the-odyssey-translated-emily-wilson-review.

Hill Collins, Patricia. 2014. *Black Feminist Thought: Knowledge, Consciousness, and the Politics of Empowerment*. 2nd edn. London and New York: Routledge.

Hogh, Philip. 2017. 'Apathie kälte Verdinglichung. Zur Gesellschaftlichen wirklichkeit moralischer Indifferenz'. In *Warum Kritik? Begründungsformen kritischer Theorien*, edited by Sven Ellmers and Hogh, 22–50. Weilerswist: Velbrück Wissenschaft.

Homer. 2011. *Odyssee*. Translated by Kurt Steinmann. Zurich: Manesse.

— 2018. *The Odyssey*. Translated by Emily Wilson. New York: W.W. Norton & Company.

Honig, Bonnie, ed. 1995. *Feminist Interpretations of Hannah Arendt*. University Park: Pennsylvania State University Press.

Horkheimer, Max. 1968. *Kritische Theorie. Eine Dokumentation, 2 Bände*. Edited by Alfred Schmidt. Frankfurt am Main: S. Fischer.

— 1978. *Dawn and Decline: Notes 1926–1931 and 1950–1969*. Translated by Michael Shaw. New York: Seabury Press.

— 1985a. *Gesammelte Schriften. Band 7. Vorträge und Aufzeichnungen 1949–1973*. Edited by Alfred Schmidt and Gunzelin Schmid-Noerr. Frankfurt am Main: S. Fischer.

— 1985b. *Gesammelte Schriften. Band 8. Vorträge und Aufzeichnungen 1949–1973*. Edited by Gunzelin Schmid-Noerr. Frankfurt am Main: S. Fischer.

— 1991. *Gesammelte Schriften. Band 6: 'Zur Kritik der instrumentellen Vernunft' und 'Notizen 1949–1969'*. Edited by Alfred Schmidt and Gunzelin Schmid-Noerr. Frankfurt am Main: S. Fischer.

— 1992. *Traditionelle und kritische Theorie. Fünf Aufsätze*. Frankfurt am Main: S. Fischer.

Hostettler, Karin. 2020. *Kritik – Selbstaffirmation – Othering. Immanuel Kants Denken der Zweckmässigkeit und die koloniale Episteme*. Bielefeld: transcript.

Ivanov, Paola and Kristin Weber-Sinn. 2017. 'Sammelwut und koloniale Gewalt'. In *Humboldt Lab Tanzania. Objekte aus den Kolonialkriegen im Ethnologischen Museum, Berlin. Ein tansanisch-deutscher Dialog*, edited by Lili Reyels, Ivanov and Weber-Sinn, 66–149. Berlin: Reimer.

Jackson, Zakiyyah Iman. 2016. 'Losing Manhood: Animality and Plasticity in the (Neo)Slave Narrative'. *Qui Parle* 25(1–2): 95–136.

— 2018. 'Theorizing in a Void'. *South Atlantic Quarterly* 117(3): 617–48.

— 2020. *Becoming Human: Matter and Meaning in an Antiblack World*. New York University Press.

— 2021. 'Against Criticism: Notes on Decipherment and the Force of Things'. In *No Humans Involved*, edited by Hammer Museum. Los Angeles: DelMonico Books.

Jaeggi, Rahel. 2014. *Kritik von Lebensformen*. Berlin: Suhrkamp.

Jafa, Arthur. 2013. *APEX* (film). https://www.moma.org/collection/works/273164.

— 2016. *Love Is the Message the Message Is Death* (film).

— 2021. *AGHDRA* (film).

James, C.L.R. 2021. *Die schwarzen Jakobiner*. Edited by Çiğdem Inan and Philipp Dorestal and translated by Jen Theodor. Berlin: Karl Dietz and b_books.

Jeffries, Stuart. 2016. *Grand Hotel Abyss: The Lives of the Frankfurt School*. New York: Verso Books.

Jelinek, Elfriede. 2009. 'Die Kontrakte des Kaufmanns'. In *Drei Theaterstücke*, 207–348. Hamburg: Rowohlt.

Jenkins, Destin and Justin Leroy, eds. 2021. *Histories of Racial Capitalism: Columbia Studies in the History of US Capitalism*. New York: Columbia University Press.

Johnson, Walter. 2003. 'On Agency'. *Journal of Social History* 37(1): 113–24.

Jones, David. 2020. 'How Can We Win'. *David Jones Media*. https://www.youtube.com/watch?v=sb9_qGOa9Go.

Jones, Kimberly. 2022. *How We Can Win: Race, History and Changing the Money Game That's Rigged*. New York: Henry Holt and Co.

Judy, R.A. 2020. *Sentient Flesh: Thinking in Disorder, Poiēsis in Black*. Durham, NC: Duke University Press.

Jung, Moon-Kie and João Helion Costa Vargas, eds. *Antiblackness*. Durham, NC: Duke University Press, 2021.

Kailouli, Nadia and Jonas Schreijäg. 2020. 'SeaWatch 3. Dokumentation'. *NDR*. https://www.ndr.de/fernsehen/SeaWatch3,seawatch688.html.

Kaiser, Birgit M. and Kathrin Thiele. 2017. 'What Is Species Memory? Or, Humanism, Memory and the Afterlives of 1492'. *Parallax* 23(4): 403–15.

Kant, Immanuel. 1999. *Was Ist Aufklärung? Ausgewählte Kleine Schriften*. Edited by Horst D. Brandt. Hamburg: Felix Meiner.

Kasmani, Omar. 2019. 'Thin Attachments'. *Capacious: Journal for Emerging Affect Inquiry* 1(4): 34–53.

— 2021. 'Thin, Cruisy, Queer'. In *Gender and Genre in Ethnographic Writing*, edited by Elisabeth Tauber and Dorothy Louise Zinn, 163–88. Cham: Palgrave Macmillan.

Kelly, Natasha A. 2016. *Afrokultur. 'Der raum zwischen gestern und morgen'*. Münster: Unrast.

Kerner, Ina. 2009. *Differenzen und Macht. Zur Anatomie von Rassismus und Sexismus*. Frankfurt am Main: Campus.

Khader, Serene J. 2019. *Decolonizing Universalism: A Transnational Feminist Ethic*. Oxford University Press.

Khalil Saucier, P. and Tryon P. Woods. 2014. 'Ex Aqua: The Mediterranean Basin, Africans on the Move and the Politics of Policing'. *Theoria: A Journal of Social and Political Theory* 61(141): 55–75.

King, Tiffany Lethabo, Jenell Navarro and Andrea Smith. 2020. *Otherwise Worlds: Against Settler Colonialism and Anti-Blackness*. Durham, NC: Duke University Press.

Kirkland, Frank M. 2018. 'Hegel on Race and Development'. In *The Routledge Companion to Philosophy of Race*, edited by Luvell Anderson, Paul C. Taylor and Linda Martín Alcoff, 43–60. London and New York: Routledge.

Klonschinski, Andrea. 2020. 'Frauen in der akademischen Philosophie in Deutschland. Eine Bestandsaufnahme'. *Zeitschrift für philosophische Forschung* 74: 593–616.

Knoch, Habbo. 2021. 'Die Zerstörung des Subjekts. Auschwitz und die bürgerliche Kälte'. In *Selbstentwürfe. Neue Perspektiven auf die politische Kulturgeschichte des Selbst im 20. Jahrhundert*, edited by Tilmann Siebeneichner. Göttingen: Wallstein.

Koselleck, Reinhart. 1973. *Kritik und Krise*. Frankfurt am Main: Suhrkamp.

— 2000. *Critique and Crisis: Enlightenment and the Pathogenesis of Modern Society*. Cambridge, MA: MIT Press.

Kramer, Sina. 2017. *Excluded Within: The (Un)intelligibility of Radical Political Actors*. Oxford University Press.

Kunst, Bojana. 2015. *Artist at Work: Proximity of Art and Capitalism*. Winchester and Washington: Zero Books.

Le Guin, Ursula K. 1997. 'The Carrier Bag Theory of Fiction'. In *Dancing at the Edge of the World*, 149–54. New York: Grove Press.

Lebeau, Vicky. 2004. 'The Unwelcome Child: Elizabeth Eckford and Hannah Arendt'. *Journal of Visual Culture* 3(1): 51–62.

Lee, Emily S., ed. 2014. *Living Alterities: Phenomenology, Embodiment, and Race*. Albany: SUNY Press.

Lennox, Sara, ed. 2016. *Remapping Black Germany: New Perspectives on Afro-German History, Politics, and Culture*. Boston: University of Massachusetts Press.

Lepold, Kristina and Marina Martinez Mateo, eds. 2021. *Critical Philosophy of Race. Ein Reader*. Frankfurt am Main: Suhrkamp.

Lepold, Kristina and Marina Martinez Mateo. 2019. 'Schwerpunkt: Critical Philosophy of Race'. *Deutsche Zeitschrift für Philosophie* 67(4): 572–88.

Lethen, Helmut. 2002. *Cool Conduct: The Culture of Distance in Weimar Germany*. Translated by Don Reneau. Berkeley: University Of California Press.

— 2018. *Verhaltenslehren der Kälte. Lebensversuche zwischen den Kriegen*. 8th edn. Frankfurt am Main: Suhrkamp.

Lettow, Susanne. 2021. 'Re-articulating Genealogy: Hegel on Kinship, Race and Reproduction'. *Hegel Bulletin* 42(2): 256–76.

Levi, Primo. 1990. *Die Untergegangenen und die Geretteten*. Translated by Moshe Kahn. Munich: Hanser.

Ley, Michael. 1997. *'Zum Schutze des deutschen Blutes . . .'. 'Rassenschandegesetze' im Nationalsozialismus*. Mainz: Philo.

Liebscher, Doris. 2021. *Rasse im Recht – Recht gegen Rassismus. Genealogie einer ambivalenten rechtlichen Kategorie*. Frankfurt am Main: Suhrkamp.

Locke, John. 1689. *Second Treatise of Government*. London: Awnsham Churchill. https://www.gutenberg.org/files/7370/7370-h/7370-h.htm.

— 1977. *Zweite Abhandlung über die Regierung*. Translated by Hans Jörn Hoffmann. Frankfurt am Main: Suhrkamp.

Loick, Daniel. 2012. *Kritik der Souveränität*. Frankfurt am Main and New York: Campus.

— 2017. *Juridismus. Konturen einer kritischen Theorie des Rechts*. Berlin: Suhrkamp.

— 2018a. *Der Missbrauch des Eigentums*. 2nd edn. Berlin: August.

— 2018b. *Kritik der Polizei*. Frankfurt am Main and New York: Campus.

— 2021. 'Daniel Loick: Benjamin and Abolition'. 24 March. https://www.youtube.com/watch?v=HtU1xldcm1I.

Lorde, Audre. 2007. *Sister Outsider*. London: Penguin Books.

— 2018. *Euer Schweigen schützt Euch nicht. Audre Lorde und die Schwarze Frauenbewegung in Deutschland*. Edited by Peggy Piesche. 2nd edn. Berlin: Orlanda.

Lorey, Isabell. 2015. *State of Insecurity: Government of the Precarious*. London: Verso.

Louisiana Channel. 2017. 'Arthur Jafa Interview: Not All Good, Not All Bad'. https://www.youtube.com/watch?v=iprTrTgXvZ8.

Macpherson, Crawford B. 1975. *The Political Theory of Possessive Individualism: Hobbes to Locke*. 6th edn. Oxford University Press.

Malkin, Irad. 1998. *The Returns of Odysseus: Colonization and Ethnicity*. Berkeley: University of California Press.

— 2001. 'The Odyssey and the Nymphs'. *Gaia. Revue interdisciplinaire sur la Grèce Archaïque* 5(1): 11–27.

Marasco, Robyn. 2015. *The Highway of Despair: Critical Theory after Hegel.* New York: Columbia University Press.

Marcuse, Herbert. 1971. 'Ein Brief an Angela Davis'. *Neue Wege* 65(12): 359.

— 2004. *The New Left and the 1960s.* Edited by Douglas Kellner. London and New York: Routledge.

Martinot, Steve and Jared Sexton. 2003. 'The Avant-Garde of White Supremacy'. *Social Identities* 9(2): 169.

Martinot, Steve. 2014. 'On the Epidemic of Police Killings'. *Social Justice* 39(4)/130: 52–75.

Marx, Karl. 1982. *Capital: A Critique of Political Economy, Volume 1.* Translated by Ben Fowkes. London: Penguin.

— 1986. *Das Kapital: Erster Band.* 30th edn. Berlin: Karl Dietz. Materla, Vanessa and Tilman Steffen. 2019. 'Carola Rackete. Die besonnene Widerständlerin'. *Die Zeit*, 2 July. https://www.zeit.de/gesellschaft/zeitgeschehen/2019-07carola-rackete-sea-watch-3-kapitaenin-seenotrettung-italien.

Maurel, Christian and Peter Rehberg. 2019. *Für den Arsch / Christian Maurel.* Translated by Tobias Haberkorn. Berlin: August.

Maurel, Christian. 2025. *The Screwball Asses and Other Texts.* Cambridge, MA: MIT Press.

Mbembe, Achille. 2017. *Kritik der schwarzen Vernunft.* Translated by Michael Bischoff. Frankfurt am Main: Suhrkamp.

McCarthy, Thomas. 2009. *Race, Empire, and the Idea of Human Development.* Cambridge University Press.

McClymont, J.D. 2008. 'The Character of Circe in the *Odyssey*'. *Akroterion*, 21 January.

McKittrick, Katherine, ed. 2015. *Sylvia Wynter: On Being Human as Praxis.* Durham, NC: Duke University Press.

Menke, Christoph. 2013. *Die Kraft der Kunst.* Frankfurt am Main: Suhrkamp.

Mettin, Martin. 2021. *Kritische Theorie des Hörens. Untersuchungen zur Philosophie Ulrich Sonnemanns.* Berlin: J.B. Metzler.

Mezzadra, Sandro. 2020. 'Abolitionist Vistas of the Human. Border Struggles, Migration and Freedom of Movement'. *Citizenship Studies* 24(4): 424–40.

Miller, Madeline. 2018. *Circe.* Boston: Little, Brown and Company.

Mills, Charles W. 2007. 'White Ignorance'. In *Race and Epistemologies of Ignorance*, edited by Shannon Sullivan and Nancy Tuana, 11–38. Albany: SUNY Press.

— 2012. 'Philosophy Raced, Philosophy Erased'. In *Reframing the Practice of Philosophy: Bodies of Color, Bodies of Knowledge*, edited by George Yancy, 45–70. Albany: SUNY Press.

— 2014. *The Racial Contract.* Ithaca: Cornell University Press.

— 2015. *Blackness Visible: Essays on Philosophy and Race.* Ithaca: Cornell University Press.

Moten, Fred. 2003. *In the Break: The Aesthetics of the Black Radical Tradition.* Minneapolis: University of Minnesota Press.

— 2013. 'Blackness and Nothingness (Mysticism in the Flesh)'. *South Atlantic Quarterly* 112(4): 737–80.

— 2017. *Black and Blur: Consent not to be a single being, Volume 1.* Durham, NC: Duke University Press.

— 2018a. *Stolen Life: Consent not to be a single being, Volume 2.* Durham, NC: Duke University Press.

— 2018b. *The Universal Machine: Consent not to be a single being, Volume 3.* Durham, NC: Duke University Press.

Mühlhoff, Rainer. 2019. 'Affective Disposition'. *In Affective Societies: Key Concepts*, edited by Jan Slaby and Christian von Scheve, 119–30. London and New York: Routledge.

Müller, Maximilian. 2017. 'Die Vietnamesische Diaspora in Berlin'. *GISCA Occasional Papers Series.*

Mussell, Simon. 2013. '"Pervaded by a Chill": The Dialectic of Coldness in Adorno's Social Theory'. *Thesis Eleven* 117(1): 55–67.

Nagel, Christine. 2020. 'Hannah Arendt. Denken ohne Geländer'. *Deutschlandfunk Kultur.* https://www.deutschlandfunkkultur.de/hannah-arendt-denken-ohne-gelaender.1024.de.html?dram:article_id=249953.

Nandy, Ashis. 2003. *The Romance of the State and the Fate of Dissent in the Tropics.* 2nd edn. Oxford University Press.

Nash, Jennifer Christine. 2019. *Black Feminism Reimagined: After Intersectionality.* Durham, NC: Duke University Press.

NDR. 2019. 'Exklusiv: Was geschah an . . .'. *Panorama.* https://www.daserste.de/information/politik-weltgeschehen/panorama/videosextern/exklusiv-was-geschah-an-bord-der-sea-watch-3-100.html.

Negri, Antonio, Maurizio Lazzarato, Paolo Virno and Thomas Atzert. 1998. *Umherschweifende Produzenten. Immaterielle Arbeit und Subversion.* Berlin: ID Verlag.

Nelson, Jill. 2001. *Police Brutality: An Anthology.* New York: W.W. Norton & Company.

Nietzsche, Friedrich. n.d. 'Nietzsche on Art: Selections from Later Writings'. https://www2.hawaii.edu/~freeman/courses/phil330/20.%20Nietzsche%20Later%20writings.pdf.

— 1974. *The Gay Science: With a Prelude in Rhymes and an Appendix of Songs.* Translated by Walter Kaufmann. New York: Vintage.

— 1995. *The Complete Works of Friedrich Nietzsche: Beyond Good and Evil.* Redwood City: Stanford University Press.

— 1997. *Daybreak: Thoughts on the Prejudices of Morality.* Edited by Maudemarie Clark and Brian Leiter and translated by R.J. Hollingdale. New York: Cambridge University Press.

— 2013a. *Die fröhliche Wissenschaft. Wir Furchtlosen.* Vol. 5 of *Philosophische Werke.* Hamburg: Felix Meiner.

— 2013b. *Jenseits von Gut und Böse / Die Geburt der Tragödie.* Vol. 1 of *Philosophische Werke.* Hamburg: Felix Meiner.

— 2013c. *Morgenröthe.* Vol. 4 of *Philosophische Werke.* Hamburg: Felix Meiner.

— 2013d. *Zur Genealogie der Moral / Götzen-Dämmerung.* Vol. 6 of *Philosophische Werke.* Hamburg: Felix Meiner.

NSU Watch. 2020. *Aufklären und einmischen. Der NSU-Komplex und der Münchner Prozess*. Berlin: Verbrecher Verlag.

Nussbaum, Martha. 1996. 'Compassion: The Basic Social Emotion'. *Social Philosophy and Policy* 13(1): 27–58.

Oberle, Eric. 2018. *Theodor Adorno and the Century of Negative Identity*. Redwood City: Stanford University Press.

Okiji, Fumi. 2018. *Jazz as Critique: Adorno and Black Expression Revisited*. Redwood City: Stanford University Press.

Okpewho, Isidore. 2002. 'Walcott, Homer, and the "Black Atlantic"'. *Research in African Literatures* 33(1): 27–44.

Olaloku-Teriba, Annie. 2018. 'Afropessimism and the (Un-)logic of Anti-Blackness'. *Historical Materialism* (26, Identity Politics). http://www.historicalmaterialism.org/articles/afro-pessimism-and-unlogic-anti-blackness.

Olney, James. 1984. '"I Was Born": Slave Narratives, Their Status as Autobiography and as Literature'. *Callaloo* 20: 46.

Osterweil, Vicky. 2020. *In Defense of Looting: A Riotous History of Uncivil Action*. New York: Bold Type Books.

Owens, Emily A. 2017. 'Promises: Sexual Labor in the Space between Slavery and Freedom'. *Louisiana History* 58(2): 179.

— 2019a. 'Keyword 7: Consent'. *Differences*, 2019.

— 2019b. 'Capitalism and Slavery Part 1, Interview by Daniel Denvir'. *The Dig*. https://www.thedigradio.com/podcast/capitalism-and-slavery-part-1.

Palmer, Tyrone S. 2017. '"What Feels More Than Feeling?": Theorizing the Unthinkability of Black Affect'. *Critical Ethnic Studies* 3(2): 31–56.

— 2020. 'Otherwise than Blackness: Feeling, World, Sublimation'. *Qui Parle* 29(2): 247–83.

Patterson, Orlando. 1982. *Slavery and Social Death: A Comparative Study*. Cambridge, MA: Harvard University Press.

Pedwell, C. 2014. *Affective Relations: The Transnational Politics of Empathy*. London: Palgrave Macmillan.

Pichl, Maximilian. 2021. *Der Moria-Komplex. Verantwortungslosigkeit, Unzuständigkeit und Entrechtung fünf Jahre nach dem EU-Türkei-Abkommen und der Einführung des Hotspot-Systems*. Frankfurt am Main: Medico International.

Piesche, Peggy. 2017. 'Der "Fortschritt" der Aufklärung. Kants "Race" und die Zentrierung des weißen Subjekts'. In *Masken, Mythen und Subjekte. Kritische Weißseinsforschung in Deutschland*, edited by Maureen Maisha Eggers, Grada Kilomba, Piesche and Susan Arndt, 3rd edn, 30–39. Münster: Unrast.

Piper, Adrian. 1996. 'Untitled Performance for Max's Kansas City'. In *Out of Order, Out of Sight, Volume I: Selected Writings in Meta-Art, 1968–1992*. Cambridge, MA: MIT Press.

Plessner, Helmuth. 2002. *Grenzen der Gemeinschaft. Eine Kritik des sozialen Radikalismus*. Frankfurt am Main: Suhrkamp.

Proglio, Gabriele, Camilla Hawthorne, Ida Danewid, P. Khalil Saucier, Giuseppe Grimaldi, Angelica Pesarini, Timothy Raeymaekers, Giulia Grechi and Vivian Gerrand, eds. 2021. *The Black Mediterranean: Bodies, Borders and Citizenship; Mediterranean Perspectives.* London: Palgrave Macmillan.

Quashie, Kevin. 2021. *Black Aliveness, or a Poetics of Being.* Durham, NC: Duke University Press.

Rancière, Jacques. 2002. *Das Unvernehmen. Politik und Philosophie.* Frankfurt am Main: Suhrkamp.

— 2006. *Die Aufteilung des Sinnlichen. Die Politik der Kunst und ihre Paradoxien.* Berlin: b_books.

— 2013. *The Politics of Aesthetics.* Translated by Gabriel Rockhill. New York: Continuum.

Rassool, Ciraj. 2015. 'Re-Storing the Skeletons of Empire: Return, Reburial and Rehumanisation in Southern Africa'. *Journal of Southern African Studies* 41(3): 653–70.

Rebentisch, Juliane. 2003. Ästhetik der Installation. Frankfurt am Main: Suhrkamp.

Reckwitz, Andreas. 2008. 'Wie bürgerlich Ist die Moderne? Bürgerlichkeit als hybride Subjektkultur'. In *Unscharfe Grenzen. Perspektiven der Kultursoziologie*, edited by Reckwitz, 197–216. Bielefeld: transcript.

Reines, Ariana. 2019. *A Sandbook.* Portland: Tin House Books.

Renault, Matthieu. 2021. 'Counter-Violence, a "Hegelian" Myth: Minor Variations on the Master–Slave Dialectic'. *Radical Philosophy* 210: 21–32.

Rinon, Yoav. 2007. 'The Pivotal Scene: Narration, Colonial Focalization, and Transition in Odyssey 9'. *American Journal of Philology* 128(3): 301–34.

Roberts, Neil. 2015. *Freedom as Marronage.* University of Chicago Press.

Robinson, Cedric J. 2000. *Black Marxism: The Making of the Black Radical Tradition.* Chapel Hill: The University of North Carolina Press.

Roediger, David R. 1994. *Towards the Abolition of Whiteness: Essays on Race, Politics, and Working Class History.* London and New York: Verso.

— 1999. *The Wages of Whiteness: Race and the Making of the American Working Class.* London and New York: Verso.

Rotkopf, Marie. 2020. 'Völkerordnung'. In *Rejected Designs for the European Flag.* Edited by Jonas von Lenthe. Berlin: Wirklichkeit Books.

Rousseau, Jean-Jacques. 2011. *Vom Gesellschaftsvertrag oder Grundsätze des Staatsrechts.* Stuttgart: Reclam.

Royal Academy of Art, The Hague. 2020. 'Lecture Recording: Denise & Valentina – KABK Studium Generale Series Wxtch Craft'. https://vimeo.com/488053466.

Salamon, Gayle. 2009. 'Justification and Queer Method, or Leaving Philosophy'. *Hypatia* 24(1): 225–30.

Salem, Sara and Vanessa Thompson. 2016. 'Old Racisms, New Masks: On the Continuing Discontinuities of Racism and the Erasure of Race in European Contexts'. *Nineteen Sixty Nine* 3(1).

Sandford, Stella. 2018. 'Kant, Race, and Natural History'. *Philosophy & Social Criticism* 44(9): 950–77.

Sandywell, Barry. 1995. *The Beginnings of European Theorizing: Reflexivity in the Archaic Age*. London and New York: Routledge.

Sarr, Felwine and Bénédicte Savoy. 2019. *Zurückgeben. Über die Restitution afrikanischer Kulturgüter*. Translated by Daniel Fastner. Berlin: Matthes & Seitz.

Schmid, Peter A. 1997. 'Bürokratie bei Karl Marx und Max Weber'. *Rote Revue. Zeitschrift für Politik, Wirtschaft und Kultur* 75(1): 40–43.

Schultz, Dagmar. 2012. *Audre Lorde. Die Berliner Jahre 1984–1992 – Dichterin, Aktivistin, lesbische Mutter*. Berlin: Salzgeber.

— 2014. 'Audre Lorde: The Berlin Years 1984 to 1992 – The Making of the Film and Its Reception'. *Feminist Studies* 40(1): 199–206.

Schwarzbach-Apithy, Aretha. 2017. 'Interkulturalität und anti-rassistische Weis(s)heiten an Berliner Universitäten'. In *Masken, Mythen und Subjekte. Kritische Weißseinsforschung in Deutschland*, edited by Maureen Maisha Eggers, Grada Kilomba, Peggy Piesche and Susan Arndt. 3rd edn. Münster: Unrast.

Sea-Watch e.V. 2019a. 'Sea-Watch fordert Anlandung der 43 geretteten Personen bis zum morgigen Weltflüchtlingstag'. Sea-Watch e.V. (blog). 19 June. https://sea-watch.org/sea-watch-fordert-anlandung-43-geretteten-weltfluechtlingstag.

— 2019b. 'Europa will keine Verantwortung übernehmen. Sea-Watch 3 fährt wegen Notlage in italienische Gewässer ein'. Sea-Watch e.V. (blog). 26 June. https://sea-watch.org/sea-watch-3-faehrt-in-italienische-gewaesser.

Sedgwick, Eve Kosofsky. 2003. *Touching Feeling: Affect, Pedagogy, Performativity*. Edited by Michèle Aina Barale, Jonathan Goldberg and Michael Moon. Durham, NC: Duke University Press.

Sellami, Samir. 2020. 'Synkopischer Widerstand. Fred Motens schwarze Reanimation der Kritischen Theorie'. *Merkur* 855.

Seshadri-Crooks, Kalpana. 2000. *Desiring Whiteness: A Lacanian Analysis of Race*. London and New York: Routledge.

Sexton, Jared. 2017. 'On Black Negativity, or the Affirmation of Nothing', interview by Daniel Colucciello Barber. *Society and Space*. https://www.societyandspace.org/articles/on-black-negativity-or-the-affirmation-of-nothing.

— 2019. 'Affirmation in the Dark: Racial Slavery and Philosophical Pessimism'. *The Comparatist* 43(1): 90–111.

— 2021. 'Trouble Consciousness'. In *Arthur Jafa: MAGNUMB*, edited by Lærke Rydal Jørgensen and Mathioc Ussing Seeberg, 72–76. Copenhagen: Louisiana Museum of Modern Art.

Sharpe, Christina. 2016. *In the Wake: On Blackness and Being*. Durham, NC: Duke University Press.

— 2018. '"And to Survive"'. *Small Axe: A Caribbean Journal of Criticism* 22(3): 171–80.

Silva, Grant. 2018. 'On the Difficulties of Writing Philosophy from a Racialized Subjectivity'. *Newsletter on Hispanic/Latino Issues in Philosophy*, October.

Slaby, Jan and Christian von Scheve, eds. 2019. *Affective Societies: Key Concepts*. London and New York: Routledge.

Slaby, Jan and Christian von Scheve. 2020. 'Affect's "Iron Cage"'. Part of the lecture series 'Mobility Affects', Berlin, 18 November. https://vimeo.com/497302618.

Slaby, Jan, Rainer Mühlhoff and Philipp Wüschner. 2019. 'Affective Arrangements'. *Emotion Review* 11(1): 3–12.

Slaby, Jan. 2019. 'Relational Affect'. In *How to Do Things with Affects: Affective Triggers in Aesthetic Forms and Cultural Practices*, edited by Ernst van Alphen and Tomáš Jirsa, 59–81. Leiden: Brill.

Sloterdijk, Peter. 1987. *Critique of Cynical Reason*. Minneapolis: University of Minnesota Press.

— 2018. *Kritik der zynischen Vernunft*. 21st edn. Frankfurt am Main: Suhrkamp.

Smallwood, Stephanie E. 2008. *Saltwater Slavery: A Middle Passage from Africa to American Diaspora*. Cambridge, MA: Harvard University Press.

Sonderegger, Ruth. 2018. 'Fragen zur Kolonialität der Europäischen Ästhetik'. In *Archive dekolonialisieren mediale und epistemische Transformationen in Kunst, Design und Film*, edited by Mara Recklies, Sophie Lembcke and Eva Knopf, 173, 251–58. Bielefeld: transcript.

— 2019a. *Vom Leben der Kritik – Kritische Praktiken – und die Notwendigkeit ihrer geopolitischen Situierung*. Vienna: Zaglossus.

— 2019b. 'Elemente einer postkolonialen Genealogie der westlichen Ästhetik'. In *Polyphone Ästhetik*, 53–68. Vienna: transversal.

— 2020. 'Eine nicht verpasste Begegnung. Zu Fred Motens Auseinandersetzung mit Theodor W. Adorno'. Edited by Sven Kramer and Gerhard Schweppenhäuser. *Zeitschrift für kritische Theorie* 50–51: 80–108.

Spigno, Alessandra and Phil Marshall. 2017. 'Labour Conditions in the Italian Tomato-Growing Sector'. RCG Research and Communications Group.

Spillers, Hortense J. 1987. 'Mama's Baby, Papa's Maybe: An American Grammar Book'. *Diacritics* 17(2): 65–81.

— 2017. 'Shades of Intimacy: Women in the Time of Revolution'. Barnard Center for Research on Women. https://www.youtube.com/watch?v=KPa7KhbuEJo.

Spivak, Gayatri Chakravorty. 1988. 'Can the Subaltern Speak?' In *Marxism and the Interpretation of Culture*, edited by L. Grossberg and C. Nelson, 271–313. Champaign: University of Illinois Press.

— 2008. *Can the Subaltern Speak? Postkolonialität und subalterne Artikulation*. Vienna: Turia + Kant.

— 2014. *Kritik der postkolonialen Vernunft. Hin zu einer Geschichte der verrinnenden Gegenwart*. Translated by Nadine Böhm-Schnitker, Doris Feldmann, Barbara Gabel Cunningham, Christian Krug and Andreas Nehring. Stuttgart: Kohlhammer.

Stakemeier, Kerstin. 2017. *Entgrenzter Formalismus. Verfahren einer anti-modernen Ästhetik*. Berlin: b_books.

Stangneth, Bettina. 2011. *Eichmann vor Jerusalem. Das unbehelligte Leben eines Massenmörders*. 2nd edn. Zurich: Arche.

Statistisches Bundesamt. 2018. 'Personal an Hochschulen'. https://www.destatis.de/DE/Themen/Gesellschaft-Umwelt/Bildung-Forschung-Kultur/Hochschulen/Publikationen/_publikationen-innen-hochschulen-personal.html.

Steyerl, Hito and Encarnación Gutiérrez Rodríguez, eds. 2003. *Spricht die Subalterne deutsch? Migration und postkoloniale Kritik*. Münster: Unrast.

Steyerl, Hito. 2007. 'Die Institution der Kritik'. *Psychologie & Gesellschaftskritik* 31(1): 71–80.

— 2012. *The Wretched of the Screen*. Berlin: Sternberg Press.

Süder Happelmann, Natascha. 2019. *Ankersentrum*. Edited by Franciska Zólyom. Berlin: Archive Books.

The Museum of Modern Art. 2019. 'Arthur Jafa: APEX – Artist Stories'. https://www.youtube.com/watch?v=-c-IpBIWNCY.

The New School. 2014. 'bell hooks and Arthur Jafa Discuss Transgression in Public Spaces at The New School'. https://www.youtube.com/watch?v=fe-7ILSKSog.

Thompson, Vanessa Eileen and Fatima El-Tayeb. 2019. 'Alltagsrassismus, staatliche Gewalt und koloniale Tradition. Ein Gespräch über Racial Profiling und intersektionale Widerstände in Europa'. In *Racial Profiling. Struktureller Rassismus und antirassistischer Widerstand*, edited by Mohamed Wa Baile, Serena O. Dankwa, Tarek Naguib, Patricia Purtschert and Sarah Schilliger, 311–28. Bielefeld: transcript

Thompson, Vanessa Eileen. 2020. 'Rassismus an der Hochschule. Intersektionale Verstrickungen und Möglichkeiten des Abolitionismus'. Lecture series 'Bildung dekolonisieren', TU Berlin, 4 November.

— 2021. 'Schwarz-feministische Kritik der Polizei'. In *X-Texte zu Kultur und Gesellschaft*, edited by Onur Suzan Nobrega, Matthias Quent and Jonas Zipf, 109–24. Bielefeld: transcript.

Tibebu, Teshale. 2011. *Hegel and the Third World: The Making of Eurocentrism in World History*. New York: Syracuse University Press.

Tinsley, Omise'eke Natasha. 2008. 'Black Atlantic, Queer Atlantic: Queer Imaginings of the Middle Passage'. *GLQ: A Journal of Lesbian and Gay Studies* 2–3(14): 191–215.

Toll, Robert C. 1974. *Blacking Up: The Minstrel Show in Nineteenth-Century America*. Oxford University Press.

Traverso, Enzo. 2016. *Left-Wing Melancholia: Marxism, History, and Memory*. New York: Columbia University Press.

Trilling, Lionel. 2008. *The Moral Obligation to Be Intelligent: Selected Essays*. Edited by Leon Wieseltier. Evanston: Northwestern University Press.

Tuck, Eve and K. Wayne Yang. 2012. 'Decolonization Is Not a Metaphor'. *Decolonization: Indigeneity, Education and Society* 1(1): 1–40.

Tuck, Eve. 2009. 'Suspending Damage: A Letter to Communities'. *Harvard Educational Review* 79(3): 409–27, 539–40.

— 2010. 'Breaking Up with Deleuze: Desire and Valuing the Irreconcilable'. *International Journal of Qualitative Studies in Education* 23(5): 635–50.

Van Gelder, Frederik. 1998. 'Trauma and Society'. https://www.amsterdam-adorno.net/fvg1998_PA_trauma_gesell_ENG.html.

Vetters, Larissa, Judith. M. Eggers and Lisa Hahn. 2017. 'Migration and the Transformation of German Administrative Law'. In *Working Papers*, edited by Max Planck Institute for Social Anthropology.

Vetters, Larissa. 2007. 'The Power of Administrative Categories'. *Ethnopolitics* 6(2): 187–209.

— 2019. 'Administrative Guidelines as a Source of Immigration Law?' *Journal of Legal Anthropology* 3(2): 70–90.

Vitale, Alex S. 2017. *The End of Policing*. London and New York: Verso.

Von der Leyen, Ursula. 2019. 'Political Guidelines for the Next Commission (2019–2024): "A Union That Strives for More: My Agenda for Europe"'. European Commission. https://ec.europa.eu/info/files/political-guidelines-new-commission_en.

— 2021. 'Rede der Präsidentin von der Leyen zur Lage der Union'. European Commission. https://ec.europa.eu/commission/presscorner/detail/de/SPEECH_21_4701.

Von Redecker, Eva. 2020a. *Revolution für das Leben. Philosophie der neuen Protestformen*. Frankfurt am Main: S. Fischer.

— 2020b. 'Ownership's Shadow'. *Critical Times* 3(1): 33–67.

Walcott, Derek. 1990. *Omeros*. London: Macmillan.

Walcott, Rinaldo. 2021. *On Property: Policing, Prisons, and the Call for Abolition*. Windsor, Ontario: Biblioasis.

Warren, Calvin L. 2018. *Ontological Terror: Blackness, Nihilism, and Emancipation*. Durham, NC: Duke University Press.

WDR. 2020. 'Carola Rackete mit Karl-Küpper-Preis ausgezeichnet'. 19 October. https://www1.wdr.de/nachrichten/rheinland/rackete-bekommt-karl-kuepper-preis-100.html.

Weber, Max. 2009. *Wirtschaft und Gesellschaft. Grundriss der verstehenden Soziologie*. Edited by Johannes Winckelmann. 5th revised edn. Tübingen: Mohr-Siebeck.

— 2019. *Economy and Society: A New Translation*. Edited and translated by Keith Tribe. Cambridge, MA: Harvard University Press.

Weheliye, Alexander G. 2014. *Habeas Viscus: Racializing Assemblages, Biopolitics, and Black Feminist Theories of the Human*. Durham, NC: Duke University Press.

Weier, Sebastian. 2014. 'Consider Afro-Pessimism'. *Amerikastudien* 59(3): 419–33.

Wekker, Gloria. 2016. *White Innocence: Paradoxes of Colonialism and Race*. Durham, NC: Duke University Press.

West, Cornel. 1977. 'Philosophy and the Afro-American Experience'. *The Philosophical Forum* 2/3(9): 117–48.

Westra, Evan. 2021. 'Virtue Signaling and Moral Progress'. *Philosophy & Public Affairs* 49(2): 156–78.

White, Deborah Gray. 2008. *Telling Histories: Black Women Historians in the Ivory Tower*. Chapel Hill: The University of North Carolina Press.

Wilderson III, Frank B. 2010. *Red, White and Black: Cinema and the Structure of US Antagonisms*. Durham, NC: Duke University Press.

— 2014. '"We're trying to destroy the world": Anti-Blackness & Police Violence after Ferguson'. ill-will-editions.tumblr.com.

Willett, Cynthia. 1995. *Maternal Ethics and Other Slave Moralities*. London and New York: Routledge.

Williams, Robert A. 2012. *Savage Anxieties: The Invention of Western Civilization*. New York: Palgrave Macmillan.

Wilson, Emily. 2018. 'Introduction'. In *Homer: The Odyssey*. New York: W.W. Norton & Company.

Winters, Joseph. 2020. 'Afropessimism's Contributions to Black Studies'. AAIHS (blog). 4 September. https://www.aaihs.org/afropessimisms-contributions-to-black-studies.

Wittke, Carl. 1930. *Tambo and Bones: A History of the American Minstrel Stage*. 3rd edn. Durham, NC: Duke University Press.

Witzgall, Susanne and Kerstin Stakemeier. 2015. *Fragile Identitäten*. Zurich: Diaphanes.

Wynter, Sylvia. 1992. 'Rethinking "Aesthetics": Notes towards a Deciphering Practice'. In *Ex-Iles: Essays on Caribbean Cinema*, edited by Mbye Cham, 237–79. Trenton, NJ: Africa World Press.

— 1995. '1492: A New World View'. In *Race, Discourse, and the Origin of the Americas: A New World View*, edited by Vera Lawrence Hyatt and Rex Nettleford, 5–57. Washington, DC and London: Smithsonian Institution Press.

— 2003. 'Unsettling the Coloniality of Being/Power/Truth/Freedom: Towards the Human, after Man, Its Overrepresentation – An Argument'. *CR: The New Centennial Review* 3(3): 257–337.

— 2013. 'Towards the Sociogenic Principle: Fanon, Identity, the Puzzle of Conscious Experience, and What It Is Like to Be "Black"'. In *National Identities and Socio-Political Changes in Latin America*, edited by Antonio Gomez-Moriana and Mercedes Duran-Cogan, 46–82. London and New York: Routledge.

Zeit Online. 2019. 'Seenotrettung. Paris zeichnet Carola Rackete und Pia Klemp aus'. *Die Zeit*, 12 July. https://www.zeit.de/gesellschaft/zeitgeschehen/2019-07/seenotrettung-carola-rackete-pia-klemp-verdienstmedaille-paris.

Zischka, Johannes. 1986. 'Die NS-Rassenideologie. Machttaktisches Instrument oder handlungsbestimmendes Ideal?'. *Europäische Hochschulschriften. Reihe 3, Geschichte und ihre Hilfswissenschaften* (274). Frankfurt am Main: Lang.

Photo: Inke Johannsen

About the author

Henrike Kohpeiß is a philosopher in Berlin, working on social and political philosophy, critical theory, affect studies, Black studies and feminist philosophy. She regularly publishes work in academic journals and criticism in magazines. She organises and hosts events in Berlin, such as the conversation series 'Feelings at the end of the world' at Volksbühne. *Bourgeois Coldness* is her first book, and was published in German in 2023 by Campus Verlag.

About the translator

Grace Nissan is the author of *The Utopians* (Ugly Duckling Presse) and *The City Is Lush with / Obstructed Views* (DoubleCross Press), as well as the translator of *War Diary* by Yevgenia Belorusets (New Directions) and *kochanie, today i bought bread* by Uljana Wolf (World Poetry Books). Their translations of Belorusets were presented in the 59th Venice Biennale, as well as in the accompanying publication *In the Face of War* (Isolarii). They are the recipient of a National Endowment for the Arts Translation Fellowship to translate the Austrian poet Ann Cotten's *Banned! An Epic Poem* into English.

Other books out with Divided

Let Them Rot by Alenka Zupančič
This brilliant account of Sophocles's *Antigone* breaks new ground for philosophy, psychoanalysis, and political and feminist theory. —Joan Copjec

Disorganisation & Sex by Jamieson Webster
Who knew the hole was what Freud had in mind when he invented psychoanalysis and wouldn't stop saying 'sex'. Take a tumble into Wonderland with Dr Webster and decide for yourself what counts as real. —Courtney Love

I have brought you a severed hand by Ghayath Almadhoun
Translated by Catherine Cobham
This book never misses the defiant beat of an exile's haunted footing across wars, seas and memory. Almadhoun turns the genocidal logic of colonialism upside down, emptying out the crumbs of humanity and civilisation. —Don Mee Choi

Wave of Blood by Ariana Reines
Her voice – which is always more than hers alone – is a dialectic between the very ancient and the bleeding edge. —Ben Lerner

Stage of Recovery by Georgia Sagri
This book observes a decade of revolutionary animism. There is no score of absolute ethics, the subject is made in anarchy. Her presence pulses in sustained relation. —Mayra A. Rodríguez Castro

How to Leave the World by Marouane Bakhti
Translated by Lara Vergnaud
What it takes to imagine social and physical freedom is what it meant to keep reading this incredible book. —Bhanu Kapil

In Pursuit of Revolutionary Love: Precarity, Power, Communities by Joy James
Revolutionary Love is umph-degree love; or love beyond measure . . . It is love that dares all things, beyond which others may find the spirit-force to survive. —Mumia Abu-Jamal